WORKING WITH CONFLICT

Skills and Strategies for Action

✪ DEDICATION

To Noora, three, and Jessica, three months, who have contributed actively to the making of this book. May they, and their generation, live in a world of peace.

WORKING WITH CONFLICT

Skills and Strategies for Action

◆ *SIMON FISHER*   ◆ *DEKHA IBRAHIM ABDI*

◆ *JAWED LUDIN*   ◆ *RICHARD SMITH*

◆ *STEVE WILLIAMS*   ◆ *SUE WILLIAMS*

Ⓩ ZED BOOKS   RESPONDING RTC Skills & Strategies for Peace TO CONFLICT

Working with Conflict: Skills and Strategies for Action
was first published in 2000 by
Zed Books Ltd, 7 Cynthia Street, London N1 9JF, UK and
Room 400, 175 Fifth Avenue, New York, NY 10010, USA
in association with
Responding to Conflict, 1046 Bristol Road, Selly Oak, Birmingham B29 6LJ, UK.

Distributed in the USA exclusively by
St Martin's Press, Room 400, 175 Fifth Avenue, New York, NY 10010, USA.

Cover & book design by Lee Robinson, Ad Lib Design & Illustration, London N19 5HT, UK

Printed and bound in the United Kingdom by Bookcraft, Midsomer Norton, Bath, UK.

The catalogue record for this book is available from the British Library.

Library of Congress Cataloging-in-Publication Data is available

ISBN 1 85649 836 0 Hb
ISBN 1 85649 837 9 Pb

✪ CONTENTS

✹ ABOUT THE AUTHORS

SIMON FISHER has been Director of Responding to Conflict (RTC) since it was founded in 1991, responsible for a range of conflict transformation training and support programmes worldwide. Born in 1948 and a teacher by profession, he has worked in many countries on education, development and peace-building issues, including Algeria, the UK, Congo (Zaire), much of sub-Saharan Africa and the South Pacific. He likes writing and, amongst other things, has co-authored a handbook for teachers. He is currently actively engaged with partners in the Balkans, Kazakhstan, Afghanistan, Sudan and West Africa and is a member of the Steering Committee for Action for Conflict Transformation, an international network of practitioners. At the same time he tries to maintain a private life as a husband and father of four.

JAWED LUDIN is the Project Officer for Afghanistan at the British Refugee Council in London, where his work involves cooperation with the British relief and development NGOs operating in Afghanistan. He has been involved in development and community peace-building work since 1994 and has worked for a number of national and international agencies in Afghanistan and Pakistan. Since 1996 Jawed has been associated with RTC and has facilitated training activities both inside and outside his region. At present he is also pursuing postgraduate studies in Politics and Sociology at the University of London.

SUE WILLIAMS has many years of experience in reconciliation and political mediation in various countries, particularly Uganda (1984–5 and 1990–91) and Northern Ireland (1987 to the present). She was Director for Policy and Process Skills at RTC until 1998, then Director of the Policy and Evaluation Unit of INCORE (the Initiative for Conflict Resolution and Ethnicity) at the University of Ulster/United Nations University. She has acted as consultant to groups involved in work on conflict in many countries, including Cambodia, Guatemala, Rwanda, Burundi, Congo and Kenya. Sue has lived in Northern Ireland since 1987.

STEVE WILLIAMS is a part-time Special Consultant for RTC, working from his home in Northern Ireland. He was a full-time course tutor on four of RTC's Working with Conflict courses between 1997 and 1999, including the 10-week course in South Africa at the end of 1997. Employed by RTC since 1994, he has held positions as Course Organiser and Tutor and as Director for Conflict-Handling Skills. During this period he worked overseas with RTC's partners in Nigeria, Cambodia and Ethiopia as well as doing training and consultancy work in Northern Ireland. Previously, he worked on extended mediation and reconciliation initiatives in Uganda, Kenya and Botswana. He made shorter visits to South Africa, and to the Middle East, Fiji, New Zealand, Australia and Sri Lanka, while gathering first-hand material for a book, *Being in the Middle by Being at the Edge: Quaker experience of non-official political mediation* (Williams Sessions, York, England, 1994), which he co-authored with Sue Williams. Born in the USA in 1951, Steve is now a citizen of both the UK and the USA.

DEKHA IBRAHIM ABDI has worked in Wajir, north-east Kenya, in various capacities: as an educationalist, as a community development worker and in conflict resolution. She has had considerable experience as a trainer and in 1997 worked with the Arid Lands Resource Management Project (ALRMP), a World Bank-funded project managed by the office of the president in Kenya. Dekha has worked with the Coalition for Peace in Africa (COPA) in South Africa (1997) and with RTC in Birmingham, UK (1995 and 1997). She is RTC's Trainer and Learning Co-ordinator and lead tutor on the Working with Conflict course. Dekha is an experienced mediator in community-based conflicts, especially with the pastoralist community in northern Kenya. She is a founder member of various peace initiatives in Wajir District and neighbouring districts of northern Kenya. Dekha has made an extensive contribution towards pastoralist development, notably in the area of developing an appropriate education system, where she has introduced the Mobile School concept.

RICHARD SMITH was RTC's International Fellow for the period April 1999 to August 2000. During this time he undertook extensive training on the Working with Conflict and Strengthening Policy and Practice courses, as well as undertaking various consultancies for RTC in Sudan and Sri Lanka. His initial experience was gained in South Africa, as an anti-apartheid activist and later through involvement in the reconstruction and reconciliation processes. He has worked with the Independent Electoral Commission and the Truth and Reconciliation Commission in South Africa, and, on a community level, with the Reconstruction and Development Programme in the Southern Cape Region. With a background in development and adult education and training, he has worked extensively in Ethiopia, Sudan, Somaliland and Eritrea. Richard is a member of the Coalition for Peace in Africa and serves on the Steering Committee of Action for Conflict Transformation, a formal network of global practitioners.

✦ ACKNOWLEDGEMENTS

THIS BOOK IS THE RESULT OF WORK BY MANY PRACTITIONERS and facilitators from all over the world, working in many languages and contexts. These pages are based upon their work in progress, and if there is credit, it should go primarily to them, and to those they are working with.

'WORKING WITH CONFLICT' REFERS TO A FIELD OF WORK in which ideas and frameworks are shared generously and adapted freely to suit different needs by people who are practically involved in this work. Responding to Conflict (RTC) has been fully part of that process. We constantly borrow, adapt, invent and share ideas and tools. This is essential if our common capacity to address conflicts creatively is to increase. However, it is often possible to lose sight of where an idea came from and therefore not to give acknowledgement where it should be given. We have credited, wherever possible, those whose work is quoted. Where we have failed to do this, please forgive us, and inform us so that future editions can be more complete.

IN PARTICULAR, THERE ARE SOME WHOSE WRITINGS AND IDEAS have been crucial to the development of RTC and our approach: John Paul Lederach, Chris Mitchell, Mari Fitzduff, Adam Curle, Paulo Freire, Sally Timmel and Anne Hope, to mention a few.

CHRIS BARBER WAS CENTRALLY INVOLVED IN THE BIRTH OF RTC and led the trustees in its early years with great wisdom and selflessness. Val Ferguson took over from Chris and has been an equally devoted and energetic chair. With the other trustees and members of the Advisory Group, they have given RTC the security we needed to grow. Nicholas and Bevis Gillett have given invaluable encouragement from the earliest, and most uncertain, moments.

A SPECIAL ACKNOWLEDGEMENT NEEDS TO BE MADE to Judith Large. Judith is a co-founder of RTC and a highly valued colleague. She helped conceptualise and give shape to RTC's approach in our early days. Her contribution to this book is great: sometimes directly, in that she helped devise and draft some of the tools and explanations, sometimes indirectly, as her creativity has influenced the orientation of the whole organisation. We thank her here and wish her well in her current work.

WE ARE GRATEFUL ALSO TO PAUL CLIFFORD who works in many countries on behalf of RTC, sharing his learning and challenging us with new ideas, especially on negotiation and mediation.

THANKS TO OUR FUNDERS, especially Joseph Rowntree Charitable Trust, Polden Puckham Foundation, Edward Cadbury Charitable Trust and the Southall Trust, for their generous and consistent support. Thanks also to the Government of the Netherlands and the Allen Lane Foundation for funding the writing, publication and dissemination of this book.

AS THE BOOK WAS BEING PUT TOGETHER certain people gave invaluable help: Bridget Walker helped redraft extensive parts of Chapters 3 and 9 and frequently raised questions about gender and rights. Mary Lou Leavitt restructured Chapter 6 and made us think a lot about active nonviolence as an approach. Both read and commented on the entire manuscript, as did Ruth Musgrave, Donna Copnall, Rosemary Tucker, Shomari Walingamina and Gwen Prince. Others gave their time for a 'road-testing' of the practical tools for analysis and strategy-building, including the entire Development Studies course in the Selly Oak Colleges Federation, and many other students at Woodbrooke College during the Autumn Term of 1999.

SPECIAL THANKS GO TO PAT PRIESTLEY, JOHN MANSFIELD, KAREN LEACH AND JACKIE MOORE, the RTC Administration and Finance team, for the efficiency and good humour with which they have helped to take the book from concept to culmination.

SPECIFIC ACKNOWLEDGEMENTS TO:
- Fahim Hakim for several drawings.
- Mari Fitzduff for her ideas on prejudice and discrimination in Chapter 4, and for allowing us to quote from her paper given at an RTC Consultation in Chapter 5.
- Shomari Walingamina for the drawing in Figure 8.2, Chapter 9.
- Oxfam Sudan for the Values Tree (page 80).
- Trevor Findlay (VERTIC) for writing about verification in Chapter 6.
- Post War Reconstruction and Development Unit, University of York (see section on Reconstruction, page 126).

IN ADDITION TO THESE PEOPLE YOU WILL FIND THE NAMES OF MANY OTHERS who have made direct contributions scattered throughout the text. Without the commitment of all of them it would not have been possible to produce this book. Our heartfelt thanks go to all contributors.

✦ PREFACE

ABOUT THIS BOOK

THIS BOOK IS A PRACTICAL TOOL. It offers ideas, methods and techniques for understanding and working with conflict. It is based on the insights of practitioners and communities from their first-hand experience in conflict situations.

WORKING WITH CONFLICT IS INTENDED FOR PEOPLE who are working for a more just and peaceful world, whatever their belief or background. Some will have labels such as aid and development, human rights, community relations, peace and justice, emergency relief, conflict resolution and prevention. Others will be working in quite different sectors, but with similar values. They will be found in every country of the world: wherever rulers and ruled, rich and poor, in-groups and out-groups confront each other; wherever there is hope that things can be better.

THE CONTENTS HAVE COME OUT OF THE COLLECTIVE WISDOM and experience of some 300 practitioners from all over the world who have worked with Responding to Conflict (RTC) since 1991. Many have been participants and tutors on our 10-week (formerly 11-week) Working with Conflict course, or other shorter courses, where through the study of each other's problems and the sharing of insights and experience, new tools and approaches have been forged to address common problems. Many of these participants have invited RTC staff to work with them: for example in various parts of Africa, in Central America, in Afghanistan and Pakistan, in Kazakhstan and other parts of the Commonwealth of Independent States, in Eastern Europe, in Cambodia, and in the South Pacific. In each place these ideas and techniques have mutated in the light of local needs and circumstances, so that the contents of this book have been and still are in a constant state of change. We have necessarily described them at a particular moment in time, but be assured that when you finally read this, they will have evolved further, and new ideas will be developing alongside them.

HOW TO USE THIS BOOK

THIS BOOK CAN ASSIST YOU TO:
• Analyse the social and political conflicts you are facing.
• Assess the capacity of your group or agency to work on a conflict.
• Evaluate the impact of your work on a conflict.
• Identify weaknesses and gaps in your current actions.
• Devise new activities and strategies appropriate to the dynamics of the situation.
• Develop essential skills.
• Influence strategic thinking in your own organisation, and others.
• Learn from what you have done, and help others to do so.
Used systematically it can help you to make sense of what is happening in the conflicts that you face, whether large or small, and to increase your ability to address them creatively and effectively.

THE BOOK IS NOT PRIMARILY A MANUAL FOR TRAINERS. However, the ideas and methods have nearly all been used in workshops and courses, and many trainers will probably use them in this way. We welcome this and hope for your feedback. Photocopying is encouraged, where necessary, with due acknowledgement.

THE BOOK DOES NOT HAVE TO BE READ FROM COVER TO COVER. It can be dipped into when the need arises. However, there is a sequence to it, which we believe is important. So, if you start with a later chapter, you may find that you are referred back to ideas and tools that were covered in earlier chapters.

THERE ARE FOUR PARTS TO THE BOOK, as you can see from the diagram facing the Introduction to each of the four parts (Analysis, Strategy, Action, Learning). We see these as a useful series of steps to have in mind, applicable to any intervention. If you read the book through, it should help you to plan and act effectively and to gain important information from it before entering the cycle again. However, you may at this moment be looking for some specific information: a method for assessing the impact of your programme on the conflicts in your area, for example, or some more detailed advice on mediation. If so, we suggest you go straight to the relevant pages, using the table of contents or the index at the back. But at whatever point you enter this cycle, as shown in the diagram, we invite you to continue with it and to incorporate the four dimensions in a systematic way.

ONE FINAL WORD: sometimes it may seem that a tool or method is too complicated to try. If you feel this at any point, we hope you will gather your courage and try it anyway. Do not worry whether you are doing it 'correctly'. There are many ways to use each method and none is objectively the best or correct version. If it works for you, then that is how it should be. Have a go! We hope you find the book both useful and inspiring. Please let us know.

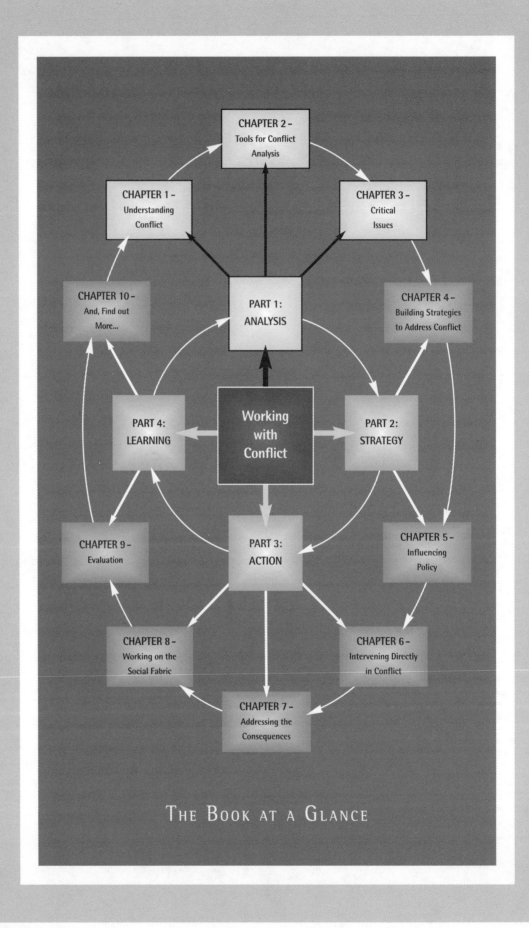

THE BOOK AT A GLANCE

✵ PART 1: ANALYSIS

THIS PART OF THE BOOK offers a FOUNDATION STONE on which any work in an area affected by conflict can be built. Before you, as an individual or an organisation, attempt to do anything, whether to address the conflict directly or to carry out other types of work, it is essential that you know as much as possible about what is going on. This is what we call 'analysis'.

Differences in viewpoint are inevitable. When people study a problem together they often assume that, with the same facts at everyone's disposal, they will all agree on a single analysis. This is not so. Differences are brought about by a range of dimensions: status, power, wealth, age, the role assigned to our gender, belonging to a specific social group, and so on. These indicators of position in society often mean that people want different things from the same situation: when their goals clash or are incompatible, we have a conflict.

CHAPTER 1 This chapter introduces basic ideas for thinking about conflict, violence and peace. It also introduces frameworks for thinking about intervention in conflict.

CHAPTER 2 Differences in perspective and goals, while often seen as a problem, can equally be seen as a resource, leading to a wider understanding of a problem and an improvement in the present situation. It is with this in mind that Chapter 2 sets out nine separate tools of analysis that can help you to find out more about what is happening in a conflict, identify areas where you need to know more, and begin to see where you can influence the situation. These tools have been used by individuals working alone, by groups of people trying to find ways of addressing the conflicts they face, and by groups from different sides in a conflict trying to understand each other. Have a go at using them. We have found that people understand them by trying them.

Chapter 2 also considers the reasons for analysing conflict: analysis can be an intervention as well as a preparation for action. In our work with people who are dealing with political and social conflicts, we have found that having a better understanding of the dynamics, relationships and issues of the particular situation helps them to plan and carry out better actions and strategies. They gain this understanding in two ways: by undertaking detailed analyses of conflicts from a variety of perspectives, and by exploring the specific issues and problems that relate to these conflicts.

CHAPTER 3 This chapter explores some of the major themes that arise when you analyse conflicts: power, culture, identity, gender, rights. These raise questions to which there is no 'right' answer, but with which you will need to grapple if you are intending to turn your analysis into a strategy and concrete actions. You will, no doubt, have other issues that are critical in your own context.

PART 1 provides the basis on which to build your strategy: a conceptual framework, a sequence of methods of analysis and an initial discussion of key issues, which are controversial yet fundamental to any serious work for peace and conflict transformation.

1 - UNDERSTANDING CONFLICT
Towards a conceptual framework

SUMMARY ■ This chapter introduces some basic ideas for thinking about conflict. The main topics discussed are:
- **Making sense of conflict**
- **Addressing conflict**
- **Differing approaches: to manage, resolve or transform conflict?**
- **Theories about different approaches to intervention in conflict**
- **Violence is more than behaviour: it also involves context and attitudes**
- **Violence and nonviolence as ways of bringing about change**
- **Peace as a process**
- **What is peace-building?**
- **How is it best to start?**

Making sense of conflict
PERCEPTIONS

People have different perspectives on life and its problems:
- We each have our own unique history and character.
- Each of us is born either male or female.
- Each of us is born into a particular way of life: a nomadic pastoralist from Northern Kenya and an urban dweller in Kuala Lumpur have radically different experiences of, and views about, the world and their place in it.
- Each of us has our own values, which guide our thinking and our behaviour and motivate us to take certain actions and to reject others.

Not surprisingly, therefore when we meet and work with others, we find that they often have a different perspective on things. Look for a moment at the picture below.

▶ **What do you see?**
▶ **And when you look again, can you see something different?**

Rather like seeing different images in the picture, people see social and political situations differently. Our backgrounds lead us to see things in a particular way.

Differences in viewpoint are inevitable, and often enriching. When people study a problem together they often assume that, with the

⊙ If you have not fought with each other, you do not know each other.
CHINA

©PETRA ROHR-ROUENDAAL

same facts at everyone's disposal, they will all agree on a single analysis. This is not so. Unanimity is even more unlikely when we consider that, in addition to these 'natural' differences, there are those brought about by a range of other dimensions: status, power, wealth, age, the role assigned to our gender, belonging to a specific social group, and so on. These indicators of position in society often mean that people want different things from the same situation: sometimes these goals clash, or are incompatible. It is then that we have a conflict.

Differences in perspective and goals are often seen as a problem that will only be resolved when we all have the same intentions, or when one view wins over the others. Alternatively, they can be seen as a resource, leading to a wider understanding of a problem, and an improvement to the present situation.

CONFLICT AND VIOLENCE ARE DIFFERENT THINGS

As basic working definitions of conflict and violence, we would suggest the following:

• **CONFLICT** is a relationship between two or more parties (individuals or groups) who have, or think they have, incompatible goals.[1]

• **VIOLENCE** consists of actions, words, attitudes, structures or systems that cause physical, psychological, social or environmental damage and/or prevent people from reaching their full human potential.

Conflicts are a fact of life, inevitable and often creative. Conflicts happen when people pursue goals which clash. Disagreements and conflicts are usually resolved without violence, and often lead to an improved situation for most or all of those involved. Which is just as well, since conflicts are part of our existence. From the micro, interpersonal level through to groups, organisations, communities and nations, all human relations – social relations, economic relations and relations of power – experience growth, change and conflict. Conflicts arise from imbalances in these relations – i.e. unequal social

status, unequal wealth and access to resources, and unequal power – leading to problems such as discrimination, unemployment, poverty, oppression, crime. Each level connects to the others, forming a potentially powerful chain of forces either for constructive change or for destructive violence.

This book focuses on the middle to higher levels: community and national. However, it needs to be read in the knowledge that events at the other levels – interpersonal and family as well as regional and global – are also crucial.

In the household, for example, child abuse and domestic violence are far-reaching in their impact, and at the global level decisions made by multinational economic bodies such as the IMF, World Trade Organisation and World Bank have a grass roots impact.

▶ **How many conflicts are you aware of at this moment?**
▶ **Can you see links between conflicts at different levels?**

If it is clear that conflict is with us whether we like it or not, it is only another step to seeing that we actually need it. There is much literature, in the business world especially, which focuses on the beneficial effects of conflict. These include making people aware of problems, promoting necessary change, improving solutions, raising morale, fostering personal development, increasing self-awareness, enhancing psychological maturity – and fun.[2]

While, from your own experience, you may want to disagree with the advantages listed above, it is intriguing to reflect on the positive contribution that conflict can make, not just within organisations but at all levels. Without it, you might imagine, individuals would be stunted for lack of stimulation, groups and organisations would stagnate and die, and societies would collapse under their own weight, unable to adapt to changing circumstances and altering power relations. It is commonly said, for example, that the Roman Empire collapsed because it was not able to adapt and change.

> ▶ Can you think of a situation, from your own experience, where conflict has made a positive contribution?
> ▶ How did conflict help to change the situation?
> ▶ Do you now agree that conflict can help to stimulate necessary change?

Addressing conflict
INTENSIFYING CONFLICT

Sometimes it is necessary to intensify conflict. For example, when people are doing well and have enough power and resources to meet their needs, they do not notice, or refuse to acknowledge, that others are disadvantaged or marginalised. In this case, conflict needs to be introduced or brought into the open so that the necessary changes can be brought about.

People working for community development and human rights will often find themselves working not to resolve a conflict, but to intensify it and make it more visible, to the point where the issue is more widely recognised and effective action begins to be taken. This may mean siding with a disadvantaged group and using strategies for empowerment. For example, in South Africa for much of the twentieth century, activists working for change were striving to bring the hidden, or latent, conflicts into the open so that they could be addressed and dealt with.

NB: In this book a clear distinction is made between:
- **INTENSIFYING CONFLICT**, which means making a hidden conflict more visible and open, for purposeful, nonviolent ends, and
- **ESCALATING CONFLICT**, which refers to a situation in which levels of tension and violence are increasing.

Some basic facets of conflict are illustrated in the diagram below (Figure 1.1).[3] Conflict is differentiated along two axes: goals and behaviours. This accords with our working definition that 'conflict is a relationship between

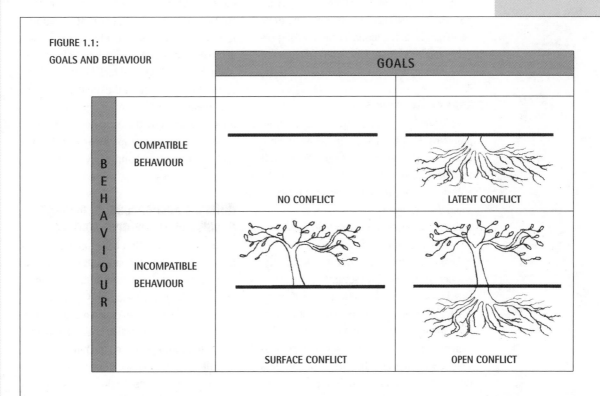

FIGURE 1.1:
GOALS AND BEHAVIOUR

		GOALS	
B E H A V I O U R	**COMPATIBLE BEHAVIOUR**	NO CONFLICT	LATENT CONFLICT
	INCOMPATIBLE BEHAVIOUR	SURFACE CONFLICT	OPEN CONFLICT

two or more parties who have, or think they have, incompatible goals'.

The four boxes in the figure show relationships between goals and behaviour and their implication in terms of conflict. The aim is to illustrate types of conflict in order to point towards different kinds of possible intervention. There is no ideal situation in this scenario, but each of the four types has its own potential and challenges.

- **NO CONFLICT**: A common perception may be that the box on the top left, NO CONFLICT, is preferable. However, any peaceful group or society, if it is to endure, must be lively and dynamic, incorporating conflicts of behaviour and goals and addressing them creatively.
- **LATENT CONFLICT** is below the surface and, as already suggested, may need to be brought into the open before it can be effectively addressed.
- **OPEN CONFLICT** is both deep-rooted and very visible, and may require actions that address both the root causes and the visible effects.
- **SURFACE CONFLICT** has shallow or no roots and may be only a misunderstanding of goals that can be addressed by means of improved communication.

SUPPRESSING CONFLICT

If a conflict is suppressed, this leads to future problems. Conflict itself can be as much a part of the solution as it is of the problem. It becomes violent when:

- there are inadequate channels for dialogue and disagreement
- dissenting voices and deeply held grievances cannot be heard and addressed
- there is instability, injustice and fear in the wider community and society.

One blockage that is often underestimated lies in the trauma and hurts that all of us carry from our past: the personal and collective experience of distress, loss, pain, and perhaps violence. While this is true of all people, it is clearly most devastating and lasting in situations of war and genocide.

These hurts can continue to destabilise us, consciously or unconsciously, if they are not acknowledged and dealt with. At their simplest we often experience them as blockages to creative thought, to relationships and to action. More drastically, they can surface in demonising attitudes towards other people or groups and act as a perceived legitimisation for destroying them, thus creating yet more hurt. The same process works at the social level. If a group or nation considers that it has been wrongly treated or victimised in the past, it will tend to remember these injustices, perhaps fearing a repeat of them, perhaps actively looking for a chance to take revenge against the perceived aggressors.

When such blockages are in place, and linked in a chain from the personal to the national, they create the conditions in which people easily resort to force. The slogan of the women's movement that 'the personal is political' applies here. When people are disadvantaged or oppressed, they experience suppressed conflicts at a personal level that can lead them to take political action at a national level. The suppression of conflicts also provides a fertile ground that can be exploited by politicians, warlords and racketeers, who may recruit the aggrieved or the disadvantaged to help them assert their power and influence at a national level by the use of coercive force. A culture of violence grows, in which conflicts are habitually handled by force.

Differing approaches: to manage, resolve or transform conflict

There is now much effort being put into resolving conflicts. Until the late 1980s most wars were fought between nation states. Now most wars are internal, civil wars and the casualties are mainly civilians. While men are more likely to be killed, 'disappeared' or coerced into military action, women and children make up the majority of those who are displaced or become refugees. Many attribute this increase in civil wars to the ending of the Cold War and the resurgence of nationalism and ethnic identity in the wake of the collapse of the 'bipolar' world order. The collapse of the Soviet socialist sphere of influence has also resulted in an unrestrained globalisation of capitalism that has had an impact on the efforts of people to build democratic societies and economies.

International financial institutions, such as the World Bank and the International Monetary Fund (IMF), now have a more influential and decisive role in the way that weaker and poorer countries operate politically, economically and socially. Economic liberalisation has often fuelled tensions and conflict within these countries. The increase of internal conflicts, along with the globalisation of conflicts beyond the control of individual countries, has also resulted from the growth of associated trends such as warlordism, political corruption and criminal economies. In a sense, the ending of the Cold War opened a valve for many global tensions that had previously been forcibly repressed.

In response to this situation there has been a major expansion in research and practical effort to reduce violent conflict. Governments and civil society alike have tried to develop answers to a problem that in many areas is hampering development or derailing it completely. New organisations have sprung up, and a new terminology is struggling to be born.

At this early stage there is lively disagreement over what words mean. Below we offer a typology, which is consistent but has no claim to be universally accepted. The terms describe the various approaches to addressing conflict. Sometimes they are seen as steps in a process. Each step taken includes the previous one (e.g. **conflict settlement** includes measures for **conflict prevention**, as appropriate). In this book we use the term **conflict transformation** more generally to describe the field as a whole.

- **CONFLICT PREVENTION** aims to prevent the outbreak of violent conflict.
- **CONFLICT SETTLEMENT** aims to end violent behaviour by reaching a peace agreement.
- **CONFLICT MANAGEMENT** aims to limit and avoid future violence by promoting positive behavioural changes in the parties involved.
- **CONFLICT RESOLUTION** addresses the causes of conflict and seeks to build new and lasting relationships between hostile groups.
- **CONFLICT TRANSFORMATION** addresses the wider social and political sources of a conflict and seeks to transform the negative energy of war into positive social and political change.

Figure 1.2 is not meant to explain 'when to do what', but rather to clarify terms. So, for example, **conflict prevention** refers to strategies that address conflict when it is still latent, in the hope of preventing an escalation into violence.

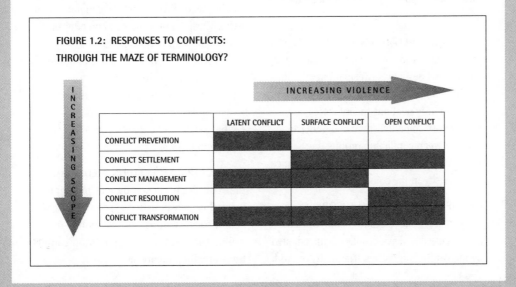

FIGURE 1.2: RESPONSES TO CONFLICTS:
THROUGH THE MAZE OF TERMINOLOGY?

INCREASING VIOLENCE

INCREASING SCOPE

	LATENT CONFLICT	SURFACE CONFLICT	OPEN CONFLICT
CONFLICT PREVENTION	■		
CONFLICT SETTLEMENT		■	■
CONFLICT MANAGEMENT	■	■	
CONFLICT RESOLUTION			■
CONFLICT TRANSFORMATION	■	■	■

Conflict resolution, on the other hand, refers to strategies that address open conflict in the hope of finding not only an agreement to end the violence (**conflict settlement**), but also a resolution of some of the incompatible goals underlying it. While **conflict transformation** is the most thorough and far-reaching strategy, it is also the one that needs the longest and most wide-ranging commitment.

The conflict in Kosovo in 1999 can serve as an example: it was an open conflict, clearly involving clashing goals and behaviours, and resulting in many deaths and much displacement. An appropriate intervention needed to address both **settlement** and **resolution.** Many of the peace attempts were aimed solely at settlement because of the serious violence. However, there were also longer-term initiatives involving groups from the different communities in dialogue over their common future. Once the war finished they provided a valuable, middle-level basis for working out future relationships and the make-up of public institutions. They were working at the longer-term task of **conflict transformation.**

Theories about the causes of conflict

To help you in considering ways of addressing conflicts, we offer the following summary[4] of the major theories about the causes of conflict, each of which points to different methods and goals.

COMMUNITY RELATIONS THEORY assumes that conflict is caused by ongoing polarisation, mistrust and hostility between different groups within a community. The goals of work based on **community relations theory** are:
- to improve communication and understanding between conflicting groups
- to promote greater tolerance and acceptance of diversity in the community.

PRINCIPLED NEGOTIATION THEORY assumes that conflict is caused by incompatible positions and a 'zero-sum' view of conflict being adopted by the conflicting parties. The goals of work based on **principled negotiation theory** are:
- to assist conflicting parties to separate personalities from problems and issues, and to be able to negotiate on the basis of their interests rather than fixed positions
- to facilitate agreements that offer mutual gain for both/all parties.

HUMAN NEEDS THEORY assumes that deep-rooted conflict is caused by unmet or frustrated basic human needs – physical, psychological and social. Security, identity, recognition, participation and autonomy are often cited. The goals of work based on **human needs theory** are:
- to assist conflicting parties to identify and share their unmet needs, and generate options for meeting those needs
- for the parties to reach agreements that meet the basic human needs of all the sides.

IDENTITY THEORY assumes that conflict is caused by feelings of threatened identity, often rooted in unresolved past loss and suffering. The goals of work based on **identity theory** are:
- through facilitated workshops and dialogue, for conflicting parties to identify threats and fears they each feel and to build empathy and reconciliation between themselves
- to jointly reach agreements that recognise the core identity needs of all parties.

INTERCULTURAL MISCOMMUNICATION THEORY assumes that conflict is caused by incompatibilities between different cultural communication styles. The goals of work based on intercultural **miscommunication theory** are:
- to increase the conflicting parties' knowledge of each other's culture
- to weaken negative stereotypes they have of each other
- ultimately, to enhance effective intercultural communication.

CONFLICT TRANSFORMATION THEORY assumes that conflict is caused by real problems of inequality and injustice expressed by competing social, cultural and economic frameworks. The goals of work based on **conflict transformation theory** are:

- to change structures and frameworks that cause inequality and injustice, including economic redistribution
- to improve longer-term relationships and attitudes among the conflicting parties
- to develop processes and systems that promote empowerment, justice, peace, forgiveness, reconciliation, recognition.

▶ Which of these theories, if any, agrees with your own approach to working on conflict?

▶ Do your goals agree with the goals given here for that theory?

▶ Do the theories help you to better understand how others are working on the same conflict?

▶ Are there other approaches used by yourself or others which do not fit into one of these theories?

▶ Can you suggest a theory to add to this list?

Violence is more than behaviour: it also involves context and attitudes

Whatever you may or may not find useful about theories, the reality is that you are trying to deal with real conflict. And that reality often includes some form of violence, which is a central obstacle when you are trying to intervene in the situation.

Most of us think of violence as behaviour. Killing, beating, torture, maiming and so on are all examples of physical violence and there is no shortage of this kind of behaviour in communities, societies and countries all over the world. Wars are a very visible and intense manifestation of this. Much violent behaviour occurs also in the private domain – for example, in families where women and children experience abuse.

VIOLENCE AS CONTEXT OR STRUCTURE

But in recent years our understanding of violence has deepened to include other, less obvious forms of violence that can be equally damaging and perhaps even more difficult to address.

People have found it unhelpful to draw a clear line between, for example, killing with a gun and killing through deprivation of food

and other essentials of life. In each case one group inflicts suffering on another. This can be deliberate, or it can result from simply not taking into account the needs of other groups. There are many **systems and structures** that operate in this way.

Many see some of the trends in international financial systems as violent **structures**, whereby one group of nations imposes deliberate suffering on others. For example, many international institutions encouraged poorer countries of Africa, Asia and Latin America to borrow large amounts of money. These debts and the conditions for repayment now being imposed by the IMF have forced many poorer countries to restructure their economies in order to pay the debts rather than meet the basic needs of their people. The effects, in terms of deaths and damaged lives, are often as serious as the effects of a war.

This situation is complicated further by the fact that economic and political leaders in the north and the south have colluded in creating these debts, with the result that they gain financially while the majority of people suffer. Wars themselves are often the result of systems deliberately fostered by those benefiting from the destruction, for example arms manufacturers, arms dealers and warlords. Wherever systems discriminate between groups, communities and nations to the point of threatening lives and livelihoods, the result is **structural or institutional violence**.

ATTITUDES AND VALUES IN RELATION TO VIOLENCE

There is, however, another deeper layer to our understanding of violence. This relates to less visible, mental processes: the feelings, attitudes and values that people hold. These are not violent in themselves but can easily become the sources of violence, or at least allow violent behaviour and violent structures to operate. Hate, fear and mistrust are feelings which can allow us to classify people as inferior, or superior, in terms of categories such as race, gender, religion, ethnicity, mental ability, physical ability,

FIGURE 1.3: BEHAVIOUR, CONTEXT AND ATTITUDE

DIRECT PHYSICAL VIOLENCE: BEHAVIOUR
- KILLING   • BEATING
- INTIMIDATION   • TORTURE

VISIBLE VIOLENCE

LESS VISIBLE VIOLENCE (UNDER THE SURFACE)

➡ **ACTION:**
VIOLENCE REDUCTION TO PROMOTE 'NEGATIVE PEACE'

➡ **ACTION:**
WORK TO CHANGE ATTITUDES AND CONTEXT, AS WELL AS VIOLENCE REDUCTION, TO PROMOTE 'POSITIVE PEACE'

SOURCES OF VIOLENCE: ATTITUDES, FEELINGS, VALUES
- HATRED   • FEAR, MISTRUST
- RACISM, SEXISM   • INTOLERANCE

STRUCTURAL OR INSTITUTIONAL VIOLENCE: CONTEXT, SYSTEMS, STRUCTURES
- DISCRIMINATION IN e.g. EDUCATION, EMPLOYMENT, HEALTH CARE
- GLOBALISATION OF ECONOMIES   • DENIAL OF RIGHTS AND LIBERTIES
- SEGREGATION (e.g. APARTHEID)

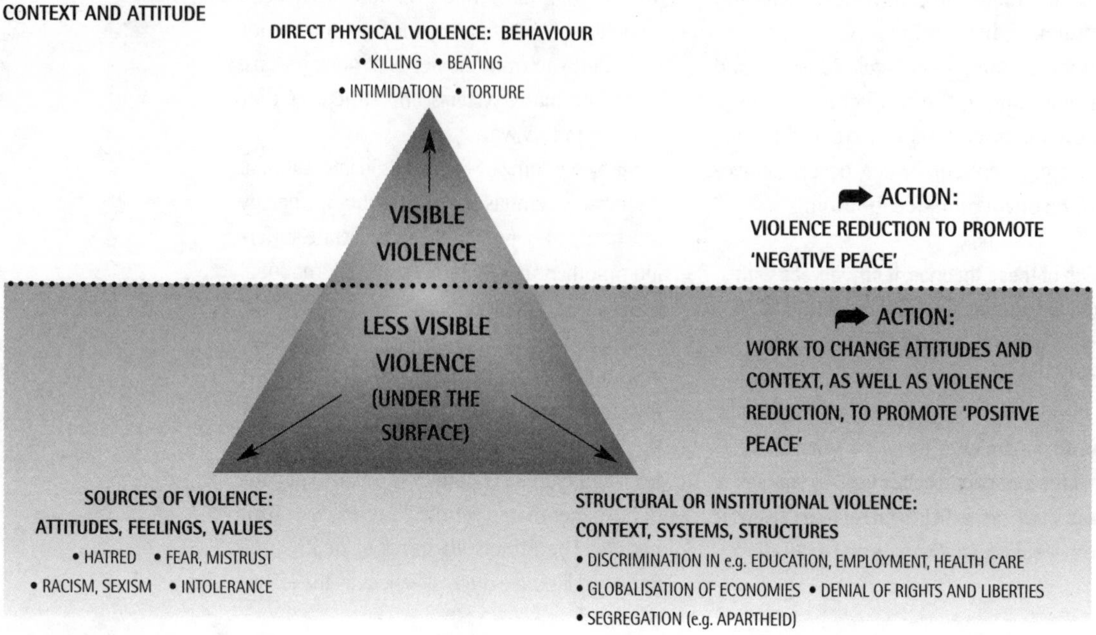

SOURCE: DEVELOPED FROM JOHAN GALTUNG, 'CULTURAL VIOLENCE', *JOURNAL OF PEACE RESEARCH*, VOL. 27, NO. 3, 1990.

---

political ideology or sexual orientation. These feelings may cause some groups of people to become intolerant of anyone who is different from themselves in any or all of these categories. From there, with the appropriate misinformation, it is a relatively small step for them to begin seeing people in other groups as less than human, and thus to participate in, or justify from the sidelines, inhuman action against them.

In Figure 1.3 these three elements (behaviour, context and attitude) are shown as interconnected. An action aimed at reducing violent behaviour, crucial as it is, needs to be complemented by actions directed at both context and attitudes if real or positive peace is to be achieved. A negative peace, the absence of violent behaviour, will not last if the other dimensions are not addressed. Action on all three dimensions is needed to promote positive peace.

This wider understanding of violence can be helpful because:

- It shows that violent behaviour and war are, in most cases, only a small part of what makes up a conflict.
- It shows the interconnectedness of all three dimensions: an intervention in one area has a ripple effect in the others.
- It prompts us to identify those people who organise and profit from violence, sometimes known as 'conflict entrepreneurs', whose interests are served by the continuation of violence.
- It points to vital entry points for conflict transformation, in both the context and the attitudes of a situation.

It also implies that those working to resolve social and political conflicts need to be clear about their own values and long-term goals.

▶ Can you identify violent structures, and attitudes which promote violence, in conflicts you are addressing?
▶ Do you see how these factors prevent real change and movement toward positive peace?

Violence and nonviolence as ways of bringing about change

In our experience of working with people from many different situations, we have found wide differences of opinion about the relative value of violence or nonviolence in bringing about change. The two broad areas of opinion are:

- **THOSE WHO ACCEPT THE NEED FOR COERCIVE FORCE**, including violent means, to compel others to comply with their wishes when all else fails. There are a range of views on precisely when violence can justifiably be used, and theories about just war have been developed to address this problem. For example, many people believe that the Second World War of 1939–45 was justified as a means to overcome the greater violence being perpetrated by Hitler and Nazi Germany against Jewish people and other ethnic minorities. However, in the current age of nuclear weapons, with the danger of a nuclear holocaust, some of these same people would say that full-scale war is no longer justifiable. There are others who believe that the use of violence is justified in order to liberate people from authoritarian and repressive regimes that are torturing and killing, and severely restricting rights and liberties. Movements with this value base often target property and try to avoid harming the people whose support they need.
- **THOSE WHO TAKE A TOTALLY NONVIOLENT STANCE** and believe that in no circumstances can violence lead to a just outcome, therefore its use cannot be justified. In practice, nonviolent actions are carried out by a mixture of those who take this absolute position and those who adopt nonviolent methods because they see them as the most likely to succeed in their situation.

A commitment to nonviolence among the leadership of Tibetan refugees, led by the Dalai Lama, has prevented an armed resistance movement developing to challenge the Chinese occupation of Tibet. On the other hand, the Palestine Liberation Organisation, faced with a similar situation, chose armed struggle.

ACTIVE NONVIOLENCE

There is another approach that falls between the two mentioned above. For those who use 'active nonviolence', force and coercion are possible, and often necessary, even though they refuse to use violence and do not want to harm other people and relationships. This kind of force aims to change a situation by making it too 'costly' – literally or psychologically – for an undesirable situation or relationship to be sustained. For example, Gandhi's campaigns in South Africa and in India or the campaign for women's suffrage were actively nonviolent and forceful in bringing about positive change. Active nonviolence seeks to reach out and enhance or awaken the common humanity of all involved in a conflict, including one's opponents. It tries to increase the potential for truthful communication, while seeking also to stop or prevent destructive behaviour by everyone involved.

In practice, of course, most social change movements use a mix of violent and nonviolent tactics. The late twentiethth century saw an explosion of movements using some variants of active nonviolence, whether for pragmatic or principled reasons – for example, the people-power revolutions of the Philippines and Eastern Europe, anti-nuclear and environmental movements in Western Europe and the United Democratic Front in South Africa (as in the extract on page 12) to mention just a few.

Peace as a process

Peace is a process: a many-sided, never-ending struggle to transform violence. Both those who accept the need for coercive force, including violence, and those who take a totally nonviolent stance, and the many others with views in between, would say that they want peace. But their ideas about what peace really is are rather different.

Stable peace is a relatively rare state. Many societies and communities are excluded from peace by a range of economic, political and social factors. Peace is often compared to

> ✪ Indeed, one perfect resister is enough to win the battle of right against wrong.
> **GANDHI**

NELSON MANDELA'S STATEMENT FROM THE DOCK
AT THE OPENING OF THE DEFENCE CASE IN THE RIVONIA TREASON TRIAL[5]

■ … I must deal immediately and at some length with the question of violence. Some of the things so far told to the Court are true and some are untrue. I do not, however, deny that I planned sabotage. I did not plan it in a spirit of recklessness, nor because I have any love of violence. I planned it as a result of a calm and sober assessment of the political situation that had arisen after many years of tyranny, exploitation, and oppression of my people by the Whites.

■ I admit immediately that I was one of the persons who helped to form Umkhonto we Sizwe, and that I played a prominent role in its affairs until I was arrested in August 1962.

■ … I, and the others who started the organisation, did so for two reasons. Firstly, we believed that, as a result of Government policy, violence by the African people had become inevitable, and that unless responsible leadership was given to canalise and control the feelings of our people, there would be outbreaks of terrorism which would produce an intensity of bitterness and hostility between the various races of this country that is not produced even by war. Secondly, we felt that without violence there would be no way open to the African people to succeed in their struggle against the principle of white supremacy. All lawful modes of expressing opposition to this principle had been closed by legislation, and we were placed in a position in which we had either to accept a permanent state of inferiority, or to defy the Government. We chose to defy the law. We first broke the law in a way which avoided any recourse to violence; when this form was legislated against, and then the Government resorted to a show of force to crush opposition to its policies, only then did we decide to answer violence with violence.

health, in that it is more easily recognised by its absence. Like health, all have access to it. However, unlike health it is contested: people disagree over what a peaceful society is.

Many people understand peace to be the absence of war. While this is, of course, vital, others see it as only a first step towards a fuller ideal, using definitions such as: an interweaving of relationships between individuals, groups and institutions that value diversity and foster the full development of human potential. Women in Taliban-controlled ('peaceful') Afghanistan, deprived of education and opportunities to work, would not take long to see the difference.

Absence of war is often described as negative ('cold') peace, and is contrasted with positive ('warm') peace, which encompasses all aspects of the good society that we might envisage for ourselves: universal rights, economic well-being, ecological balance and other core values.

There are always those who fear peace. Many have good reason to do so: they will lose wealth, status and power as result of what

FAHIM HAKIM

they have done. Oxfam in the Horn of Africa developed the concept of 'dynamic stability' to describe its vision of a peace in which conflicts would still occur, but violence would be absent.

What is peace-building?

The United Nations distinguishes between several different kinds of intervention to bring about peace. In addition to **humanitarian aid** or **emergency assistance**, designed to provide

From understanding to analysis: elders mapping relationships in their village, Sudan (right) and a workshop on conflict in Birmingham, England (below).

✪ Nkochi
tahukokotaka
babele.
Two people
facing each other
cannot pull a rope.
BEMBE, CENTRAL
AFRICA

the immediate means of survival for populations at risk, the main categories of intervention are:

- **PEACE-MAKING:** interventions designed to end hostilities and bring about an agreement using diplomatic, political and military means as necessary.
- **PEACE-KEEPING:** monitoring and enforcing an agreement, using force as necessary. This includes verifying whether agreements are being kept and supervising agreed confidence-building activities.
- **PEACE-BUILDING:** undertaking programmes designed to address the causes of conflict and the grievances of the past and to promote long-term stability and justice.

Peace-building is not primarily concerned with conflict behaviour but addresses the underlying context and attitudes that give rise to violence, such as unequal access to employment, discrimination, unacknowledged and unforgiven responsibility for past crimes, prejudice, mistrust, fear, hostility between groups. It is therefore low-profile work that can, at least in theory, continue through all stages of a conflict. But it is likely to be strongest either in later stages after a settlement and a reduction in violent behaviour or in earlier stages before any open violence has occurred. Peace-building is most often used to describe work that has peace-enhancing **outcomes**, and it attaches great importance to **how** things happen. In other words, it is about **the process** as well as the activity itself and its outcomes.

For example, the rebuilding of a bridge in Kabul after it was destroyed in fighting might have best been described simply as reconstruction. However, the UN agency involved saw the opportunity and set out deliberately to develop the peace-building potential of the situation by involving the previously conflicting sides jointly in the planning, the physical work and future maintenance and control.

PEACE IS HERE AND NOW – LET IT BEGIN WITH ME

If you are trying to influence the conflicts in which you work and to build peace and social justice in your community, you need to look at the groups and organisations you work with, and each of their activities, in the same light. Do they contain examples of people striving for peaceful cooperation? If so, there is a good chance that you can spread that vision further. If they demonstrate the opposite (unaccountable leadership, unjust or confused procedures, reputation-seeking...), the likelihood is that these opposite tendencies will be reinforced.

❯ **Looking frankly at your group or organisation, what do you see?**

❯ **Do you see people who have the capacities, skills and qualities to work for peace and justice?**

❯ **Do you see any obstacles in the way the group operates?**

❯ **Do you see your organisation having a positive role in promoting change in your community, society or nation?**

Much is possible if there is the will to make a difference. Conflicts can be influenced and steps to peace and justice can be achieved, bearing in mind that HOW you work is as important as WHAT you do. As Gandhi said: 'We must BE the change we wish to SEE in the world.'

How is it best to start?

STOP: 'Think before you act'
This is a crucial principle in working with conflict – provided that circumstances allow. Do your analysis before you take action. If your intention is to intervene in conflict and try to influence it for the better, your analysis should be undertaken from different viewpoints and perspectives.

LOOK: 'Put your own house in order'
Take a good look at yourself and your organisation and consider whether you may need to change in order to be able to intervene effectively in the conflict. Addressing this is a

vital and continuing area of work, whatever your intentions for influencing the wider society. Tools explained in Chapter 5 may be helpful for this step.

 LISTEN: 'What do others say and what does your own intuition tell you?'
Try to imagine what might happen in the future: in three or six months' time, or further ahead. It is easier to take effective action, and perhaps to prevent violence, if you can anticipate and plan for any obstacles or changes that might arise.

 PROCEED: 'Start out from where you are and begin some new action'
Your current work can provide an entry point to work for peace and justice. There is no need to create special labels and categories, indeed it is often wiser not to. Also keep in mind that there are always many allies and collaborators out there who can help you on this journey, if only you can see them as such, and not as rivals or 'roadblocks' in the way of your progress.

The following chapter sets out some methods of analysing conflicts. It invites you to try some of them out and then move on to methods of building a strategy and taking action.

NOTES

1. Chris Mitchell, *The Structure of International Conflict*, Macmillan, London, 1981, chapter 1.

2. Dean Tjosvold, *The Conflict-Positive Organisation: Stimulate Diversity and Create Unity*, Addison Wesley, 1992.

3. We first encountered this diagram when working with Dr Hizkias Assefa, who is now based at Eastern Mennonite University, Harrisonburg, Virginia, USA.

4. This list is adapted from Working with Conflict course notes on 'Conflict Theories' by Hugo van der Merwe, Johannesburg, South Africa,1997, and from a paper by Marc Ross, 'Creating the conditions for peacemaking: theories of practice in ethnic conflict resoluton', *Ethnic and Racial Studies*, 2000.

5. African National Congress website: www.anc.org.za/ancdocs/history/

2-TOOLS FOR CONFLICT ANALYSIS

SUMMARY ■ In this chapter we begin by looking at the reasons for analysing conflict – analysis can be an intervention as well as a preparation for action.

We then set out nine specific tools for conflict analysis that can help you to:
- find out more about what is going on in a conflict
- identify areas where you need to know more
- begin to see ways in which you can influence the situation.

Introduction

In our work with people who are dealing with political and social conflicts we have found that gaining a better understanding of the dynamics, relationships and issues of the situation helps them to plan and carry out better actions and strategies. People gain this understanding in two ways:
- by carrying out a detailed analysis of the conflict from a variety of perspectives
- by exploring the specific issues and problems that relate to it.

In this chapter we explain and illustrate a number of practical tools and techniques that people have found useful in analysing the situations they are trying to address. They have been used by individuals working alone, by groups of people trying to find ways of addressing a conflict they were faced with, and by groups from different sides in a conflict who were trying to understand each other. Have a go at using these tools and techniques yourself. We have found that it is often only by trying them out in practice that people fully understand how they can help.

In Chapter 3 we shall examine some of the issues and themes that have arisen from analyses already carried out. These may also be issues for you, although you will probably identify others as you begin to analyse your own particular situation.

What is conflict analysis?

For many of those who are engaged in practical work on conflict, the concept of conflict analysis can seem quite remote from their own experience. It is sometimes seen as requiring objectivity and neutrality rather than personal experience and strong emotion. This is not our understanding of the concept. We see conflict analysis as a practical process of examining and understanding the reality of the conflict from a variety of perspectives. This understanding then forms the basis on which strategies can be developed and actions planned.

Conflict analysis can be done with the help of a number of simple, practical and adaptable tools and techniques. Some of the tools presented here are ones that we and our colleagues have invented, while others have been borrowed from other sources.

The tools and techniques explained in this chapter are not rigid processes. We would encourage you to adapt them, as necessary, to the particular circumstances being analysed. Don't feel that you have to follow our suggested steps if they don't seem to work in your own context. It is important to be as creative as possible in the approach you take.

WHY DO WE NEED TO ANALYSE CONFLICT?
- To understand the background and history of the situation as well as current events.
- To identify all the relevant groups involved, not just the main or obvious ones.
- To understand the perspectives of all these groups and to know more about how they relate to each other.
- To identify factors and trends that underpin conflicts.
- To learn from failures as well as successes.

Conflict analysis is not a one-time exercise. It must be an ongoing process as the situation

❂ Chuluke chuluke mwa njuchi umanena iyo yakuluma.
Bees can be many, but you must know the one that has stung you.
MALAWI

is developing, so that you can adapt your actions to changing factors, dynamics and circumstances.

Tools for analysing conflict situations

Some of the tools and techniques we suggest for conflict analysis may already be familiar to you from other sources. However, as you will see, here they have been adapted and used in new ways. Other tools may be unfamiliar to you, but all have been tried and used repeatedly and successfully in our courses and programmes, by people involved in many different types of conflict situation. In many cases groups have adapted the tools to suit a particular need. The examples given are based on the real experience of people around the world who have used the tools, adapting them to their own needs. Therefore each example is based on the perceptions of the people who worked on it.

On the following pages we shall explain nine of these tools for conflict analysis and illustrate how they have been used in specific cases:

- STAGES OF CONFLICT
- TIMELINES
- CONFLICT MAPPING
- THE ABC (ATTITUDE, BEHAVIOUR, CONTEXT) TRIANGLE
- THE ONION (OR THE DOUGHNUT)
- THE CONFLICT TREE
- FORCE-FIELD ANALYSIS
- PILLARS
- THE PYRAMID

The order in which you use the tools can be flexible, according to the situation you are analysing. Often they are best used in combination, with one tool highlighting certain factors or issues or points in time, which are then analysed with other tools. Remember that all the examples used reflect the perceptions of the people who drew them up. They are not meant to be the 'right' or only analysis. Your own

analysis, and that of the people you work with, will be informed by your own experiences, perceptions and values and may well be different. The tools presented here do not claim to be scientific, but they do open the way to inclusive and effective action.

ADAPTABILITY OF TOOLS

The tools have been applied effectively by groups of men and women from very different social backgrounds and varying levels of education – with pen and markers on paper, with chalk on a board or drawing with sticks in the dirt, using words, symbols and objects to represent the people, events or ideas concerned. We would encourage you to adapt the tools, as appropriate and necessary, in order to analyse the situation you are trying to address. We would be very pleased to hear about your adaptations. We are glad to receive any suggestions about how the tools can be used more effectively, so that we can pass them on to others.

PARTICIPATION

The tools can also be used to assist groups in developing a common understanding of a particular situation. This is useful when the analysis is being undertaken as a basis for action. By working together on the tools, individual members of an organisation or group can each see how the situation is understood from the viewpoint of the group as a whole, on the basis of the collective perceptions of its members. Where the group is made up of people from both sides of a conflict, the tools can provide a way for each side to begin to understand and respect the perspective of the other, while at the same time deepening its own analysis of what is happening.

LANGUAGES

These tools have been translated for use by colleagues in various parts of the world, so many of them are also available in French, Spanish, Russian, Khmer, Farsi, Somali and other languages (please contact RTC for more information).

**ROSALBA OYWA / GULU, UGANDA –
FOLLOWING A CONFLICT ANALYSIS WORKSHOP FOR COMMUNITY MEMBERS**

■ The main output I saw from the analysis was that it drew people together, because, to begin with, everybody saw that they were all being affected, whatever side they belonged to. Whether they sympathise with rebels, whether they are government supporters, whether they belong to any religious denominations, whether they call themselves anything – all of them are being affected in a similar way, so there is no point in them thinking that, by doing this, I am gaining, because there is no gain in this war. That was the key realisation.

Stages of conflict

Conflicts change over time, passing through different stages of activity, intensity, tension and violence. It is helpful to recognise these stages and use them together with other tools to analyse the dynamics and events that relate to each stage of the conflict.

The basic analysis comprises five different stages, which generally occur in the order given here (although there may be variations in specific situations) and may recur in similar cycles. These stages are:

• **PRE-CONFLICT:** This is the period when there is an incompatibility of goals between two or more parties, which could lead to open conflict. The conflict is hidden from general view, although one or more of the parties is likely to be aware of the potential for confrontation. There may be tension in relationships between the parties and/or a desire to avoid contact with each other at this stage.

• **CONFRONTATION:** At this stage the conflict has become more open. If only one side feels there is a problem, its supporters may begin to engage in demonstrations or other confrontational behaviour. Occasional fighting or other low levels of violence may break out between the sides. Each side may be gathering its resources and perhaps finding allies with the expectation of increasing confrontation and violence. Relationships between the sides are becoming very strained, leading to a polarisation between the supporters of each side.

• **CRISIS:** This is the peak of the conflict, when the tension and/or violence is most intense. In a large-scale conflict, this is the period of war, when people on all sides are being killed. Normal communication between the sides has probably ceased. Public statements tend to be in the form of accusations made against the other side(s).

• **OUTCOME:** One way or another the crisis will lead to an outcome. One side might defeat the other(s), or perhaps call a cease-fire (if it is a war). One party might surrender or give in to the demands of the other party. The parties may agree to negotiations, either with or without the help of a mediator. An authority or other more powerful third party might impose an end to the fighting. In any case, at this stage the levels of tension, confrontation and violence decrease somewhat with the possibility of a settlement.

• **POST-CONFLICT:** Finally, the situation is resolved in a way that leads to an ending of any violent confrontation, to a decrease in tensions and to more normal relationships between the parties. However, if the issues and problems arising from their incompatible goals have not been adequately addressed, this stage could eventually lead back into another pre-conflict situation.

Figure 2.1 on the following page gives an example of how this tool was used to look at stages of conflict in Central and Western Uganda as compared to stages occurring in

**STAGES OF
CONFLICT**
WHAT IS IT?
▶ *A graphic that shows the increasing and decreasing intensity of conflict plotted along a particular timescale.*
PURPOSE
▶ *To see the stages and cycles of escalation and de-escalation of conflict.*
▶ *To discuss where the situation is now.*
▶ *To try to predict future patterns of escalation with the aim of preventing these from occurring.*
▶ *To identify a period of time to be analysed later using other tools.*
WHEN TO USE IT
▶ *Early in a process of analysis to identify patterns in the conflict.*
▶ *Later to help in the process of strategy-building.*
VARIATION
▶ *Analyse stages from the viewpoints of different sides or different parts of a country in conflict.*
▶ *Use a fire analogy, seeing these stages as the increasing and decreasing intensity of a fire. (See* Playing With Fire *by Nic Fine & Fiona Macbeth – details in Chapter 10.)*

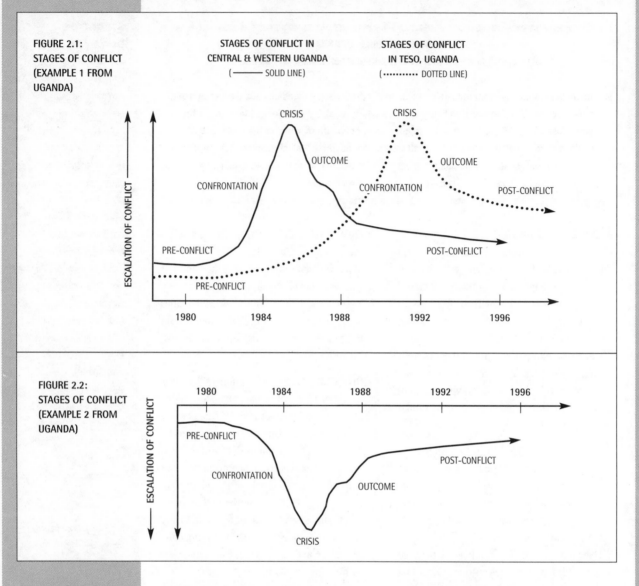

**FIGURE 2.1:
STAGES OF CONFLICT
(EXAMPLE 1 FROM
UGANDA)**

STAGES OF CONFLICT IN
CENTRAL & WESTERN UGANDA
(—— SOLID LINE)

STAGES OF CONFLICT
IN TESO, UGANDA
(·········· DOTTED LINE)

CRISIS

CRISIS

OUTCOME

OUTCOME

POST-CONFLICT

CONFRONTATION

CONFRONTATION

PRE-CONFLICT

POST-CONFLICT

PRE-CONFLICT

ESCALATION OF CONFLICT

1980   1984   1988   1992   1996

**FIGURE 2.2:
STAGES OF CONFLICT
(EXAMPLE 2 FROM
UGANDA)**

1980   1984   1988   1992   1996

ESCALATION OF CONFLICT

PRE-CONFLICT

CONFRONTATION

POST-CONFLICT

OUTCOME

CRISIS

the Teso region of Northeast Uganda during the same time period.

This example illustrates the fact that the conflict was more intense (and perceived as such) in Central and Western Uganda during 1984–6, whereas the confrontation and crisis occurred later (1988–92) in the Teso region. So, while one part of the country felt relatively peaceful, another was in the midst of violent war and extreme insecurity, and vice versa. This suggests the need to analyse both of these periods in order to understand the conflict from the perspective of both parts of the country.

A variation in the use of this tool is to show the escalation of conflict in a downward direction, as a negative movement in the situation, and the de-escalation in the upward direction. Figure 2.2 uses this method to show the stages for Central and Western Uganda.

Timelines

In principle, a timeline is a very simple tool. It is a graphic that shows events plotted against time. It lists dates (years, months or days, depending on the scale) and depicts events in chronological order. You could use this method

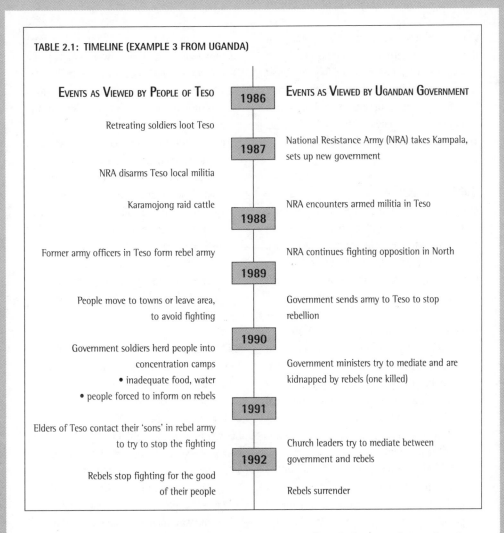

TABLE 2.1: TIMELINE (EXAMPLE 3 FROM UGANDA)

EVENTS AS VIEWED BY PEOPLE OF TESO		EVENTS AS VIEWED BY UGANDAN GOVERNMENT
	1986	
Retreating soldiers loot Teso		
	1987	National Resistance Army (NRA) takes Kampala, sets up new government
NRA disarms Teso local militia		
Karamojong raid cattle		NRA encounters armed militia in Teso
	1988	
Former army officers in Teso form rebel army		NRA continues fighting opposition in North
	1989	
People move to towns or leave area, to avoid fighting		Government sends army to Teso to stop rebellion
	1990	
Government soldiers herd people into concentration camps • inadequate food, water • people forced to inform on rebels		Government ministers try to mediate and are kidnapped by rebels (one killed)
	1991	
Elders of Teso contact their 'sons' in rebel army to try to stop the fighting		Church leaders try to mediate between government and rebels
	1992	
Rebels stop fighting for the good of their people		Rebels surrender

to show a succession of events in your own life, for example, or the history of your country. In this case, you can use timelines to show the history of a conflict.

In a conflict, groups of people often have completely different experiences and perceptions: they see and understand the conflict in quite distinct ways. They often have different histories. People on opposing sides of the conflict may note or emphasise different events, describe them differently, and attach contrasting emotions to them.

The aim of using timelines in this way is not to try to arrive at a 'correct' or 'objective' history but to understand the perceptions of the people involved. For this reason, the different events described by opposing groups are an important element in understanding the conflict.

The timeline is also a way for people to learn about each other's history and perceptions of the situation. And in discussing their different perceptions of the conflict, and the events that each group commemorates, they will develop a richer understanding of their shared situation.

USING A TIMELINE

A timeline as we use it here is not primarily a research tool, but a way to prompt discussion and learning. In conflict it is to be expected that people will disagree about which events are important and how to describe them. We aim to reach a point where the parties in a conflict can accept that others may have valid perceptions, even if these are opposed to their own.

Table 2.1 outlines an example of how this tool was used to look at events in Uganda as

TIMELINE
WHAT IS IT?
▶ A graphic that shows events plotted against a particular time-scale.
PURPOSE
▶ To show different views of history in a conflict.
▶ To clarify and understand each side's perception of events.
▶ To identify which events are most important to each side.
WHEN TO USE IT
▶ Early in a process, along with other analytical tools.
▶ Later in the process to help in strategy-building.
▶ When people disagree about events, or don't know each other's history.
▶ As a way of helping people to accept their own perspective as only part of the 'truth'.
VARIATIONS
▶ Used by the parties themselves and shared with each other.
▶ Followed by a discussion about events that are highlighted by each side.
▶ Adding a line for peace initiatives during the same time period.

viewed by the people of the Teso region and by the national government. Note how each side remembers different events and has a different interpretation of events. In constructing timelines from different perspectives of your own conflicts, you too may find this to be the case. Try doing this and see whether you agree.

Conflict mapping

Mapping is a technique used to represent a conflict graphically, placing the parties in relation both to the problem and to each other. When people with different viewpoints map their situation together, they learn about each other's experiences and perceptions.

HOW TO MAP A CONFLICT SITUATION

1. Decide **what** you want to map, **when**, and from what **point of view**. Choose a particular moment in a specific situation. If you try to map the whole of a regional political conflict in detail, the result may be so time-consuming, so large and so complex that it is not really helpful.

   It is often useful to do several maps of the same situation from a variety of viewpoints and see how the different parties might perceive it. Trying to reconcile the differing viewpoints is the reality of working on the conflict. It is a good discipline to ask whether those who hold a particular view would actually accept your description of their relationships with the other parties.

2. **Don't forget to place yourself and your organisation on the map.** Putting yourself on the map is a reminder that you are part of the situation, not above it, even when you analyse it. You and your organisation are perceived in certain ways by others. You may have contacts and relationships that offer opportunities and openings for work with the parties involved in the conflict.

3. Mapping is dynamic — it reflects a particular point in a **changing situation** and points towards **action**. This kind of analysis should offer new possibilities. What can be done?

Who can best do it? When is the best moment? What groundwork needs to be laid beforehand, what structures built afterwards? These are some of the questions you should ask as you are carrying out the mapping.

4. In addition to the 'objective' aspects, it is useful to map the **issues** between parties that are in conflict. Why does the conflict exist? These can be put in a box, as we have done in the following examples, or you may have a better way of showing what the issues are.

   It may also be useful to think about the position of the conflicting parties. What are their views of the other groups involved in the situation?

EXAMPLES OF CONFLICT MAPPING

Here we look at three examples of Conflict Mapping:

■ The first example, Figure 2.3, shows what a basic conflict map might look like. Try making a map of a situation you are currently working on. Some questions you might ask are:
• Who are the main parties in this conflict?
• What other parties are involved or connected in some way, including marginalised groups and external parties?
• What are the relationships between all these parties and how can these be represented on the map? Alliances? Close contacts? Broken relationships? Confrontation?
• Are there any key issues between the parties that should be mentioned on the map?
• Where are you and your organisation in relation to these parties? Do you have any special relationships that might offer openings for working on this conflict situation?

■ A second example, this time of a conflict within a family, is shown in Figure 2.4. The primary conflict examined here is between a father and daughter, over whether or not to go ahead with an arranged marriage. Notice the thickness of the line that is used to represent

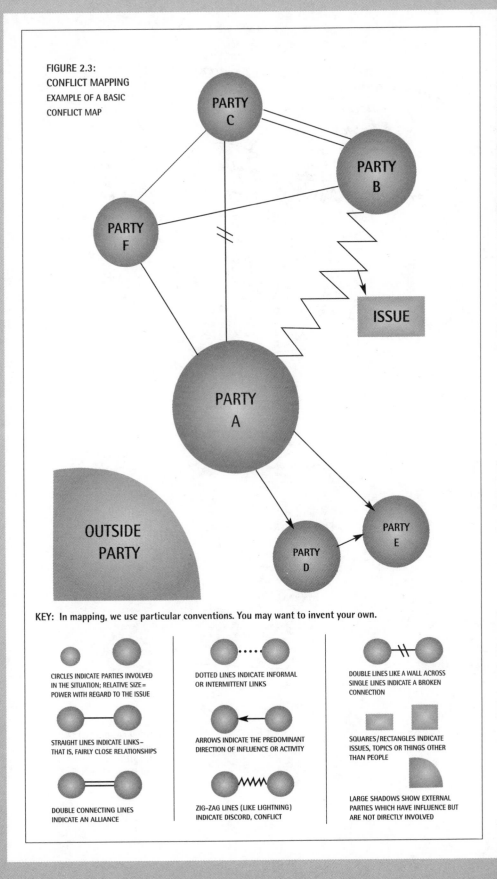

FIGURE 2.3:
CONFLICT MAPPING
EXAMPLE OF A BASIC
CONFLICT MAP

PARTY C

PARTY B

PARTY F

ISSUE

PARTY A

PARTY D

PARTY E

OUTSIDE PARTY

KEY: In mapping, we use particular conventions. You may want to invent your own.

CIRCLES INDICATE PARTIES INVOLVED IN THE SITUATION; RELATIVE SIZE = POWER WITH REGARD TO THE ISSUE

DOTTED LINES INDICATE INFORMAL OR INTERMITTENT LINKS

DOUBLE LINES LIKE A WALL ACROSS SINGLE LINES INDICATE A BROKEN CONNECTION

STRAIGHT LINES INDICATE LINKS – THAT IS, FAIRLY CLOSE RELATIONSHIPS

ARROWS INDICATE THE PREDOMINANT DIRECTION OF INFLUENCE OR ACTIVITY

SQUARES/RECTANGLES INDICATE ISSUES, TOPICS OR THINGS OTHER THAN PEOPLE

DOUBLE CONNECTING LINES INDICATE AN ALLIANCE

ZIG-ZAG LINES (LIKE LIGHTNING) INDICATE DISCORD, CONFLICT

LARGE SHADOWS SHOW EXTERNAL PARTIES WHICH HAVE INFLUENCE BUT ARE NOT DIRECTLY INVOLVED

CONFLICT MAPPING

WHAT IS IT?
▶ *A visual technique for showing the relationships between parties in conflict.*

PURPOSE
▶ *To understand the situation better.*
▶ *To see more clearly the relationships between parties.*
▶ *To clarify where the power lies.*
▶ *To check the balance of one's own activity or contacts.*
▶ *To see where allies or potential allies are.*
▶ *To identify openings for intervention or action.*
▶ *To evaluate what has been done already.*

WHEN TO USE IT
▶ *Early in a process, along with other analytical tools.*
▶ *Later, to identify possible entry points for action or to help the process of strategy-building.*

VARIATIONS
▶ *Geographical maps showing the areas and parties involved.*
▶ *Mapping of issues.*
▶ *Mapping of power alignments.*
▶ *Mapping of needs and fears.*
▶ *As a human sculpture to bring out feelings and relationships.*

FIGURE 2.4: CONFLICT
MAPPING / EXAMPLE 2
CONFLICT WITHIN THE FAMILY

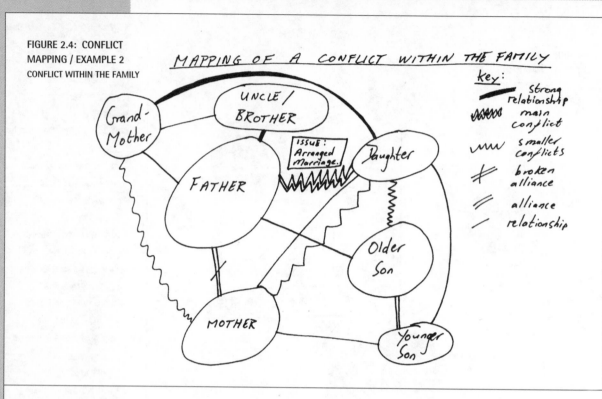

MAPPING OF A CONFLICT WITHIN THE FAMILY

key:
— strong relationship
〰〰〰 main conflict
⌁⌁⌁ smaller conflicts
⫽ broken alliance
∥ alliance
/ relationship

ISSUE: Arranged Marriage.

FIGURE 2.5: CONFLICT
MAPPING / EXAMPLE 3
AFGHANISTAN, OCTOBER 1999

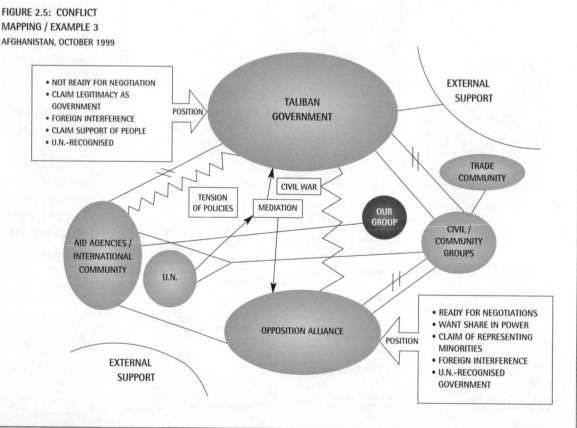

POSITION
• NOT READY FOR NEGOTIATION
• CLAIM LEGITIMACY AS GOVERNMENT
• FOREIGN INTERFERENCE
• CLAIM SUPPORT OF PEOPLE
• U.N.-RECOGNISED

TALIBAN GOVERNMENT

EXTERNAL SUPPORT

TRADE COMMUNITY

TENSION OF POLICIES

CIVIL WAR

MEDIATION

OUR GROUP

CIVIL / COMMUNITY GROUPS

AID AGENCIES / INTERNATIONAL COMMUNITY

U.N.

OPPOSITION ALLIANCE

POSITION
• READY FOR NEGOTIATIONS
• WANT SHARE IN POWER
• CLAIM OF REPRESENTING MINORITIES
• FOREIGN INTERFERENCE
• U.N.-RECOGNISED GOVERNMENT

EXTERNAL SUPPORT

the strength of the relationship between the grandmother and the daughter, the broken relationship between the mother and father, and the ways in which the two brothers are divided over who to support in the conflict despite the bond between them. This example shows how the technique of mapping can be adapted to suit a range of situations.

Although this is an example of how mapping can be used to represent parties within a family dispute, it is a technique that can also be used to depict large-scale conflicts – for example, conflict between the members of a community, or even a national or international conflict.

■ The third example, Figure 2.5, shows a mapping analysis of Afghanistan from the perspective of a small, locally based NGO. It illustrates the conflict between the Taliban government and the opposition forces within Afghanistan. Looking at the mapping, it is easy to identify the main parties involved in the context, as well as the relationships between them. While the conflict relationship between the Taliban and the opposition (represented by the bold jagged line) is the core issue in the context and the basis for the civil war, certain other relationships are also important and need to be brought into focus when analysing this situation.

You can draw boxes, as shown, to indicate the viewpoints of the main parties. This will show how they see the context differently, and thus help you to find entry points for action to address the conflict. The other, less powerful parties, such as the civil groups and the trade community, may not appear to be influencing the situation directly, but by including them in your map you are making sure that all possible means of intervention are considered. The organisation from whose perspective this map is drawn has been placed on the map where it sees itself in the context – 'our group'. It is related to the aid agencies and has strong links with civil and community groups. (We will come back to this example in Chapter 4 to examine how a map such as this can be used to identify entry points for taking action.)

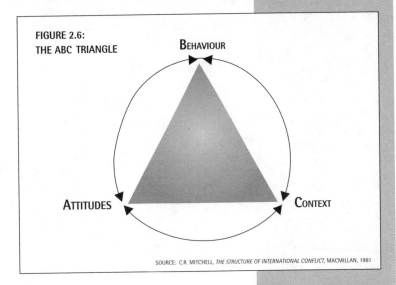

**FIGURE 2.6:
THE ABC TRIANGLE**

BEHAVIOUR

ATTITUDES   CONTEXT

SOURCE: C.R. MITCHELL, *THE STRUCTURE OF INTERNATIONAL CONFLICT*, MACMILLAN, 1981

Mapping on its own, however, cannot provide all of the answers. As with all these tools, it only provides partial insight into the nature of a conflict. Often it is the issues underlying the observed relationships that lie at the root. The following tools offer some insight into how to begin to uncover those underlying causes.

The ABC Triangle

This analysis is based on the premise that conflicts have three major components: the **context** or situation, the **behaviour** of those involved and their **attitudes**. Figure 2.6 represents these graphically as the corners of a triangle.

These three factors influence each other, hence the arrows leading from one to another. For example, a context that ignores the demands of one group is likely to lead to an attitude of frustration, which in turn may result in protests. This behaviour might then lead to a context of further denial of rights, contributing to greater frustration, perhaps even anger, which could erupt into violence. Work that is done to change the context (by making sure that demands are acknowledged), to reduce the level of frustration (by helping people to focus on the long-term nature of their struggle) or to provide outlets for behaviours that are not violent will all contribute to reducing the levels of tension.

ABC TRIANGLE
WHAT IS IT?
▶ *An analysis of factors related to Attitude, Behaviour and Context for each of the major parties.*
PURPOSE
▶ *To identify these three sets of factors for each of the major parties.*
▶ *To analyse how these influence each other.*
▶ *To relate these to the needs and fears of each party.*
▶ *To identify a starting point for intervention in the situation.*
WHEN TO USE IT
▶ *Early in the process to gain a greater insight into what motivates the different parties.*
▶ *Later to identify what factors might be addressed by an intervention.*
▶ *To reveal how a change in one aspect might affect another.*
VARIATIONS
▶ *After listing issues for each of the 3 components, indicate a key need or fear of that party in the middle of the triangle.*

TABLE 2.2: ABC ANALYSIS OF INTERNAL ORGANISATIONAL CONFLICT –
EXAMPLE: CONFLICT BETWEEN CAPITAL-BASED STAFF AND PROVINCIAL FIELD STAFF OF AN ORGANISATION IN CAMBODIA

I. CAPITAL CITY PERSONNEL:

BEHAVIOURS
B

CITY VIEW OF PROVINCIAL PEOPLE
Not smart, coarse manners
Don't know how to communicate
No initiative, no ideas
Do nothing constructive
Work hard but unproductive

CITY VIEW OF THEMSELVES
Sophisticated
Act with long-term vision
Participatory approach
Sometimes too impatient

KEY NEED: A SHARED APPROACH

ATTITUDES A

CITY VIEW OF PROVINCIAL PEOPLE
Tough, obstinate
Don't want to change
Hierarchical, narrow outlook
Resentful, pitiable
Always think they are right
Jealous, resistant

CITY VIEW OF THEMSELVES
Modern, open-minded
Can see the big picture
Sensitive to the needs of others
Occasionally superior

C CONTEXT

CAPITAL CITY PERSONNEL
More high school graduates in the capital
Education system better in the capital
Higher education institutions all city based
Longer history of NGO work in the capital
Political/military security better in the capital
Better communication systems in the capital
Opportunities for recreation better in the capital
More Khmer returnees based in the city
Easier living conditions in the capital
More job opportunities in the capital
Cost of living higher in the capital
More foreign passport holders in the city
Wider exposure to outside views in the capital
Salaries are below expectations

II. PROVINCIAL FIELD STAFF:

BEHAVIOURS
B

PROVINCIAL VIEW OF CITY PEOPLE
Talk a lot; are always right
Look down on us
Always stay in hotels, not homes
Afraid of the countryside
Avoid the provinces
Bossy and arrogant

PROVINCIAL VIEW OF THEMSELVES
Hardworking
Care about people
Resist interference
Dealing with reality
Trying their best

KEY NEED: A SHARED APPROACH

ATTITUDES A

PROVINCIAL VIEW OF CITY PEOPLE
Proud
Inattentive, ignorant
Spoilt
Dismissive
Think they are superior

PROVINCIAL VIEW OF THEMSELVES
Aware of the reality
Traditional
Know what is needed
Resent outside involvement
Feel marginalised by city
Feel unrespected

C CONTEXT

PROVINCIAL FIELD STAFF
More political oppression in the provinces
Inattentive, ignorant
Military presence strong and 'felt' in the provinces
Personal security better in in provinces
Limited capacity in the provinces
Salaries are higher in the capital
All salaries are below expectations
Better communication systems in the city
More Khmer returnees based in the city
Easier living conditions in the capital.
More job opportunities in the capital

HOW TO USE THIS TOOL

1. Draw up a separate ABC Triangle for each of the major parties in the conflict situation.
2. On each triangle, list the key issues related to **attitude**, **behaviour** and **context** from the viewpoint of that party. (If the parties are participating in this analysis, then they can each make a triangle from their own perspective.)
3. Indicate for each party what you think are their most important needs and/or fears in the middle of their own triangle. This will be YOUR perception.
4. Compare the triangles, noting similarities and differences between the perceptions of the parties.

In the case of any given conflict, different parties have different experiences and contrasting perceptions. For these reasons, they are likely to attribute the conflict to different causes. One side may , for example, claim that the root problem is injustice, while another side may feel that it is insecurity. Each group is focused on the issues that concern it most, and particularly the areas where it is suffering most. All of these causes and issues are real and important, and all will have to be addressed before the conflict can be resolved and the situation improved. Meanwhile, a great deal of energy may go into attacking those who see different causes or concentrate on different issues. One challenge is to try to help everyone involved to see that all the different issues are part of the problem, although certainly some will be more urgent or important than others.

In using the ABC Triangle it is important to be sure about whose perception the analysis is based upon. You could do the analysis entirely on your own perception of the realities in the conflict if you are closely involved in it. Otherwise, it will be important to put yourself in the shoes of each of the main parties and look at the issues in the conflict as they see it in terms of 'context', 'behaviour' and 'attitude'.

Table 2.2 analyses the tension between rural and urban members of an international aid agency in Cambodia. While the context is similar for both groups they emphasise different things and each views the behaviour and attitudes of the other quite differently.

The Onion

Figure 2.7 is based on the analogy of an onion and its layers. The outer layer contains the **positions** that we take publicly, for all to see and hear. Underlying these are our **interests** – what we want to achieve from a particular situation. Finally, at the core are the most important **needs** we require to be satisfied. It is useful to carry out this Onion analysis for each of the parties involved.

In times of stability, when relationships are good and trust is high, our actions and strategies may stem from our most basic **needs.** We may be willing to disclose these needs to others and to discuss them openly, if we trust the others. And through analysis and empathy, they may be able to grasp our needs even before we disclose them.

In more volatile or dangerous situations, when there is mistrust between people, we may want to keep our basic needs hidden. To inform others of them would reveal our vulnerability and perhaps give them extra power over us. But if we hide things from the other side,

THE ONION
WHAT IS IT?
▸ A way of analysing what different parties to a conflict are saying.
PURPOSE
▸ To move beyond the public position of each party and understand each party's interests and needs.
▸ To find the common ground between groups that can become the basis for further discussions.
WHEN TO USE IT
▸ As part of an analysis to understand the dynamics of a conflict situation.
▸ In preparation for facilitating dialogue between groups in a conflict.
▸ As part of a mediation or negotiation process.
VARIATIONS
▸ Some groups prefer to see the graphic as a doughnut rather than an onion.

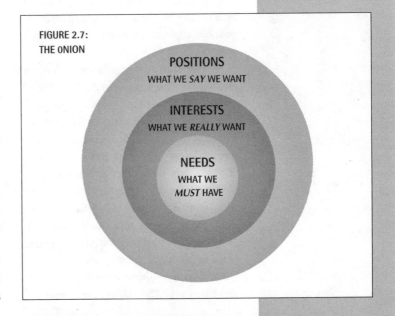

FIGURE 2.7:
THE ONION

POSITIONS
WHAT WE *SAY* WE WANT

INTERESTS
WHAT WE *REALLY* WANT

NEEDS
WHAT WE *MUST* HAVE

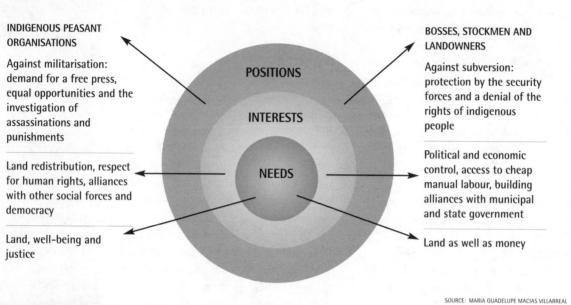

FIGURE 2.8: THE ONION – AN EXAMPLE FROM CHIAPAS, MEXICO

INDIGENOUS PEASANT ORGANISATIONS

Against militarisation: demand for a free press, equal opportunities and the investigation of assassinations and punishments

Land redistribution, respect for human rights, alliances with other social forces and democracy

Land, well-being and justice

POSITIONS

INTERESTS

NEEDS

BOSSES, STOCKMEN AND LANDOWNERS

Against subversion: protection by the security forces and a denial of the rights of indigenous people

Political and economic control, access to cheap manual labour, building alliances with municipal and state government

Land as well as money

SOURCE: MARIA GUADELUPE MACIAS VILLARREAL

they are also less likely to be able to grasp our needs through analysis or empathy, as a result of lack of knowledge and because mistrust changes people's perceptions of each other.

Thus, in a situation of conflict and instability, actions may no longer come directly from needs. People may look at the more collective and abstract level of **interests** and base their actions on these. When those interests are under attack, they may take up and defend a **position** that is still further removed from their basic needs.

This type of analysis is useful for parties who are involved in negotiation, to clarify for themselves their own needs, interests and positions. Then, as they plan their strategies for the negotiation, they can decide how much of the interior 'layers' – interests and needs – they want to reveal to the other parties involved.

As suggested above, people may choose to reveal more when the level of trust has risen. But, even if they are slow to do this to the other side(s), at least they will gain awareness of the needs that are most important to them – enabling them to identify those interests on which they might be willing to compromise.

Thus, in the example shown in Figure 2.8 one group of people (indigenous peasant organisations) has a **need** for land, well-being and justice. Their **interest** is in land redistribution, respect for human rights, alliances with other social forces and democracy. But, because of the crisis in which they are involved, what they express publicly is their **position** – they are against militarisation and demand a free press, equal opportunities and the investigation of assassinations and punishments.

The second group of people (bosses, stockmen and landowners) also have a **need** for land, in addition to money. Their **interest** is in political and economic control, access to cheap manual labour, and building alliances with the state and municipal government. Their publicly expressed **position** is strongly against subversion, protection by the security forces and denial of the rights of indigenous people.

It is easy to see how groups that are locked into defending their positions will find it very difficult to find any common ground. This might, then, mean that that their actual needs are not met, and are unlikely to be met in the future.

The point of the Onion is to show graphically the possibility of peeling away as many as possible of the layers that build up as a result of conflict, instability and mistrust, in order to try to meet the underlying needs that form the basis of people's individual and group actions.

A long-term goal is to improve communication and trust to the point where people can reveal their own real needs and also understand and try to meet each other's needs. However, even before this point is reached people can be challenged to examine whether their actions and strategies are a good way to further their own interests and meet their own needs.

The Conflict Tree

This tool is best used within groups – i.e. collectively rather than as an individual exercise. If you are familiar with the 'Problem Tree' from development and community work, you will recognise that we have borrowed and adapted this for use in conflict analysis.

In many conflicts there will be a range of opinions concerning questions such as:
• What is the core problem?
• What are the root causes?
• What are the effects that have resulted from this problem?
• What is the most important issue for our group to address?

The Conflict Tree offers a method for a team, organisation, group or community to identify the issues that each of them sees as important and then sort these into three categories: (1) core problem(s), (2) causes and (3) effects.

HOW TO USE THIS TOOL

1. Draw a picture of a tree, including its roots, trunk and branches – on a large sheet of paper, a chalkboard, a flipchart, on the side of a building or on the ground.

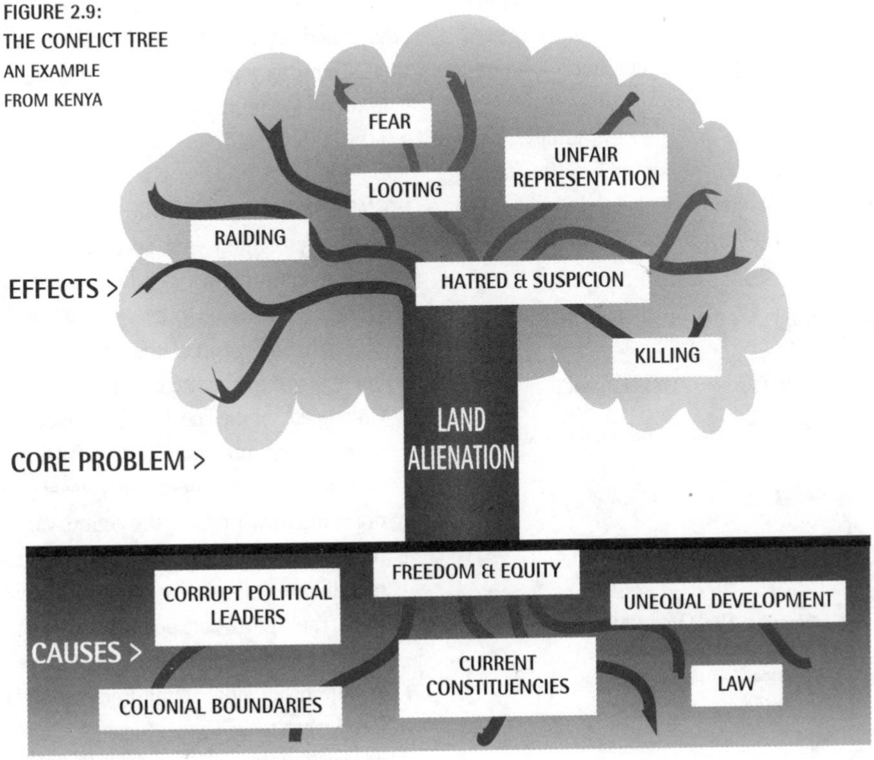

THE CONFLICT TREE

WHAT IS IT?
▸ A graphic tool, using the image of a tree to sort key conflict issues.

PURPOSE
▸ To stimulate discussion about causes and effects in a conflict.
▸ To help a group to agree on the core problem.
▸ To assist a group or a team to make decisions about priorities for addressing conflict issues.
▸ To relate causes and effects to each other and to the focus of the organisation.

WHEN TO USE IT
▸ With a group having difficulty in agreeing about the core problem in their situation.
▸ With a team who need to decide about which conflict issues they should try to address.

VARIATIONS
▸ Can be used to explore values. See Chapter 5 for more on this.

FIGURE 2.9:
THE CONFLICT TREE
AN EXAMPLE
FROM KENYA

EFFECTS >

FEAR
LOOTING
UNFAIR REPRESENTATION
RAIDING
HATRED & SUSPICION
KILLING

CORE PROBLEM >

LAND ALIENATION

CAUSES >

FREEDOM & EQUITY
CORRUPT POLITICAL LEADERS
UNEQUAL DEVELOPMENT
CURRENT CONSTITUENCIES
COLONIAL BOUNDARIES
LAW

WHAT IS IT?

▸ A tool for analysing both positive and negative forces in a conflict.

PURPOSE

▸ To identify those forces which either support or hinder a plan of action or a desired change.

▸ To assess the strength of these forces and our own abilities to influence them.

▸ To determine ways of increasing the positive forces or decreasing the negative forces.

WHEN TO USE IT

▸ When planning an action or strategy, to clarify the forces that might support or hinder what you intend to do.

• While implementing a strategy of change, to assess the strength of other forces and your ability to influence these.

2. Give each person several index cards, or similar paper, on which to write a word or two, or draw a symbol or picture, indicating a key issue in the conflict as they see it.

3. Invite people to attach their cards to the tree:
 • **on the trunk**, if they think it is the core problem,
 • **on the roots**, if they think it is a root cause,
 • **on the branches**, if they see it as an effect.

4. After all the cards have been placed on the tree, someone will need to facilitate a discussion so that the group can come to some agreement about the placement of issues, particularly the core problem.

5. An optional next step is to ask people to visualise their own organisation as a living organism (e.g. a bird, a worm, ivy) and place this on the tree in relation to the issues it is currently addressing. Is current work focusing mainly on the consequences, the roots, or the core problem?

6. If an agreement has been reached, people may want to decide which issues they wish to address first in dealing with the conflict.

7. This process may take a long time and need to be continued in further group meetings.

The Conflict Tree pictured in Figure 2.9 on page 29 is what the tree looked like after names of issues or problems were added by members of a community in Wajir, Northeast Kenya.

They agreed that, in their situation, 'Land Alienation' was the core problem, with other issues being either causes or effects.

You will find when you try this tool that many issues can be seen as both causes and effects of the conflict. For example, scarcity of food is often a cause of conflict between groups, but it is also often the consequence of normal cultivation being disrupted by violence. This can form the basis for a useful discussion about the cycle of violence and the way in which communities can become trapped by conflict. There is no reason why, graphically, the same issues cannot appear in both places.

Force-Field Analysis

This tool can be used to identify the different forces influencing a conflict. Whenever you are taking some action to bring about change, there will be other forces that are either supporting or hindering what you are trying to achieve. This tool offers a way of identifying these positive and negative forces and trying to assess their strengths and weaknesses. It can also help you to see more clearly what is maintaining the status quo.

HOW TO USE THIS TOOL

1. Begin by naming your specific objective, i.e. the action you intend to take or the change you desire to achieve. Write this objective at the top of the page and draw a line down the centre of the page.

2. On one side of the line, list all the forces that seem to support and assist the action or change that is to happen. Next to each one draw an arrow towards the centre, varying the length and/or thickness of the arrow to indicate the relative strength of each force. These arrows are pointing in the direction of the desired change.

3. On the other side of the line, list all the forces that seem to restrain or hinder the desired action or change from happening. Next to each one draw an arrow pointing

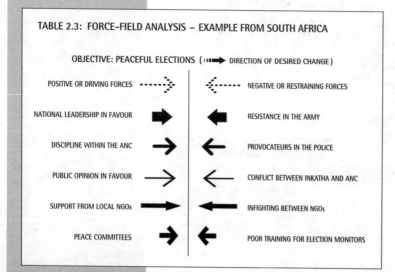

TABLE 2.3: FORCE-FIELD ANALYSIS – EXAMPLE FROM SOUTH AFRICA

OBJECTIVE: PEACEFUL ELECTIONS (▐▬▶ DIRECTION OF DESIRED CHANGE)

POSITIVE OR DRIVING FORCES			NEGATIVE OR RESTRAINING FORCES
NATIONAL LEADERSHIP IN FAVOUR			RESISTANCE IN THE ARMY
DISCIPLINE WITHIN THE ANC			PROVOCATEURS IN THE POLICE
PUBLIC OPINION IN FAVOUR			CONFLICT BETWEEN INKATHA AND ANC
SUPPORT FROM LOCAL NGOs			INFIGHTING BETWEEN NGOs
PEACE COMMITTEES			POOR TRAINING FOR ELECTION MONITORS

back towards the centre, against the direction of desired change. Again, the length and/or thickness of each arrow can indicate its relative strength.

4. Now, consider which of these forces you can influence, either to strengthen the positive forces or to minimise in some way the negative forces, so as to increase the likelihood of the desired change taking place.

5. You may want to review your plan of action and make modifications to your strategy in order to build upon the strengths of positive forces, while also trying to minimise, or remove, the effects of the negative ones.

Table 2.3, left, is an example of Force-Field Analysis, based on a particular situation in one part of South Africa during the period leading up to the national elections in 1994.

In this table the estimated strength of each force is indicated by the thickness of the arrows. After the analysis had been carried out, the following strategies were suggested:
• National political leadership to exercise more control over local membership, and also over negative elements in the army and police.
• Bring representatives of Inkatha and the ANC together in Peace Committees.
• Include members of the army and the police in Peace Committees at all levels.

• Mobilise public support through national media campaign.
• Provide better training for election monitors – recruit more of them with the help of NGOs.

Pillars

This graphic tool is based on the premise that some situations are not really stable, but are 'held up' by a range of factors or forces – the 'pillars'. If we can identify these pillars and try to find ways to remove them or minimise their effect on the situation, we will be able to topple a negative situation and build a positive one.

HOW TO USE THIS TOOL

1. Identify the unstable situation (conflict, problem or injustice) and show this as an inverted triangle standing on one point.
2. Next identify the forces or factors seeming to maintain this situation. Show them as the 'supporting pillars' on both sides of the triangle.
3. Consider how each of these pillars might be weakened or removed from the situation. Briefly list your strategies for each pillar.
4. Also consider what stable situation could replace this unstable one.

The example in Figure 2.10 is from Afghanistan. The problem to be analysed and addressed is

PILLARS

WHAT IS IT?
▸ *A graphic illustration of elements or forces that are 'holding up' an unstable situation.*

PURPOSE
▸ *To understand how structures are sustained.*
▸ *To identify factors that are maintaining an undesirable situation.*
▸ *To consider ways to weaken or remove these negative factors, or perhaps to change them to more positive forces.*

WHEN TO USE IT
▸ *When it is not clear what forces are maintaining an unstable situation.*
▸ *When a situation seems to be 'stuck' in a kind of structural injustice.*

VARIATIONS
▸ *Draw the changes that have already happened, and what would sustain the future you hope for.*

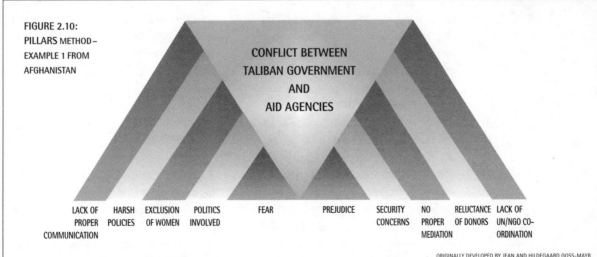

FIGURE 2.10:
PILLARS METHOD –
EXAMPLE 1 FROM
AFGHANISTAN

CONFLICT BETWEEN
TALIBAN GOVERNMENT
AND
AID AGENCIES

LACK OF PROPER COMMUNICATION — HARSH POLICIES — EXCLUSION OF WOMEN — POLITICS INVOLVED — FEAR — PREJUDICE — SECURITY CONCERNS — NO PROPER MEDIATION — RELUCTANCE OF DONORS — LACK OF UN/NGO CO-ORDINATION

ORIGINALLY DEVELOPED BY JEAN AND HILDEGAARD GOSS-MAYR

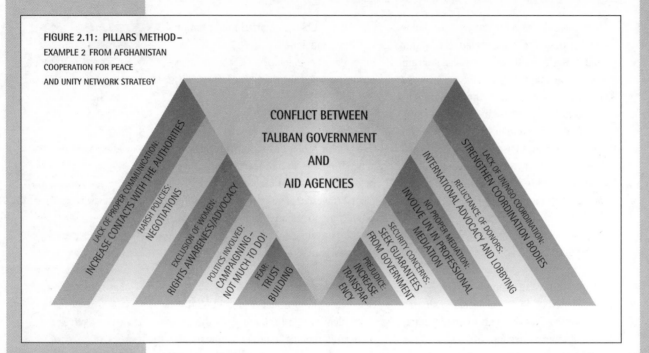

FIGURE 2.11: PILLARS METHOD –
EXAMPLE 2 FROM AFGHANISTAN
COOPERATION FOR PEACE
AND UNITY NETWORK STRATEGY

CONFLICT BETWEEN
TALIBAN GOVERNMENT
AND
AID AGENCIES

LACK OF PROPER COMMUNICATION:
INCREASE CONTACTS WITH THE AUTHORITIES

HARSH POLICIES:
NEGOTIATIONS

EXCLUSION OF WOMEN:
RIGHTS AWARENESS/ADVOCACY

POLITICS INVOLVED:
CAMPAIGNING –
NOT MUCH TO DO!

FEAR:
TRUST
BUILDING

PREJUDICE:
INCREASE
TRANSPAR-
ENCY

SECURITY CONCERNS:
SEEK GUARANTEES
FROM GOVERNMENT

NO PROPER MEDIATION:
INVOLVE UN IN PROFESSIONAL
MEDIATION

RELUCTANCE OF DONORS:
INTERNATIONAL ADVOCACY AND LOBBYING

LACK OF UN/NGO COORDINATION:
STRENGTHEN COORDINATION BODIES

the conflict between the Taliban authorities and the aid agencies. On one side the pillars holding up the conflict are mostly those caused by, or relating to, the authorities, e.g. harsh policies, exclusion of women, and fear. On the other side, there are pillars representing lack of coordination, security concerns and prejudice, which pertain directly to the aid agencies. Some of the pillars might be more crucial than others, and some are more difficult to influence than others. It may be that work will have to be done by colleagues at other levels to influence, for instance, the politics concerning the situations and policies of the donor countries. However, the situation will improve if any of these pillars is weakened or removed.

Having looked at the pillars that support the conflict, problem or unjust situation, the next step is to devise definite actions or strategies that could address each pillar and weaken or remove it. The Cooperation for Peace and Unity Network in Afghanistan, who analysed the situation, proceeded as in Figure 2.11. In this example, there is one suggested solution for each problem. In fact, you could think of many other options and suggest more ways of tackling each problem. One possible way of using

this tool is to list the pillars separately and then brainstorm in your group the solutions to each.

It is not necessary to make decisions about possible actions at this stage. You will probably still be doing more analysis, and you should consider further options from the following chapters before taking action. However, the Pillars tool can help you to see at a glance how feasible it is to intervene. While it may be starkly evident that little can be done about some of the problems, and although some of the solutions suggested may be beyond your capabilities, this diagram does provide an opportunity for you to consider which other individuals and organisations could become allies, and to learn of constructive actions already taking place.

The Pyramid

This tool is needed when you start to analyse conflicts that have more than one level. With this method, you identify the key parties or actors at each level. In Figure 2.12 we have used three levels, but in your situation there may be only two, or alternatively you may wish to use more than three levels.

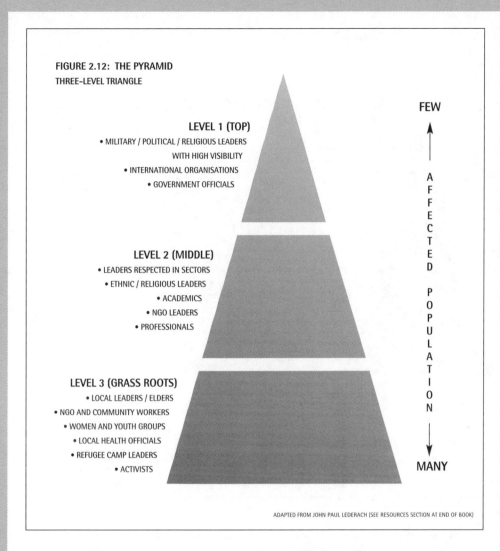

FIGURE 2.12: THE PYRAMID
THREE-LEVEL TRIANGLE

FEW

LEVEL 1 (TOP)
• MILITARY / POLITICAL / RELIGIOUS LEADERS
WITH HIGH VISIBILITY
• INTERNATIONAL ORGANISATIONS
• GOVERNMENT OFFICIALS

A
F
F
E
C
T
E
D

P
O
P
U
L
A
T
I
O
N

LEVEL 2 (MIDDLE)
• LEADERS RESPECTED IN SECTORS
• ETHNIC / RELIGIOUS LEADERS
• ACADEMICS
• NGO LEADERS
• PROFESSIONALS

LEVEL 3 (GRASS ROOTS)
• LOCAL LEADERS / ELDERS
• NGO AND COMMUNITY WORKERS
• WOMEN AND YOUTH GROUPS
• LOCAL HEALTH OFFICIALS
• REFUGEE CAMP LEADERS
• ACTIVISTS

MANY

ADAPTED FROM JOHN PAUL LEDERACH (SEE RESOURCES SECTION AT END OF BOOK)

As you consider each of the levels in the diagram and relate them to your own situation, you may find that most of your work is aimed at only one level. This can make it difficult to bring about lasting change because of the effect of the other levels on your context.

This type of analysis helps you to locate critical resource people who are strategically placed and embedded in networks that connect them vertically within the setting and horizontally in the conflict. These are people who have the ability to work with counterparts across the lines of division, therefore they can be key allies for working within the various levels as well as working simultaneously at all levels.

We will return to this analysis in Chapter 4 when we consider strategies for action.

THE PYRAMID –
AN EXAMPLE FROM GUATEMALA

Luis R. Dávila S. is Co-Director of the Research Council for Central American Development, and a former Working With Conflict course participant. In Figure 2.13 (p. 34) he illustrates how his NGO used the Pyramid to move on from analysis to build an inclusive strategy in Guatemala.

Context

In 1996, the Government and the Guatemalan National Revolutionary Unity (URNG) signed the last of the peace accords in Guatemala City. The signing of this agreement put an end to internal armed conflict, which had lasted for over three decades and cost at least 100,000

THE PYRAMID
WHAT IS IT?
▶ A graphic tool showing levels of stake-holders in a conflict.
PURPOSE
▶ To identify key actors, including leadership, at each level.
▶ To decide at which level you are currently working and how you might include other levels.
▶ To assess what types of approaches or actions are appropriate for work at each level.
▶ To consider ways to build links between levels.
▶ To identify potential allies at each level.
WHEN TO USE IT
▶ When analysing a situation that seems to include actors at various levels.
▶ When planning actions to address a multi-level conflict.
▶ When deciding where to focus one's energy.
VARIATIONS
▶ Use a triangle for each level (because each level has its own elite, middle and lower levels).
▶ Use with mapping to explore the different levels involved.

FIGURE 2.13: THE PYRAMID
EXAMPLE FROM GUATEMALA

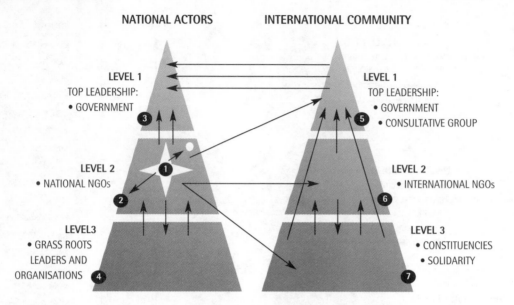

KEY

1. Our position among middle-range leaders/NGOs at the national level.

2. Identification of our relations and capacity to have influence alongside other NGOs who were significant at the national level.

3. Relations, research, studies, follow-up, proposal and pressure on government offices, mainly with regard to international cooperation, fulfilment of joint agreements and follow-up on the use of funds meant for social compensation and foreign debt. The Guatemalan Government, finally, was the centre of pressure.

4. Accompaniment to promote socioeconomic development and to strengthen the organisational capacities of grass roots organisations through training workshops, informative talks, political analysis, assistance with addressing social needs and community problems, and so forth.

5. Monitoring and lobbying the international community – especially the Consultative Group (a group of governments and intergovernmental organisations who supported the peace process in Guatemala). Our main task was to provide information from the perspective of civil society sectors regarding progress in implementation of the accords as well as to give advice on the allocation of international cooperation funds. The international forum was also used by different civil society groups to highlight those policies which tend to increase poverty and the link between these and the demands of multilateral financial organisations.

6. Dialogue, alliances and coordination with international NGOs to make efforts and financial resources more effective. This encourages international NGOs to put pressure on their own governments, to influence their policies for aid and cooperation, and to inform and motivate their constituencies.

7. Constant information to solidarity groups in support of international NGOs regarding the definition of their aid and cooperation policies, and pressure on government officials about related topics.

lives. This agreement marked the beginning of a reconstruction and reconciliation process in the country, and laid the basis for transformation to a more inclusive nation. These peace accords recognise that sustaining peace will require fundamental changes in society.

What we have covered and where we are going next

In this chapter we have offered the reader a range of tools and frameworks for analysing conflict situations:

- STAGES OF CONFLICT
- TIMELINES
- CONFLICT MAPPING
- THE ABC (ATTITUDE, BEHAVIOUR, CONTEXT) TRIANGLE
- THE ONION (OR THE DOUGHNUT)
- THE CONFLICT TREE
- FORCE-FIELD ANALYSIS
- PILLARS
- THE PYRAMID

As we have said, some of these have been adapted from other sources and some we have invented ourselves. All of them have been used, tested and sometimes modified by people from a wide range of different countries who are dealing with a variety of political and social conflicts.

They are not intended to be a rigid formula, but rather flexible and practical aids to help you in understanding the complexities of a particular situation in order to then build more effective strategies for addressing the conflicts you are concerned about.

We therefore encourage you to be creative in the way that you use these tools. They are often more effective when used in a variety of combinations – for example, applying an analysis of Stages with Mapping, ABC Triangles and a Pyramid – in order to explore from various perspectives different aspects of and factors in any given situation .

➲ *This kind of multi-dimensional analysis can help enhance your understanding of the situation and suggest a variety of entry points for action. Eventually, in Chapters 4 and 5, we will explore possible strategies for taking action. However, we want first, in Chapter 3, to address some of the critical issues that arise whenever any serious analysis is being made of human relations and the ensuing conflicts which can then occur.*

3-CRITICAL ISSUES

SUMMARY ■ This chapter deals with some of the major issues that arise when you analyse conflicts: power, culture, identity, gender and rights. These are issues to which there is no 'right answer' but which you need to grapple with, especially if you are intending to turn your analysis into a strategy and concrete actions.

Introduction

In trying out the tools introduced in the previous chapter, you will have noticed that there is a great deal more to analysing conflicts than identifying the key components: the parties and their positions, relationships and so on. As you look at the interaction between parties in dispute and dig deeper into the dynamics of conflicts, certain themes keep raising their heads. Sometimes they are explicitly named as conflict issues (e.g. 'this is a conflict over identity'), at other times they are in the background, exercising silent influence. It is important that you identify the most influential of these and begin to clarify your own ideas in relation to them.

- **POWER** Power is a vital ingredient in any human problem: often a conflict centres on the search for more of it, or a fear of losing it. If you used the conflict mapping tool in Chapter 2 (p.22), you may have illustrated the different parties with circles of varying sizes to correspond to their relative power in the situation. What factors did you consider when deciding that some parties had more power than others? Did this exercise highlight a power imbalance in the situation? Often people in conflict assume that they do not have the power to bring about change, or peace. But what are the real sources of power? How can empowerment help? How can people use power to their advantage?

- **CULTURE** Culture does much to determine the way people think and act. They honour their own culture, and often seek to maintain it in the face of outside influences. But how do they keep what is good in their cultures in the face of change in the world outside – in the area of gender for example, or rights? How can they reinvigorate traditional methods of addressing conflict, while adapting them to the needs of modern conflicts? If you carried out a force-field analysis (p.30) in Chapter 2, you may have found customary forces and modern forces pushing against each other. Or perhaps you found they were sometimes pushing in the same direction. What cultural factors do you see in the situations you wish to address?

- **IDENTITY** Culture provides people with a sense of belonging, an identity. But in conflicts people's sense of who they are can change and become fuel for escalation. At the same time, the way others see them can change and make them subject to inducement or attack. Can they develop a stronger idea of who they are, independently of what others wish them to be? The Onion analysis (p.27) in Chapter 2 may have highlighted some identity needs and interests in your context. Or, the ABC Triangle (p.25) might have clarified some attitudes and behaviours related to identity that need to be addressed. You may have used the Conflict Tree (p.29) to explore a group's understanding of their core problem, which they might see as a threat to some aspect of their identity – e.g. land alienation was the core problem for a community of nomadic herders in the example cited to illustrate the use of this tool.

- **GENDER** An understanding of gender is fundamental to making sense of the dynamics of conflict and addressing conflict constructively.

❂ He who doesn't know the extent of his power falls down and receives bruises. **ETHIOPIA**

While considering perceptions in Chapter 1 (p.5), did you identify differing perceptions of gender roles in your context? Men and women do have different social roles and different sources of power and influence. What are the implications of these differences for your actions to address conflict and to mitigate the effects of violence?

- **RIGHTS** And finally, rights are a vital dimension of social and political conflict. Abuse of rights, and the struggle to eliminate this abuse, lies at the base of many violent conflicts. The Universal Declaration of Human Rights attempts to provide a basis for establishing a common set of values and a common measure for social justice, regardless of culture or context. But these are often contested. Do people have to agree on basic rights before they can move forward? This is a question that may need to be asked when you are doing the Strategy Circle exercise in Chapter 4 (p.73).

All of the above themes can provide an invaluable area for growth and for the strengthening of relationships in any group or organisation if they are dealt with openly and with sensitivity. Equally, they can be explosive if kept suppressed. Each could easily have a separate book written about it. This is not an attempt to cover all these issues comprehensively, but we try here to highlight key aspects of each of them. Please refer to Chapter 10 for suggestions as to other resources in relation to each issue.

Power

'Power' has a number of meanings: force, legitimacy, authority or the ability to coerce. You probably sense that power influences your life continually. You know from experience how the relative power of different parties in a conflict affects the outcome. Yet it is frustratingly intangible: money you can count, power you cannot.

In the post-Cold War world, power is seen less and less in terms of centralised state structures.

You can see more readily how domestic problems spill over into international ones, how small groups can have loud voices, how rapidly old forms change, and how people's lives are interconnected. There is scope for broadening our view of power.

It is important to explore the different dimensions of power that are present in any situation, and to maximise those aspects that are most available to you. A rough equality of power between groups helps to ensure an acceptance that law and justice regulate society, rather than violence and vengeance. An effective parliamentary system is based on the assumption that, by dividing power fairly between elected representatives, a balance of power between social groups can be created. In this way the rule of law is legitimated and oppression of minorities becomes harder to implement.

POWER EXPRESSED THROUGH RELATIONSHIPS

Power does not exist in a vacuum, as an object or quantity. All power is present in, and based on, relationships: parent to child, government to governed, citizen to fellow citizen, landowner to peasant, factory manager to worker.

Another quality of power is that it does not always rely on active force. So a parent may listen to a child's plea for more freedom but never discuss it. A government may receive petitions from its citizens but never include their cause on any official agenda. Whoever has control of an agenda has control of the argument, or the absence of it. So communication, anticipation and awareness are in themselves alternative sources of power.

The Internet has already shown its huge capacity for sharing information and linking people across the world. It has become a way for even small organisations to speak to thousands of others, and for ordinary people to gain access to information that was previously beyond their reach. For example, more and more governments are now placing official documents on the Web. As more people across the world have access to the Internet, their

FAHIM HAKIM

collective power and the possibilities for joint action increase enormously.

POWER OF VETO

Equally, in a complex set of relationships it is not only the perceived leader who holds power, but any individual or group who can say no or block a given proposition. For example, cleaners may veto management's attempt to falsely impress factory inspectors by refusing to do extra cleaning work on the day of an inspection. Or a minority group in society may veto the government's wish to keep an issue off the agenda by holding public meetings or demonstrations to publicise and raise awareness about the issue.

Veto power is, of course, limited. It may be, for example, that veto holders dare not use their veto because the risks are too great: the costs to them are too high. This is clear in situations of grave inequality and extreme fear where protests or refusal to comply would be met with extreme violence.

· However, relationships and resources are key areas to look to, either when examining the need for power, or trying to understand where it really lies.

HARD AND SOFT POWER

Theorists in conflict resolution have found it useful to distinguish between:

- **COERCIVE** or **'HARD' POWER** (the ability to command and enforce) and
- **PERSUASIVE** or **'SOFT' POWER** (the ability to bring about cooperation, to provide legitimacy and to inspire).

Hard power is dominant in violent conflicts, as armies and militias struggle for victory. Soft power, on the other hand, is vital for genuine peacemaking and peace-building. Some thinkers have divided the idea of soft power into two types:

- **EXCHANGE POWER** (where compromise and bargaining are the rule) and
- **INTEGRATIVE POWER** (where the main strategies are persuasion and problem-solving).

Integrative power, aiming to deal with underlying issues, needs more time but is likely to be the most effective approach for a long-term transformation of the situation. In many conflicts all these strategies are used together: force is employed to make the space, and create the willingness for initial bargaining and compromise, followed by longer-term talks aimed

✿ The pen is mightier
than the sword.
ENGLAND

FAHIM HAKIM

at a settlement which is owned by all sides and therefore more durable. In practice it seems that the use of violent, hard power often makes that longer-term outcome much more difficult.

SOURCES OF POWER

If power is so varied in nature, and so dependent on the situation and relationship in question, there are great possibilities for civil society and individual communities to increase the power at their disposal in order to influence a given relationship or situation. In a recent Working with Conflict course, participants brainstormed the following list of sources of power available to them:

✔ Money	✔ Structures
✔ Relationship	✔ Charisma
✔ Credibility	✔ Location
✔ Access to resources	✔ Competence
✔ Tradition	✔ Communication
✔ Morality	✔ Knowledge
✔ Skills/expertise	✔ Partnership
✔ Information	✔ System
✔ Authority	✔ Sustainability
✔ Position	✔ Exchange visit
✔ Legitimacy	✔ Security
✔ Experience	✔ History
✔ Networks	✔ Personal qualities

Some of these sources of power can exert a lot of influence in certain situations:

- **AUTHORITY (or POSITION)** This is the power that an individual or group has by virtue of their role. For example, a man regarded as 'head of the household' has power over women, children and younger men. This form of power is backed up by rules, norms (accepted behaviours), resources and perhaps a means of enforcement such as police or army. Customary and modern systems often give different degrees of power to particular roles (e.g. elders). Membership of a class, caste or race can give one person power over others in this way.

- **ACCESS TO RESOURCES** This power arises from having control over the supply of resources such as materials, technology, finance, and ownership of the means of production, distribution and exchange. If one group depends on another for a scarce resource (such as water), it is, to some extent, in the other group's power.

- **NETWORKS** 'It's not what you know but who you know that counts.' Social connections are an important source of power. Networking – developing personal contacts – is a key skill and a means of exercising influence.

- **SKILLS/EXPERTISE** Technical expertise (e.g. in maintaining computers) and process knowledge (how to get things done) are both power-givers. Without these, organisations and armies fail. Initiatives for change and peace depend on these services being amply provided.

- **INFORMATION** Accurate information is crucial if good decisions are to be made. In conflicts the control and manipulation of information is a major weapon. Those who control, or expand, the flow of information have much potential influence.

- **PERSONAL QUALITIES** The power of a personality lies in a combination of attributes such as intelligence, confidence, determination, charm, charisma, energy, sincerity, background, 'track record' of effective work. These can increase credibility and influence in the eyes of others.

POWER AND ACCOUNTABILITY

As you discover more sources of power, it is vital to realise that you need also to increase your accountability for the way this power is exercised. Otherwise you risk simply mirroring the structures you are trying to change. This means finding ways of reporting to, and being questioned by others: colleagues, other members of networks and so on.

Typical ways in which people try to avoid being accountable for the use of power are:
- withholding information
- making hidden threats
- refusing to acknowledge or 'own' the power they have
- communicating poorly or not at all.

Think about the sources of power that are available to you:
➤ **Could you use these more effectively in dealing with conflict situations?**
➤ **Do you feel you are sufficiently accountable for the power that you have and use?**

Culture

Culture has been defined as: *The particular practices and values common to a population living in a given setting. It is a shared, collective product that provides a repertoire of actions and a standard against which to evaluate the actions of others.*[1]

Culture is not something we have at birth. We learn it during our childhood and youth from parents, family, elders, teachers, religious leaders and the media. Likewise, culture is not static, though it may sometimes seem to be. It changes over the course of time through the influence of various internal and external forces.

CULTURE AS A FACTOR IN CONFLICT

When we are dealing with social and political conflict, culture is often raised as a factor that must be recognised and addressed. It is argued that culture determines the way that we act, the manner in which we relate to others and even the way we think about and perceive the events happening around us. Therefore anyone working on conflicts must have an understanding of the cultural contexts of the parties involved, especially in cases where the parties are from different cultures.

Marc Ross argues that there is, in fact, a 'culture of conflict', which he defines as 'a society's configuration of norms, practices and institutions that affect what people enter into disputes about, with whom they fight, how disputes evolve, and how they are likely to end.'[2] In practical terms, this suggests that, in order to work effectively on conflict, you must understand the societal values, norms, accepted practices and community institutions of the particular parties and groups involved in the particular situation.

Methods for analysis and intervention must be sensitive to cultural factors. But, at the same time, you and your co-workers may need to question cultural assumptions that may be obstacles to resolving conflict and possibly even causes of conflict.

CULTURE AS A RESOURCE FOR PEACE-BUILDING

The traditions, structures, processes and roles that exist in any culture can be very helpful in

✪ Hay merukisina dugwa aghwahiti. IIt is not only a herd of cattle that is controlled.
BARABAIG, TANZANIA

our efforts to address conflict and build peace. In many places there are methods for dealing with interpersonal and intercommunal conflict that have been practised for centuries. In some cases 'modern' culture has ignored these or replaced them with more professional or technical methodologies.

But many grass roots practitioners now recognise that traditional approaches may be very relevant and have positive aspects that can be combined with more 'modern' methods. For example:

- People working on trauma healing in Liberia have combined counselling skills with traditional ways of communal storytelling to create a programme in which so-called 'victims' and 'perpetrators' of violence meet to share their experiences and begin to rebuild relationships that will allow them to live together.
- In Somaliland, the near-total collapse of government as a result of war has been an opportunity for people to rebuild structures and processes of governance, which are still based on the traditional leadership roles of clan elders, but adapted to be more inclusive of women and youth.
- Women in many countries, who draw on their traditional roles as mothers – which their culture would normally see as a private domain (based in the home) – and who then enter the public arena, sometimes cross political boundaries in their call for peace or justice (for example, groups such as Mothers for Peace and Mothers of the Disappeared).
- In Guatemala, a group of former armed opponents of government have become centrally involved in creating and sustaining a multi-level negotiation process that is based upon traditional ways of dialogue in the cultures represented.

These are just a few of the many examples we come across in which practitioners are drawing upon the strengths that exist within their own cultures as resources for building peace.

CULTURE, COMMUNICATION AND DISAGREEMENT

Ways and patterns of communication are formed and influenced by culture. If the parties concerned are from contrasting cultural backgrounds, they may have quite different ways of communicating but fail to recognise these differences, as illustrated by the following example:

A CULTURAL MISUNDERSTANDING

During one of our Working with Conflict courses, a South African man was having a dialogue with a woman from Eastern Europe. He, in his natural cultural style, was standing very close to her and looking directly into her eyes while speaking. She, having a very different cultural expectation about normal conversation, perceived his manner as aggressive and intimidating. In her own cultural style, she was continually backing, trying to put more distance between them, and also averting her eyes from looking directly at his. He perceived her behaviour to indicate that she was not interested, or at least not understanding, the point he was trying to make, and this caused him to continue moving closer to her and to make his point even more forcefully. As you can imagine, people observing this incident found it quite amusing, but it did illustrate quite starkly how differences in cultural communication patterns can lead to serious misunderstanding and an escalation of conflict. In this case, the tutors intervened and helped them to analyse what had been happening.

In cross-cultural conflict work, we need to understand the different ways in which each culture expresses disagreement. Even in an apparently single-culture context, it is important that people learn how to communicate disagreement in ways that do not aggravate the conflict. Within the same culture women and men often communicate in very different ways, as do people from different social classes.

Culture can also give greater power to certain ways of communicating. Often, during colonial times, indigenous groups were forced to adopt 'Western' methods in order to interact with each other and with authorities, while their traditional ways were ignored: for example, customary marriages were often not accepted by the state, forcing couples to undergo civil marriages to make them 'legitimate.' In many cultures too, women and the 'lower' classes have had to adopt the language and communication methods of powerful male elites, simply to be acknowledged or listened to.

Work on communication needs to take account of these dynamics and to acknowledge the value of different styles of communicating. For example, in many societies 'gossip' has a significant role as a means of social and information exchange, whereas in others it is frowned upon as unreliable and often provocative.

HUMAN RIGHTS AND CULTURE

Another area where the role of culture is frequently raised is that of human rights. In discussions about human rights with people coming from a variety of different cultures, many will argue that the concept of human rights is intrinsically Western and therefore not of any great significance with respect to their own cultural situations. The opinion they express is that rights are not universal and absolute, but must be considered in relation to culturally accepted ways of relating and acting. This issue arises frequently with regard to the rights of women in cultures where women and men have very distinct roles in society.

There are areas where women often do not enjoy the same rights as men in the same social group – as within the family and in laws regulating inheritance and the right to own property. Even when these rights are enshrined in law, custom may prohibit women from actually benefiting from them. This raises the question of how a universal culture of human rights can be reconciled with the need to respect cultural differences. We will address this in the section on Human Rights later in this chapter.

RELIGION AND CULTURE

It seems clear that while the world's religions provide inspiration and consolation for many, their claim to offer a path of absolute truth is rarely borne out by their adherents' behaviour.

In many cases religious believers show little variance in behaviour from the mainstream in their own culture. For example, the churches in Rwanda before and up to 1994 had preached peace and reconciliation, and even organised programmes to promote these outcomes, yet priests, nuns and ordinary churchgoers alike participated actively in the genocide.

Down the centuries Christian leadership has shown a tendency to reflect the values of the historical and cultural context: thus the scriptures have at various times been used to justify slavery, racism and women's subordination on the one hand, and liberation, theology and pacifism on the other.

Religion and culture are often key elements in political movements, in what are described by Yusuf Bangura[3] as 'culturalist groups':

CULTURALIST GROUPS

Culturalist groups emerge when a community sharing both religious and ethnic affinities perceives itself as a powerless and repressed minority within a state dominated by outsiders. The mobilisation of the opposition group's culture (of which religion is an important part) is directed towards achieving self-control, autonomy or self-government. Examples include Tibetan Buddhists in China; Sikhs in India; Muslim Palestinians in Israel's occupied territories; followers of Louis Farrakan's organisation, the Nation of Islam, in the United States; and Bosnian Muslims in ex-Yugoslavia. In each case, the religion followed by the ethnic minority provides part of the ideological basis for action against representatives of a dominant culture – whom the minority perceives as aiming to undermine or to eliminate their minority culture.

So, in working on conflict, it is important to recognise that, when religion is associated with a particular culture, it can exercise power and control in particular situations. Likewise, strong attitudes of religious and cultural intolerance may fuel the escalation of violence.

However, it is also important to recognise that religion, when people adhere to its ideals, can have a positive influence on conflicts. There are examples in every age and in all religions of people who have stood out for the basic values of their religion, often at great personal cost, Martin Luther King, Gandhi and the Dalai Lama being amongst the more prominent in recent times. There are many others – both women and men, not so well known – who have also found in their religion a set of principles and values of tolerance, truth and humanity that have led them to take risks for promoting peace and justice in the midst of violent conflict.

Take a moment to think about the issue of culture in conflicts you have experienced:
➤ **Can you identify this as a significant factor, either positive or negative?**
➤ **Can you see ways for a diversity of different cultures to be better valued and respected, in order to promote peace and justice?**

Identity

You may have often asked yourself the question 'Who am I?' If so, the responses have probably been many and varied. One person's response was: 'I am a woman, a mother, a wife, a daughter, a Somali, a Muslim, a Kenyan, a nomad, a health worker, a peace organiser, a conflict resolver, a development worker, a trainer.' All of these responses are true about the person concerned, because all are aspects or components of her identity. Some will be more important than others, depending upon how she perceives her own identity, but also depending upon place and circumstances.

Different aspects of our identities are given greater emphasis in different contexts. For example, at home this person may emphasise her identity as mother and wife, while at work the emphasis may be on other aspects, such as health worker, trainer or conflict resolver.

IDENTITY IS FORMED IN RELATIONSHIPS

Identity is heavily influenced by relationships with others, and by the dominant culture. In the case cited above, the woman may have to struggle against the primary identity ascribed by her culture, or against the fixed ideas of others at her workplace about the role and status of women. In Britain women are frequently

FAHIM HAKIM

asked 'Are you Miss or Mrs?' Men are less likely to be asked about their marital status.

The tendency humans have to put individuals and groups into categories is, essentially, a way of enabling them to survive in a world where they do not have the time to make individual assessments of everyone. However, this **stereotyping** is often inaccurate and misleading, based as it is on imperfect information and filtered through individuals' backgrounds and life experience. It is very vulnerable to media influence.

People belonging to ethnic minorities worldwide are subject to a similar process, whereby the majority community tends to impose an identity on them on the basis of their colour or other characteristics. An RTC colleague in eastern Congo constantly lives in fear for his life because he is tall, thin and has an angular nose. In his area strangers assume, wrongly, that he is a member of the Banyamulenge group, who are in violent conflict with others in the area, and he is frequently attacked as a result. This kind of stereotyping, which leads to discrimination against certain groups, is covered in more detail, along with suggested actions, in the section on 'Prejudice' in Chapter 6 (p. 98).

Enormous problems arise when people treat each other on the basis of the stereotype alone. Race and gender are both categories frequently used to classify whole groups and justify inhuman or inequitable treatment. Governments, when needing to escape from a predicament of their own making, have used this mechanism to blame, or **scapegoat**, a whole group and justify their punishment. From Jews in 1930s Germany to educated Cambodians in the 1970s, examples of this abounded in the twentieth century and are unlikely to cease in the twenty-first.

IDENTITY AND CONFLICT

Identity in relation to conflict situations has many dimensions. In particular, your sense of identity can change rapidly in response to threats, real or contrived. Human needs to belong and to be secure conspire to make you vulnerable as the context changes around you and leaders promise to protect those needs – provided you do as they say. People who thought of themselves as 'Yugoslav' in 1988 became 'Bosnian' as the state broke up, then 'Muslim' as Bosnia itself fragmented. As fear grows, people adopt labels which they think will give them the greatest security: ethnicity, nationality and religion all become potential mechanisms for the exploitation of fear and the urge for power.

It is important that people become confident in their sense of who they are, so that others cannot impose an identity on them. Phrases such as 'a culture of resistance' and 'increasing immunity to exploitation' are being used by those activists who are working to empower populations to reject attempts to label them and thus determine their behaviour. Equally, people can be encouraged to treat others on the basis of the identities they choose for themselves, rather than on the basis of stereotypes. For more about this topic, refer to 'Confidence-building' in Chapter 6 (p. 112) and 'Education for Peace and Justice' in Chapter 8 (p. 142).

THINKING ABOUT IDENTITY

In order for you to work on identity issues with others, it is crucial that you have a clear sense of your own identity. As you better understand and recognise the different components of your own identity, you are correspondingly better able to expand your choice of strategy and action, whether within conflicts or outside them. In Figure 3.1 on the following page, we offer you two different frameworks for exploring the different parts of your identity.

Using **Framework A**, first, identify those parts of your identity which relate to:

- **CULTURE**: language, ethnicity, way of life, community values and customs, etc.

- **KINSHIP**: family roles and relationships, qualities inherited from parents, clan identity, etc.

- **EDUCATION**: level of schooling, degrees or qualifications, skills training, non-formal learning, experience, etc.

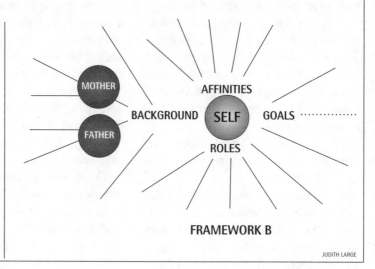

FIGURE 3.1: ASPECTS OF IDENTITY

CULTURE

KINSHIP

SELF

EDUCATION

FRAMEWORK A

BRIDGET WALKER

MOTHER

FATHER

AFFINITIES

BACKGROUND **SELF** GOALS

ROLES

FRAMEWORK B

JUDITH LARGE

We have chosen these three areas, but there may be others that are more useful for you.

Another way of thinking about aspects of your identity is illustrated in **Framework B**. Draw a similar diagram for yourself, listing the different parts of your identity on lines extending from Self in each category:

• **BACKGROUND:** Where do you come from? What identity have you inherited (e.g. German, Zulu, Muslim, Christian, high caste, working class)?

• **ROLES:** What roles or positions do you have? Who are you when you are working (e.g. a mother, husband, teacher, administrator, human rights worker, chairperson)?

• **AFFINITIES:** Who are you when you are relaxing and enjoying recreation in non-working time (e.g. a football player, pianist, potter, mountain climber, poet)?

• **GOALS:** What are you aiming to be, to do or to achieve in your life? How would you describe yourself in relation to your personal goals and values, and how do you try to put these into practice (e.g. as a peacemaker, promoter of justice, entrepreneur, spiritual seeker, learner)?

Having thought about your identity using one of these frameworks, then consider:

❯ **What is the most important aspect of your identity now? Why is this?**

❯ **How has your sense of identity changed in, say, the last five years?**

❯ **What might make this change in the future?**

TYPES OF COLLECTIVE IDENTITY

We often describe our identities according to particular groups that we belong to or associate with. **Ethnicity**, or ethnic identity, refers to the group with which we share a particular language, culture, religion and/or race. **Nationality**, or national identity, refers to the group with whom we share a territory or 'nation'. So, for example, a woman in Colombo might say that her ethnicity is either 'Sinhalese' or 'Tamil', while her nationality is 'Sri Lankan'. However, this distinction between ethnicity and nationality is often quite blurred.

In his book *Ethnic Conflicts and the Nation-State,* Rodolfo Stavenhagen lists the following criteria[4] for identifying ethnic groups:

1. '**LANGUAGE** is a powerful indicator of ethnic and national identity ... When a dominant language (spoken by a dominant ethnic group)

displaces other tongues, then the ethnic identity of the subordinate groups changes.'

2. 'RELIGION has historically been an important marker of ethnic identity. In urban industrialised society people interact independently of religion; their ethnic identities may not be related to religion at all, or only weakly. But in those societies in which religion intervenes in…public life, it may become a …determinant for ethnicity.'

3. 'TERRITORY is the basis of the economic and political structures which are considered fundamental units in the life of ethnic groups and nations. The majority of the thousands of ethnic groups in the world are identified with some territory which is not only their vital environment, but also their real or mythical land of origin.'

4. 'SOCIAL ORGANISATION…refers to the complex web of institutions and social relations that provide consistency to an ethnic group over and beyond the personal identity of its individual members… Social organisation establishes the boundaries of a group; it is the framework within which "we" and "they", "insiders" and "outsiders" are distinguished.'

5. 'CULTURE is often seen to include factors mentioned above (language, religion and social organisation). Other elements are: (1) material aspects of culture, that is, cultural artefacts, and (2) value systems, symbols and meanings, norms, mores, and customs, which are shared by members of an ethnic group.'

6. 'RACE [is] a particularly significant marker of ethnic identity [because] it commonly refers not only to the biological attributes of the individuals (e.g. skin colour, facial features, body build and so on), but also to the supposed social, cultural and psychological qualities that are associated with them…Not all ethnic differences are racial differences, but ethnic distinctions tend to be stronger and longer lasting to the extent that they include racial criteria.'

Our experience is that many conflicts are labelled as 'ethnic conflicts', suggesting that ethnicity is the cause. However, as analysis deepens it becomes clear that this is far too simple a view. Certainly, people seek to meet their essential needs through belonging to groups. However, in many conflicts, ethnicity has been the *method* by which people have been mobilised in support of a particular leader or movement. For this to happen, a population must first feel insecure or afraid, and then be persuaded that a particular group or leader can offer them safety.

Consider the identities of conflicting parties in a situation you are trying to address:
➤ **Do you respect their different identities?**
➤ **Do you model this respect of identity in your interactions with the parties?**
➤ **Do you see ways in which you can help them to better understand and respect their differing identities?**

Gender

Gender is a dynamic of human relations that reaches to the heart of society, and therefore to conflict. Yet it is often overlooked. In RTC's work with mixed groups of women and men, an awareness of gender and gender roles has become a crucial element. More widely, we have come to see that a gender perspective is essential for any work that aims to influence social relations.

In defining gender, we quote from the Oxfam Gender Training Manual:[5]

A WORKING DEFINITION OF GENDER

People are born female or male, but learn to be girls and boys who grow into women and men. They are taught what the appropriate behaviour and attitudes, roles and activities are for them, and how they should relate to other people. This learned behaviour is what makes up gender identity and determines gender roles.

The gender roles of women and men differ to some extent in all societies. These roles may vary in different societies and across different communities within the same society. (In some farming communities, for example, it may be normal for women to plough the fields, whereas in others this would be considered a man's job). Factors such as class (social position, wealth), age and education will also influence gender roles.

Gender roles are not static, but change over time or in response to sudden traumatic events such as violent conflicts or war. For example, women often lose their homes and their menfolk during war and have to take on new roles, becoming the family 'breadwinners' and the community spokespersons or representatives. Subsequently, men may experience a loss of identity if, having to give up the role of fighter, they can then find no productive activity to take its place. An ex-combatant in Nicaragua said: 'I don't really know who I am any more. I used to be a fighter and now no one will even give me a job. I used to feel that I was respected by others.'[6]

GENDER AND CONFLICT

For many reasons, largely due to their differing roles and responsibilities, women and men may have varying perspectives on a particular conflict, different needs and perhaps competing interests. It is important, therefore, to bring an awareness of gender to many of our activities: to our analysis of social and political conflict, to our assessment of the impact of violent conflict, and to identifying appropriate strategies for action and possible groups or actors to link with or support.

Analysing political and social conflict from a gender perspective means looking beyond the public face of the conflict to understand what is happening at different, perhaps deeper, levels within families and community groups. Consequently, we must understand the differing roles and responsibilities of women and men, and the kind of support they may need. Men may be a target, because of their gender,

for coercion into armed movements. Women may be faced with new responsibilities for maintaining their families in the absence of their male partners and may themselves become targets for violence.

We also need to be aware that gender roles may be in the process of change. When this is the case, these changes can be perceived as both an opportunity and a threat.

Where women are seen as guardians of the honour of a community, their roles and movements may become more restricted. Much will depend on the power relations within communities, where the authority resides and the relative subordination of different sectors such as women and young people.

Violence against women has deep roots in many societies. For example, the idea of what it means to be masculine is formed, in many societies, in opposition to the definition of femininity, so that violence against women and children is seen as the rightful exercise of authority. This raises questions about how boys, in particular, are socialised, in the family and more widely.

Open conflict may bring into the public sphere the violence of a relationship that was previously hidden within the family. This is a manifestation of 'hard' power (see 'Hard and Soft Power', p.39).

'Soft' power is sometimes overlooked or underestimated because it is exercised by those who are not generally regarded as powerful. When women organise and negotiate around issues such as food shortages or childcare or the disappearance of their menfolk, they are building strong links that have the potential for future peace-building. In Nicaragua, for example, women overcame their political differences for the sake of their children, in order to work together on common concerns and needs.

A crucial factor in analysing political and social conflict is to find out directly the views of those who often do not have a voice: women and children, members of minority groups, and people with disabilities.

Before moving on, take a moment to reflect on this subject from a practical perspective. Think of your own community or another which you know well.

▶ **List the different activities carried out. Are they done mainly by men, by women or by both? – e.g. teaching, office work, health care (doctors, nurses, community health workers, traditional healers), farming (who cares for which livestock, who ploughs, who weeds), hunting, participation in cultural or religious activities, law enforcement and so on.**

▶ **Are all the essential activities listed? Were any of the following missed out: shopping, preparing food, cooking, cleaning, childcare, collecting water?**

▶ **How would you rank all these listed activities in terms of their status and in terms of their necessity for human well-being? Where do power ('hard' and 'soft') and responsibility lie?**

▶ **Would you say that there is 'equity' (fairness) in the division of responsibilities?**

▶ **Do those with the responsibilities also have the power?**

In situations of conflict your answers to the above questions are likely to change, as women take on increasing responsibilities in the community and as men adopt roles connected directly with pursuing hostilities or defence against these. Overall, many would accept the assertion that women are acquiring more responsibilities in many areas, but are often not acquiring the authority and decision-making power to go with them. As a colleague remarked to us: 'Women hold up more than half the world and usually go unrecognised.'

▶ **What does the cartoon on the right say to you about men, women and conflict?**

▶ **Do you agree with it?**

GENDER AND VIOLENCE

The impacts of violent conflict have a gender dimension which must be analysed in each case. Generally men are more likely to be killed and women to be widowed and left to manage their families. The impacts on children are also often gender-differentiated. Boys may be coerced into armed movements, girls may be abducted by those same movements for sexual slavery. Men and women, boys and girls alike are subject to torture and sexual abuse.

The ability of survivors to cope with what they have endured depends not only on their own capacities but also on the support they receive from their communities. Gender may play a significant role. After the struggle for independence in Bangladesh, many women who had been raped were regarded as a liability by their communities. In Eritrea women who had been fighters found it hard to reintegrate after having moved out of their traditional gender roles. (A male fighter, when asked why he had chosen a peasant girl rather than a co-fighter as a wife, said that he did not want to marry 'a man'.) During the civil war in Chad, women looked after families without their husbands and in the process acquired more autonomy and personal self-confidence. Public perceptions of women also changed, and it is claimed that women are now respected for the essential role they play in the survival of their families and communities.[7]

Violent conflict often results in displacement. UNHCR estimates that 80 per cent of refugees and displaced people are women and children.

FAHIM HAKIM

✪ Women hold up half the sky.
CHINA

There are several reasons why men are absent: they may have gone to fight (either willingly or as a result of coercion), they may have gone into hiding to avoid the killers or the fighting, they may have left to seek better opportunities, or they may have been killed or 'disappeared' in the violence.

Displacement results in loss at a number of levels. There is the material impact of loss of home and the destruction of infrastructure, of roads and bridges, of land and livestock and the means of survival. There is the impact on a community when its social fabric has been ripped apart and needs to be remade, and there is the psychological impact, in terms of trauma both to the individual and to the wider social group.

Relief responses have often focused on material inputs, which have sometimes disadvantaged the women they were intended to support. For example, workers in a camp for people displaced by war in Sudan pointed out that the relief programmes 'blatantly hand the power over traditional women's affairs to men ... running food distribution, water programmes, blanket, jerry-can and other distributions ... reassigning the traditional women's responsibilities of food and shelter provision to men'.[8]

The psychosocial impact of violent conflict will vary according to context and factors such as age and gender. The reintegration of fighters into civil society may be hard for them and for the communities who have learned to live without them. In Cambodia, where half the population died or was exiled in the Pol Pot years and both family and community relations were systematically broken down, there is a need to rebuild the trust that was destroyed. Children who have known nothing but war and instability in refugee-camp life have to learn not only the usual curriculum of education, but also how to reconstruct and re-create community.

Arising out of these gender issues there are many implications for strategies and actions. Some of these are taken up in Parts 2 and 3 of this book.

Rights
WHAT ARE HUMAN RIGHTS?

The concept of human rights is based on certain values and has ancient roots. However, defining rights, and agreeing on what they are, forms the subject of continuing debate.

HUMAN RIGHTS – ONE DEFINITION

'Human rights are concerned with the dignity of the individual – the level of self-esteem that secures personal identity and promotes human community.'[9]

The development of the international framework of human rights has been influenced by the political context of the time. The two International Covenants (addressing civil and political rights on the one hand and economic, social and cultural rights on the other) became representative of the different priorities of the West and the East respectively in the years of the Cold War.

Civil and political rights, often called 'first generation rights', reflect a Western traditional liberal view of the rights of the individual in society to life, liberty and freedom of opinion and expression. Economic, social and cultural rights, known as 'second generation rights', include rights to basic necessities such as food and shelter, and to social services such as health and education. The economic collapse of the Eastern-bloc countries has led to an erosion of these rights, which were previously guaranteed by the state. There is then a set of 'third generation' or collective rights, for example those of minorities and marginalised groups. There is still much disagreement about whether these rights apply equally to everyone and, if they are genuine rights, who is responsible for enforcing them.

Internationally, the protection and enforcement of human rights depends on the acceptance and implementation of these conventions by individual states.

MAJOR HUMAN RIGHTS CONVENTIONS

In addition to the Universal Declaration of Human Rights, signed in 1948, there are a number of other conventions,[10] including the following:

- **Convention on Prevention and Punishment of the Crime of Genocide, 1948**
- **Convention on the Status of Refugees, 1951**
- **Covenant on Economic, Social and Cultural Rights, 1966**
- **Covenant on Civil and Political Rights, 1966**
- **Convention on the Elimination of all forms of Discrimination Against Women, 1979**
- **Convention Against Torture and other Cruel, Inhuman or Degrading Treatment or Punishment, 1984**
- **Convention on Rights of the Child, 1989**

The majority of countries have signed up to these conventions. However, there are notable and important exceptions:

- The USA has not ratified the conventions on the Rights of the Child, on Discrimination Against Women or on Economic, Social and Cultural Rights.
- Neither Switzerland nor Afghanistan has accepted the Convention on Discrimination Against Women.
- Nearly half of the world's nations have refused to accept the Convention against Torture and Degrading Punishment.

BASIC RIGHTS

While the field of human rights and the phrase itself remain a subject for debate, the expression 'basic rights' has been introduced to suggest that there are core rights without which other rights cannot be accessed or enjoyed. These basic rights include:

- the right not only to life but to a livelihood
- the right to protection from violence
- the right to safe water, food and shelter
- the right to health and education
- the right for both women and men to have a say in their future.

Development agencies such as Oxfam have moved from a basic needs approach to a basic rights approach in their work with poor women and men, because they recognise that denial or abuse of these rights is a basic cause of poverty and exploitation. Some key aspects of a rights-based approach are:

- The protection and provision of basic rights should become a legal obligation of the state or the international community, not of a voluntary charity.
- Empowerment and capacity-building are as important as the provision of goods and services.
- Goals must be 100 per cent – no one's rights can be ignored. (For example, even though a child health programme may have vaccinated 80 per cent of children, the fact that 20 per cent of children have still not been vaccinated is seen as a continuing violation of their right to basic health care.)

RIGHTS AND SOCIAL RELATIONS

Social or cultural difference, class, caste and ethnicity may all be factors in the use or abuse of power, and with it the denial or violation of rights. Rights, in theory guaranteed under the constitution of a state, may in practice not be accessible to men and women who belong to a marginalised group or who are intimidated by the powerful from claiming their rights.

Women are not a minority group, but their subordinate status, their limited access to the public domain, and their political marginalisation have meant that they experience wide-scale abuse of their rights at every level and still face obstacles in obtaining redress. The Convention on the Elimination of all forms of Discrimination Against Women (CEDAW, 1979) makes provision for the rights of women, and the Vienna Conference (1993) stated unequivocally that 'the human rights of women are an inalienable, integral and indivisible part of universal human rights'. The UN Conference on women at Beijing two years later promised to ensure 'the full implementation of the human rights of women and the girl child as an inalienable,

> Man cannot live by bread alone.
> **THE BIBLE** (AUTHORISED VERSION)

integral and indivisible part of all human rights and fundamental freedoms'. But not all states are signatories of CEDAW. Whole populations of women may experience denial of their rights on cultural grounds, and individual women continue to be abused at home and abroad, in peace and in war.

The rights of women may be violated throughout their life cycle: from the moment of conception (by abortion of female foetuses in preference for males), through malnutrition in childhood (by preferential feeding of boys), through denial of education to girls, through early, and at times forced, marriage, or through domestic violence and dowry death.[11] In war and armed conflict, women are targeted for rape and sexual assault; cultural norms may mean that if they survive, they are likely to suffer further abuse or ostracism from their communities.

RIGHTS AND DISABILITY

The UN regards disability as a rights issue. It adopted a World Programme of Action concerning disabled persons in 1992, and in 1993 produced the Standard Rules on the Equalization of Opportunities for Persons with Disabilities. These rules provide an international instrument with a system for monitoring. However, there is no international system to enforce them; implementation of the rules depends upon individual governments.

RIGHTS AND CONFLICT

Rights have become a foundational issue for those involved in development and relief responses, and they are also a crucial issue in conflict-related work. For many poor people the violation of their basic rights is an everyday occurrence. All conflict analysis needs to look at structural violence and explore the position and perception of the stakeholders regarding rights and freedoms. The struggle of marginalised groups for their rights may lead to necessary conflict; how that struggle and conflict is perceived will depend on the perspectives of the different parties.

Here are some points to consider:

▶ **RIGHTS OF THE INDIVIDUAL, RIGHTS OF THE GROUP AND RIGHTS OF THE SOCIETY AS A WHOLE: Are there times when these levels of rights might clash? Can you think of examples from your own experience? How do you think that these differences could be resolved?**

▶ **RIGHTS AND CULTURE: Are there times when rights might clash with culture? Can you think of examples? How do you think that these differences could be resolved?**

▶ **RIGHTS AND EQUALITY: In your own country, community, organisation and family, is there a recognition that rights are the same for everyone? Do you believe in and promote this equality of rights in the way that you relate to and work with people of all races, cultures, nationalities, religions, genders, ages and abilities?**

The violation of rights is widespread and lies at the root of many conflicts. Denial of rights will ultimately be opposed and such opposition often begins as a nonviolent protest, but, in the face of denial and violent repression, may become armed struggle. History suggests that an official peace does not bring a cessation of violence. Indeed, women may experience further violence when men come home from war frustrated and bearing guns, and peacekeeping forces may have an impact that includes the spread of sexually transmitted diseases and an increase in the sex trade.

It has been said that if we want peace we must first seek justice. To understand what justice means, we need to think of the rights of women, children, prisoners, disabled people and all those who are marginalised. Opponents in a conflict may discover that they are committed to similar principles of peace and justice, but have different priorities or ways of achieving them. A rights agenda can form one basis for building a future together.

▶ **How can the recognition of rights become part of your approach to transform conflict?**

▶ Do rights give you ways to frame your intentions and aspirations, and a standard against which to compare what you are actually doing?

Conclusion

All the issues that we have considered in this chapter are likely to have an influence on the conflict you are concerned with. It is important for you and those with whom you work to be aware of them and to know what you think about them.

The underlying factors of a conflict are likely to include issues of access to wealth and power, justice and distribution of resources, and a context in which weak or contested state institutions and international structures are impoverished in favour of richer nations and multinational corporations. In order to begin to address these factors, rather than upholding myths about 'the enemy', populations need to have access to different sources of reliable information.

❯ Parts Two and Three of this book offer a range of practical strategies and actions for transforming conflicts and building peace in situations that you and your colleagues are addressing.

NOTES

1. Marc Howard Ross, *The Culture of Conflict*, Yale University Press, New Haven and London, 1993, p. 21.

2. Ibid., p. 183.

3. Yusuf Bangura, *The Search for Identity: Ethnicity, Religion and Political Violence*, Occasional Paper no. 6, World Summit for Social Development, UNRISD (United Nations Research Institute for Social Development), 1995, p. 16.

4. Quoted from Rodolfo Stavenhagen, *Ethnic Conflicts and the Nation-State*, Macmillan, 1996, pp. 25–32.

5. Suzanne Williams, Jan Seed & Adelina Mwau (1994), *The Oxfam Gender Training Manual*, Oxfam (UK and Ireland), p. 4.

6. Patricia Ardon, 'Conflicts in Central America', Internal Oxfam Document, 1997.

7. Achta Djibrine Sy, 'Conflict and the Women of Chad', in *Focus on Gender*, vol. 1, no. 2, Oxfam (UK and Ireland), 1993.

8. Bridget Walker, in *Women and Emergencies*, Oxfam UK and Ireland, internal document, 1994.

9. Abdul Aziz, *Human Rights in Islamic Perspectives*, Praeger Publishers, 1980.

10. For details of these, consult the website of the UN High Commissioner for Human Rights–see Chapter 10 (p. 179).

11. Winin Pereira, *Inhuman Rights*, The Other India Press, India, 1997.

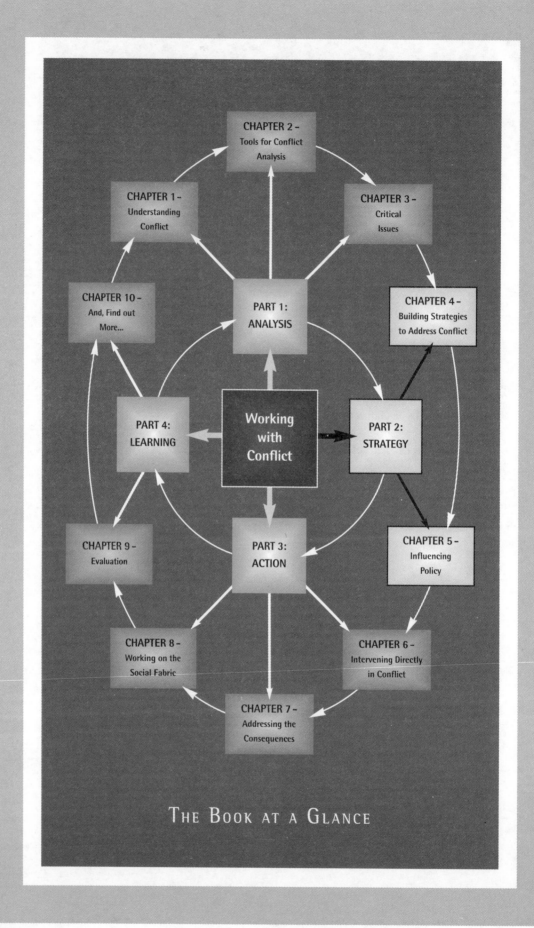

THE BOOK AT A GLANCE

⊛ PART 2: STRATEGY

AS A READER OF THIS BOOK you are probably keen to take action on the conflicts you face. But the hard fact is that you can make things worse, and take unnecessary risks, if you do not take time to analyse the situation. We are not talking about a profoundly theoretical, near-perfect analysis that can only be achieved, if at all, in the shelter of a university or other 'ivory tower' of learning, but a substantial understanding of the situation and the issues – enough to enable you to decide what action to take. Because the situation is urgent, you will do what you can and then analyse the impact of the action. You will go from analysis to action and back again.

However, before taking action it is important to develop a strategy: a series of coherent steps leading to your overall goal, which you can test and change as events unfold.

CHAPTER 4 This chapter introduces a number of tools that can assist you in thinking about strategies for action. These focus on the work being done at different levels, and by different actors, and provide a framework within which you can place the work you are already doing and identify possibilities for future work.

CHAPTER 5 It is vital to bring others with you as you develop your ideas, and to listen to them as well as persuade. Chapter 5 suggests ways of helping your organisation to rethink its role in relation to conflict and begin to adjust its policies and practices. An individual working alone, without a group or organisation, is unlikely to make a significant impact on any social or political conflict. We suggest that, following on from the steps you have taken to develop a strategy to address conflict, you also consider developing a strategy to influence the policies of your organisation.

There is another dimension to policy work which is just as important. It is hard enough to change the way one's own organisation operates, but even more difficult to change the way other organisations do their work. Yet, the more analysis you do, the more you realise how crucial it is to influence others. These could be organisations working at the same level as yours or those operating at other levels, nationally or internationally, for example, who have an effect on what you do or on the people you work with. This is something to bear in mind as you consider your own organisation's orientation and capacity. (See pp. 100 and 101 on lobbying and campaigning.)

4-BUILDING STRATEGIES TO ADDRESS CONFLICT

SUMMARY ■ This chapter begins by suggesting reasons why it is important to make a strategy, and to keep it up to date as your thinking and your interventions unfold. It then offers six tools that provide different approaches to building a strategy.

Introduction

Why analyse conflict situations? If your answer is 'in order to change them', you are like most of the people involved with RTC. One could, of course, make a career out of analysis by aiming for a perfect, objective analysis, or by seeking to become the acknowledged expert on a particular situation. But if you are primarily interested in practical action, you will aim for a solid understanding of the situation and the issues, good enough to help you decide what to do. Because the situation is urgent, you will do what you can and then analyse the impact of the action. You will be going from analysis to action, and back again.

However, before taking action it is important to have a strategy, otherwise you just have a series of uncoordinated actions that may lead nowhere. Strategy-making follows analysis. This is the decision-making stage. Having analysed fully the conflict situation you are dealing with, you now have a fair degree of accumulated knowledge about the context and the dynamics of the problem you are addressing. You now need to identify what can be done and how you can do it.

FROM ANALYSIS TO STRATEGY

This is a decisive step, moving from looking at the situation to trying to influence it. Analysis can reveal possibilities for action. Each person and each group will have certain opportunities, depending on their place in the situation and their particular abilities. The tools of analysis have revealed aspects of the problem which can now form the basis for strategy-making. New ways of seeing what you already know about your situation can help you decide where to begin.

You need to remember that you are likely to be dealing with a multi-headed monster. However complete your analysis may be, it is still important to look further. For instance, you may decide, on the basis of your analysis, that you have identified the root cause of the conflict, and therefore assume that by addressing that root cause you will bring the conflict to an end. In our experience, however, this is rarely the case. The dynamic of protracted social and political conflict is such that people join it at different moments and for different reasons. It ends up looking much more complex, with many layers and many root causes. Even identifying and addressing the very central original cause will no longer resolve the conflict, because so many other layers of causality remain.

Looking at the example of Northern Ireland illustrated in Figure 4.1 on the following page, it is clear that the root causes of the conflict in the 1960s had to do with civil rights (voting, election districts) and access to employment and housing. By the 1980s two of those three areas (civil rights and housing, but not yet employment) had been addressed with some degree of success. However, by then the conflict had more to do with people's sense of identity and the preservation of their culture. And always there were people fighting for political sovereignty, for their religion and for different borders. At each step there were people who joined the conflict because they had suffered, or to avenge those killed. So the conflict continued. Only when **all** these issues had at least begun to be addressed, when people believed that a solution could someday be found in each area, would the conflict be able to move towards a lasting settlement.

❂ If many threads are bound together, they can tie up a lion. **ETHIOPIA**

FIGURE 4.1: PERCEPTIONS OF ROOT CAUSES OF CONFLICT
NORTHERN IRELAND IN THE 1960s AND 1980s

NORTHERN IRELAND
IN THE 1960s

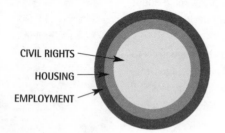

CIVIL RIGHTS
HOUSING
EMPLOYMENT

NORTHERN IRELAND
IN THE 1980s

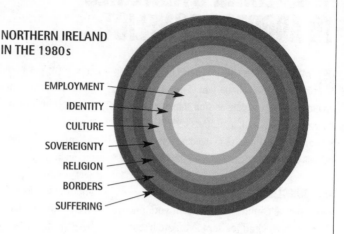

EMPLOYMENT
IDENTITY
CULTURE
SOVEREIGNTY
RELIGION
BORDERS
SUFFERING

SO MUCH TO DO

This kind of analysis seems to complicate the problem, revealing so many layers and perspectives that it seems impossible to resolve the whole situation. The positive aspect of this complexity, however, is that everyone can find something to do which may help. And if many people work on different aspects of the conflict and coordinate their activities to achieve maximum results, there is a real likelihood of improvement.

WORKING TOGETHER

A glance at any complicated and challenging context can lead to feelings of being overwhelmed and powerless. But you are not on your own. What allies can you think of? The evidence from many different and difficult places is that situations do change: South Africa, Guatemala and Northern Ireland all looked unchangeable for many years. Change did not come easily, but it did come, thanks to the combined work of many organisations. Engagement with conflict is definitely an area of synergy: the effect of all the initiatives is somehow much greater than the sum of them.

There are always individuals, organisations and institutions involved in one way or another in activities that contribute to conflict transformation and peace-building. Often they will have different labels, e.g. development, education, income generation, rights, peace, health. But if you look behind the labels you will find people who share your values and vision for the future. As we think in this way new partnerships suggest themselves – even, perhaps especially, with those you have up to now seen as rivals, who may respond positively to suggestions of joint action on particular issues.

HOW TO USE THIS CHAPTER

The tools and techniques presented in this chapter can help you look at a question from a variety of viewpoints, and so enable you to develop a coherent and inclusive strategy. Each needs, of course, to be adapted to meet the actual situation.

Our experience indicates that good results can be obtained by using these tools and techniques in sequence, in such a way that each step builds on results already achieved. We would therefore recommend that you use the following tools in the order in which they are given, basing the process on a problem that you have already analysed using the tools in Chapter 2:

• **VISIONING:** Start by exploring your vision of how you would like the future to be in your area. Articulating your vision is a reminder that the greatest motivation is the hope of a better society in the future. People's primary stimulation comes not from the negative aspects they are working to remedy, but from the positive elements they hope to build.

- **MULTI-LEVEL TRIANGLES:** This tool builds on the pyramid analysis in Chapter 2 (p.32). It can enable you to identify key actors at each level of your situation, and to explore the connections between them as well as the power relationships between the levels.

- **MAPPING FOR ENTRY POINTS:** This begins with the map produced in Chapter 2 (p.23) and goes on to look for opportunities. If you want to intervene in a conflict, this tool may give you new ideas as to what could be done and with whom you might cooperate to achieve it.

- **THE GRID:** Use the grid to form a more detailed picture of specific kinds of work that can be carried out, and of what is already being done and where there are gaps. This may provide you with further ideas of who might undertake new work, what you could do next and how different groups can work together.

- **THE WHEEL:** Use the wheel to identify how different aspects of your work complement each other. This tool can help you to explore ways of undertaking short-term work that will also contribute to a longer-term vision and vice versa.

- **AID AND CONFLICT:** This section invites you to consider the actual and potential impact of programmes dealing with the forces for violence and for peace in a specific situation, and to consider how to maximise your support for 'local capacities for peace'.

- **THE STRATEGY CIRCLE:** Finally, the strategy circle brings together many of the tools and techniques described in this book. Focusing on your own context, it offers a comprehensive means to elaborate a strategy for action. But keep it under review, as the associated case study suggests.

Visions: building and sharing

The fact that you are reading this book probably means that conflict is an issue for you. It may perhaps have been your choice to work in the midst of conflict, but for most of us conflict came and found us while we were trying to do something else. No one would wish for acute social or political conflict as a permanent fixture in a society, so concentrating on severe conflict is something we hope not to have to do in future. Our intention is to correct the problems and then get on with other things.

Some of the motivation for this work comes from problems that force themselves into the spotlight. People find energy and creativity to improve a situation which they see as urgent and terrible. They focus their attention on understanding the problem in order to create a real solution to it. In addition, however, motivation comes from the vision that draws people towards the future. This is the positive pull, the motivation that complements the negative push brought about by the unacceptable face of current reality. People rise in the morning and get through the day in the hope of moving closer to their vision for the future, the better society they hope to build for their children and grandchildren.

A CLEAR VISION OF ONE'S OWN, AND TO SHARE

To remind yourself of the hopes and dreams that motivate you:

1. Take some time to reflect by yourself. Free up your imagination. Visualise the future you want to achieve in your community or society. Do not worry if it seems too unreal or overambitious. That is *your* vision! Try not to use words – instead, think in images. Draw your vision. (It may help to think of several timeframes, perhaps 5, 10 years and 50 years.)

2. Think back over all the years you have been working for social change. What are the consistent values that underlie your vision? To begin with, ask yourself 'Why are we doing this? What are we trying to achieve?'

VISIONING

WHAT IS IT?

▸ A reminder that one works for things, and not only against them.

▸ A way to explore one's hopes and values, and share them with others.

WHEN TO USE

▸ When feeling alone, powerless, dispirited.

▸ When groups disagree about aims.

▸ When planning new work or strategies.

▸ To notice positive changes.

HOW TO USE

▸ Alone, within groups, or between groups.

VARIATIONS

▸ Begin by challenging small groups to come up with a shared vision.

AN EXAMPLE OF A VISION – drawn by a participant of a Working With Conflict course

Then ask yourself 'Why are we trying to achieve it? What difference are we hoping to make?' and finally, 'Why are we trying to make this difference?' Keep asking 'why' until you reach the values underlying the work you do.

3. Share your vision and your values with others. This may help to clarify them, and at the same time add to what you can see. It may also help you to discover common values that underlie different aspects of your work.

4. Consider whether different people share visions and values that are the same or compatible. To what extent could you build a future together? You could try drawing a shared vision of the future in 10 years' time.

5. Your vision is the point of departure for you, so make it the basis for your actions. Does your current work contribute to your vision in a practical way? Or does it in some ways work against it? What changes could you make to bring your current work and your vision into harmony?

6. The next step is to think about the obstacles that are preventing you from reaching your vision. What entry points can you find to overcome them? You can use the analysis tools in Part 1 to help with this. (See also the Values Tree, p.80.)

Multi-level triangles

This is a tool that was invented during one of our 'Working With Conflict' courses in order to better illustrate and understand the kind of complex multi-level situations that many course participants were analysing.

Multi-level triangle analysis builds on the pyramid analysis begun in Chapter 2 (p.32). It combines multiple pyramids (3-level triangles) in a way that helps one to see the multiple levels of actors within each grouping or party, as well as the ways in which these groups of actors relate to each other both within the same level (horizontally) and between levels (vertically).

HOW TO USE THIS TOOL

1. Decide on two or more vertical levels in the situation (e.g. local, national, international, or family, community, regional).

2. Starting with level 1 (e.g. local), draw triangles to represent the key parties or groups at that level. Place them horizontally, with the size of each triangle representing the strength (in terms of influence, numerical size or political power, for example). Those that are allied with each other could be grouped together on the same side, with some triangles overlapping to indicate shared interests or even shared membership.

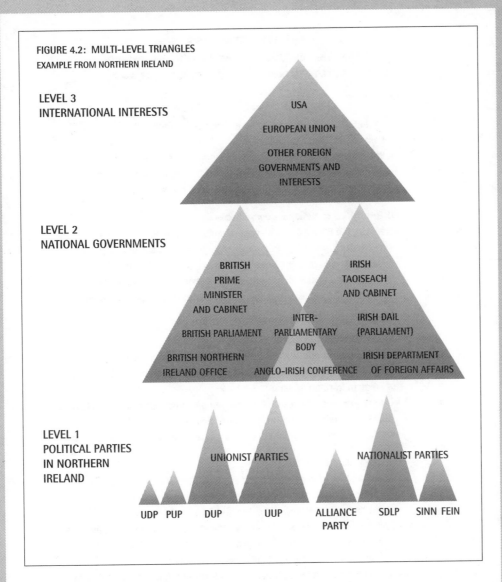

FIGURE 4.2: MULTI-LEVEL TRIANGLES
EXAMPLE FROM NORTHERN IRELAND

LEVEL 3
INTERNATIONAL INTERESTS

USA

EUROPEAN UNION

OTHER FOREIGN
GOVERNMENTS AND
INTERESTS

LEVEL 2
NATIONAL GOVERNMENTS

BRITISH
PRIME
MINISTER
AND CABINET

IRISH
TAOISEACH
AND CABINET

BRITISH PARLIAMENT

INTER-
PARLIAMENTARY
BODY

IRISH DAIL
(PARLIAMENT)

BRITISH NORTHERN
IRELAND OFFICE

ANGLO-IRISH CONFERENCE

IRISH DEPARTMENT
OF FOREIGN AFFAIRS

LEVEL 1
POLITICAL PARTIES
IN NORTHERN
IRELAND

UNIONIST PARTIES

NATIONALIST PARTIES

UDP   PUP   DUP   UUP   ALLIANCE   SDLP   SINN FEIN
PARTY

MULTI-LEVEL TRIANGLES

WHAT IS IT?
▶ A graphic illustration of key actors within and between levels in a situation.

PURPOSE
▶ To identify these key actors at each level.
▶ To include in your analysis actors who seem to be outside the situation but are active at another level.
▶ To understand the power relationships within and between levels.
▶ To see the ways in which conflicts occur within and between levels.

WHEN TO USE IT
▶ When analysing a complex multi-level conflict situation.
▶ When a simple mapping and/or 'pyramid' analysis is not adequate.

VARIATIONS
▶ Use shapes other than triangles.
▶ The pattern does not have to be symmetrical (as in the example).
▶ Use conventions of mapping to show relations.

3. Within each triangle it may be helpful to indicate the top, middle and bottom level actors within that group.

4. Repeat steps 2 and 3 for each of the other vertical levels, e.g. national and international.

5. At each higher level, the triangles can be placed above and in contact with those they relate to or are allied with at the level below.

6. Having made this graphic illustration of the multi-level relationships, you might then try to describe the specific conflicts that exist within and between the levels. You can also list what strategies are being used or might be used to address these conflicts.

Figure 4.2 relates to the political situation in Northern Ireland as it was in mid-1995. Level 1, representing the political parties in Northern Ireland, shows the range of Unionist and Nationalist parties, with the Alliance Party in the middle and the parties that relate to armed paramilitary groups on the two extremes. Level 2 represents the British and Irish governments, with the overlapping area representing the Anglo-Irish Conference and the British–Irish Inter-Parliamentary Body. Level 3 represents the international interests that relate to the political situation in Northern Ireland.

A detailed list of the conflicts identified by this example of using the multi-level triangle

MULTI-LEVEL TRIANGLES –
APPLIED TO THE POLITICAL SITUATION IN NORTHERN IRELAND
IDENTIFIED CONFLICTS AND STRATEGIES TO ADDRESS THEM

WITHIN LEVEL 1: Political parties in Northern Ireland (NI)

Conflicts:
- about identity and nationality
- over resources and access to employment, education, housing, etc.

Strategies:
- carrying perceptions and understandings between opposing groups
- arranging cross-party meetings on economic and social issues

WITHIN LEVEL 2: National governments

Conflicts:
- between the British and Irish governments about policies and practices for governance, policing, courts, prisons, employment, education, etc in NI
- between members of the British parliament and the Irish Dail about attitudes and perceptions as well as policies and legislation for Northern Ireland

Strategies:
- Anglo-Irish Agreement, resulting in Anglo-Irish Conference and Secretariat
- British–Irish Inter-Parliamentary Body

WITHIN LEVEL 3: International interests

Conflicts:
- within the EU about their policies in relation to Northern Ireland
- among politicians and lobbying groups in the USA about American policies in relation to Northern Ireland

Strategies:
- discussions and debates in the European parliament and within the European political groupings about their attitudes and concerns in relation to NI
- conferences in the USA that present a range of political viewpoints from NI

BETWEEN LEVELS 1 & 2

Conflicts:
- about the lack of consultation and participation for NI parties in political processes and decisions being made by the two governments
- about the nature and level of police and British army activity in NI

Strategies:
- informal meetings between Unionists and members of the Irish Government
- conferences and other gatherings of Northern Ireland politicians together with British and Irish politicians to discuss policies for NI
- meetings between political parties and British Northern Ireland Office in relation to concerns about police, army and prisons affairs

BETWEEN LEVELS 1 & 3

Conflicts:
- among NI parties about the extent of international involvement they want
- related to support from the USA and elsewhere for armed groups in NI

Strategies:
- facilitation of contacts between international groups and NI political parties
- visits by NI politicians to the USA and elsewhere to share their views

BETWEEN LEVELS 2 & 3

Conflicts:
- between the British Government and various levels of government in the USA about fair employment policies in NI
- between the two governments and the European Union (EU) about the nature and extent of involvement by the EU in the affairs of Northern Ireland

Strategies:
- opportunities for dialogue and discussion between the two governments and the relevant groups and politicians in the USA
- discussion of differences between each of the two governments and the EU

tool, together with the strategies to address them, is set out on page 62 opposite.

Mapping for entry points

Our vision of the future and our values can motivate us and give us direction. If you used the vision-building suggestions on p.59, you may have felt this quite strongly. But equally, you will not have forgotten the many obstacles preventing you from realising your vision. This form of mapping can help you begin to find entry points to deal with these obstacles.

HOW TO USE THIS TOOL

If you are unsure which problem to focus on, it may be helpful to first use the Conflict Tree (see p. 29) to clarify your thinking and then map the situation as you see it. The example we use here builds on the Afghanistan example shown in Chapter 2.

1. Take a previous map you have created, or map a new situation you wish to address.
2. Where and how have you mapped yourself and your organisation in relation to other parties?
3. In analysing the map you have made, look for possible entry points, such as structures that need to be changed or created, issues you wish to address, marginalised groups that could play a positive role, or blockages to communication that could be unblocked.
4. Is the timing right, and do you have the right contacts, to work on the conflict itself? Can you help matters by linking disconnected parties?

   BLOCKAGES: Notice where specific blockages exist between parties, i.e. broken relationships between parties that used to be linked, or gaps between parties that have never had any lines of communication between them. Are these blockages between parties at the same level in the conflict, or are they at different levels? What links already exist between the parties at different levels? Can you build on these links, or introduce new ones between groups? Are

there other groups who could do this work more effectively?

   MARGINALISATION: Are there parties or groupings who do not seem to have good contact with anyone? What connections seem possible, or useful to the parties involved? Are there other groupings in the broader society who could make links with these people?

5. What contacts or possible openings for making contact do you have on either side of the blocked relationships? If you have access on only one side, do you have colleagues or partner organisations that might have access to key people on the other side? Remember that groups are made up of people who may see things differently. Can you break down each group and find individuals within them with whom you can work? Think also about the levels on which you and others are working. Are there gaps that could be filled? (See the Multi-Level Triangle and Grid tools on pp. 60 and 64.)
6. Is this the right time, and are you in a position, to work on structures or issues?

   STRUCTURES: Would a different structure (perhaps an inter-party parliamentary group or a community development steering committee) be the best way to improve the situation? Which conflicting parties and which other groupings could you work with to bring about this change?

   ISSUES: Are there issues that are not being dealt with at all? If no one seems to be thinking about the needs of victims or the importance of a bill of rights, for example, you might want to start a series of community discussion meetings, or bring an experienced speaker from abroad to chair a radio panel, or produce a comic book to get people thinking about the issue.
7. What would you hope to achieve if you decided to intervene in this way? What specific action might be possible or appropriate at this stage in the conflict? Who else might be available and willing to work with you on this action?

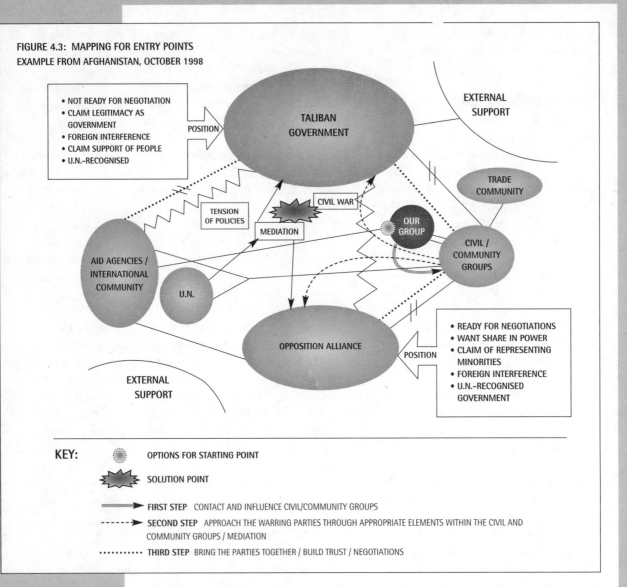

FIGURE 4.3: MAPPING FOR ENTRY POINTS
EXAMPLE FROM AFGHANISTAN, OCTOBER 1998

- NOT READY FOR NEGOTIATION
- CLAIM LEGITIMACY AS GOVERNMENT
- FOREIGN INTERFERENCE
- CLAIM SUPPORT OF PEOPLE
- U.N.-RECOGNISED

POSITION

TALIBAN GOVERNMENT

EXTERNAL SUPPORT

TRADE COMMUNITY

TENSION OF POLICIES

CIVIL WAR

MEDIATION

OUR GROUP

CIVIL / COMMUNITY GROUPS

AID AGENCIES / INTERNATIONAL COMMUNITY

U.N.

OPPOSITION ALLIANCE

POSITION

- READY FOR NEGOTIATIONS
- WANT SHARE IN POWER
- CLAIM OF REPRESENTING MINORITIES
- FOREIGN INTERFERENCE
- U.N.-RECOGNISED GOVERNMENT

EXTERNAL SUPPORT

KEY:

OPTIONS FOR STARTING POINT

SOLUTION POINT

FIRST STEP CONTACT AND INFLUENCE CIVIL/COMMUNITY GROUPS

SECOND STEP APPROACH THE WARRING PARTIES THROUGH APPROPRIATE ELEMENTS WITHIN THE CIVIL AND COMMUNITY GROUPS / MEDIATION

THIRD STEP BRING THE PARTIES TOGETHER / BUILD TRUST / NEGOTIATIONS

8. How would you propose to get started? What would be the first step in your plan of action? Share your analysis and proposed action with others and get their reactions and feedback to what you are suggesting.
9. Return to your map and indicate your proposed action.

The conflict map presented in Figure 4.3 is taken from the second example on page 24). At that stage it was an analysis of the situation showing the parties involved or influential in the conflict. As a step forward beyond analysis, the map could also be used as above, to point to strategies for action. It is very natural that people whose backgrounds and capacities are different will suggest different entry points for the same conflict. You will need to use the other tools in this chapter, as well as those in Chapter 5, to determine which entry points will be most effective.

The Grid: ideas for work on conflict

The Grid offers an excellent means of identifying multiple possibilities for action on conflict. To draw up a grid, begin by listing the kinds of work in your situation which target the conflict itself, entering them on the top row of your grid. The following list gives a variety of suggestions, which, according to their relevance to your situation, can be cut or added to.

CATEGORIES OF WORK RELATING TO CONFLICT[1]

- **CONFLICT MANAGEMENT WORK** is aimed at developing and offering a range of alternative approaches for handling disputes non-violently and effectively. The methods might include customary or traditional methods, joint problem-solving, negotiation, mediation, arbitration.

- **PEACE EDUCATION AND TRAINING** is designed to educate people about concepts and skills for dealing with conflict and for promoting peace. This work includes courses and workshops offered in schools and other educational institutions, as well as workshops and practical courses which might be offered in a variety of other locations, such as community associations, religious organisations, workplaces, professional associations and political institutions.

- **MUTUAL UNDERSTANDING WORK** is designed to decrease ignorance, suspicion, prejudice and stereotyping between individuals and groups who are in conflict with each other. The emphasis is on improving communication and understanding through various programmes that bring people in contact to listen to each other and to discuss their differences.

- **SUPPORT FOR MARGINALISED GROUPS** aims to enhance the confidence, capacities for positive action and power of excluded groups in a society. This can be done, for example, by designing special assistance programmes or establishing partnerships with vulnerable groups, e.g. disabled people, religious and racial minorities, victims of war, gypsies.

- **ANTI-INTIMIDATION WORK** is designed to decrease various types of threats, harassment

and verbal abuse that are directed against members of particular ethnic, religious or political groups. Intimidation occurs when people of a particular group are forced to leave their homes or their jobs because of the fear of harm from another group. Anti-intimidation work is aimed at helping people to feel safe and secure where they live and work.

- **CULTURAL TRADITIONS WORK** is designed to affirm and develop cultural confidence and acceptance of cultural diversity within a society. This work is based on a belief that feelings of alienation can result from the exclusion or denial of a particular culture. It also suggests that the development of cultural confidence can contribute to the capacity of a community to enter into negotiations with other communities without feeling too insecure about its own culture.

- **JUSTICE AND RIGHTS WORK** is designed to develop collectively agreed principles of justice and rights in society. There is an emphasis on enabling conflicting groups to see issues of justice and rights as common concerns which they share and which can be of benefit to all, rather than seeing OUR rights as more important than THEIR rights.

- **POLITICAL OPTIONS WORK** is designed to facilitate political discussion within and between conflicting groups. This work enables people to listen to those whose preferred political options are different from their own. It is aimed at trying to develop alternatives that can satisfy the valid political aspirations of the majority of people from all these differing groups.

LISTING SECTORS/LOCATIONS/LEVELS IN WHICH THIS WORK CAN BE DONE

On the left column of your grid, list the sectors, locations or levels where work on conflict might be done. Again, this is only a suggestion, and you should use only those items that are relevant to your own situation. You can also add other sectors, target groups, locations/levels to your list, as necessary.

THE GRID

WHAT IS IT?

▶ A graphic that shows work on conflict being carried out with different groups within a society: the types of work, where it takes place and who is doing it.

PURPOSE

▶ To appreciate how much is being done already.

▶ To clarify where there are gaps: work not being done, sectors not being helped.

▶ To identify possibilities for new work, joint work and mutual support.

WHEN TO USE IT

▶ When groups seem to be competing.

▶ At moments of despair that nothing seems to be happening.

▶ At times of rapid change, when needs might not be noticed.

VARIATIONS

▶ Begin by identifying your area of work, and related areas; think about the work you do now, and the work you might do in the future.

▶ When used by the active agencies, or by the community, it often prompts broader discussion/research.

▶ It is interesting to see examples from very different situations, and to ask: 'Could we work in that way?'

- **COMMUNITY GATHERING PLACES:** market-places, community/residents' associations

- **WORKPLACES:** offices, factories, businesses, industries

- **RELIGIOUS AND CULTURAL INSTITUTIONS:** with leaders as well as grass roots members

- **EDUCATIONAL INSTITUTIONS:** schools, colleges, universities, adult education centres

- **PROFESSIONAL ASSOCIATIONS AND TRADE UNIONS:** teachers, social workers, journalists

- **LEGAL/JUSTICE SYSTEM:** courts, judges, lawyers

- **SECURITY SERVICES:** police, military, prisons

- **POLITICAL INSTITUTIONS:** traditional leaders and institutions, i.e. rulers, chiefs, elders, clans; also political parties, local government, state government, federal government, international level actors, e.g. OAU, OAS, UN, NATO.

Once you have created your own grid, you can fill in the boxes to indicate what work is

TABLE 4.1: CONFLICT GRID
EXAMPLE FROM CAMBODIA

ROMDUOL

already being done to improve the conflict situation, in each case including the programme and/or agency that is carrying out the work. Begin with your own organisation and then go on to include other work that you are aware of. Be sure to include the work of existing institutions such as elders, the government and community organisations. You may want to ask others to help you fill in the boxes.

Having done that, note any boxes that are still empty, or where work is ineffective, and consider whether this is a type of work, and a location/level of work, that your organisation, or someone else, might be able to undertake in the future.

For example, a small organisation that was involved in conflict management training realised, after their grid analysis, that their training programmes were substantially limited to staff members of aid agencies (workplaces and professional associations). So, they decided to explore the possibility of offering training in rural areas (community centres) where a range of other people could also be trained.

Table 4.1, left, shows a grid that has been adapted to include a key. It is from a community group working in Phnom Penh, Cambodia.

The Wheel

The Wheel, as shown in Figure 4.4, is a graphic representation of some general aims and areas of work on conflict, and how they relate to each other.

Notice how conflict cuts across the three areas of need that a society may have. It can affect the basic needs of a community (such as food, water, housing or health), it can affect the ability of a community to develop further, and it can also impact on the wider institutions and norms of a society.

In addition, any of these three areas can become a source of conflict: for example, conflict over resources in times of scarcity, conflict that arises when one group feels disadvantaged by the development of another, and conflict

that is perpetuated as a result of a breakdown in social values and the existence of a culture of violence.

In order to improve the situation, these three dimensions will all have to be dealt with – by interventions aimed primarily at immediate material needs, including the consequences of conflict; by others addressing development needs; and by others aimed at building the long-term peace.

Nearly all programmes can include an element that builds up the social fabric of the society. For example, the provision of emergency shelter on its own would target short-term material needs only, but making this part of a consistent policy for social and economic development (e.g. by providing building skills and helping to establish new industries for widows and the disabled) would increase its effect in both depth and breadth.

RAISING QUESTIONS

The wheel can be used to describe and raise questions about the work of a particular organisation and the dimension(s) which it intends to address.

In the past, an organisation may have concentrated its efforts on addressing the material consequences of conflict. This analysis allows it to look at ways of carrying out longer-term

THE WHEEL

WHAT IS IT?

▶ A tool to show how different aims and areas of work relate to each other.

PURPOSE

▶ To check which areas are being neglected.

▶ To show how different aspects of work fit together.

WHEN TO USE IT

▶ When you seem to be in a new stage of conflict.

▶ When there is disagreement about what should be done.

HOW TO USE IT

▶ List the types of work you are doing and enter them into the wheel. Which areas are you focusing on? Does your programme have aspects that are building peace? Are they integrated into your other work?

VARIATIONS

▶ For policy or practical action.

▶ 'Areas of work' can vary with the situation.

▶ Can be inverted, to show that the social fabric is the inner and most important layer.

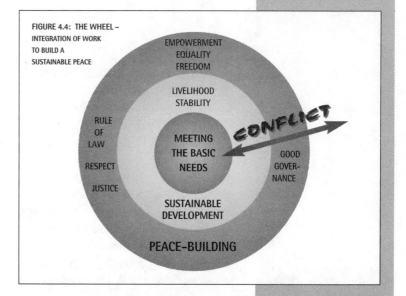

FIGURE 4.4: THE WHEEL – INTEGRATION OF WORK TO BUILD A SUSTAINABLE PEACE

EMPOWERMENT EQUALITY FREEDOM

LIVELIHOOD STABILITY

RULE OF LAW

MEETING THE BASIC NEEDS

CONFLICT

GOOD GOVERNANCE

RESPECT

JUSTICE

SUSTAINABLE DEVELOPMENT

PEACE-BUILDING

projects to address underlying issues within the social fabric of the society. In the future, the organisation may then decide to engage in areas that address the conflict directly, with the aim of restoring peace.

Using the wheel as a graphic model of the situation raises the question of whether all the areas of need are being adequately addressed. For example, it may become apparent that nearly everyone is addressing the direct consequences of the conflict. If that is the case, then more work needs to be done in other areas, to resolve the immediate conflict and to bring about long-term changes within the society. Is there sufficient capacity to address conflict, wherever it may occur, in your programme or beyond?

Carrying out a wheel analysis may raise the question: What is the actual impact of my programme? The material that follows, on **Aid and Conflict**, can help in providing the answer. The **Wheel** can usefully be combined with the **Grid** to formulate a picture of what is currently being undertaken in a situation and which areas still need to be addressed. This can be both a positive and a negative experience – on the one hand reminding you of all the work that is already under way and where your own efforts fit into this, and on the other presenting a challenge by showing where further work is needed.

Aid and conflict
DO AID/DEVELOPMENT ORGANISATIONS CONTRIBUTE TO VIOLENT CONFLICT?

Aid and emergency relief are often provided with the best of motives. However, there are always unintended consequences. Agencies believing their work to be neutral, even outside the conflict, may well influence the situation without realising it. There is now a lot of evidence that aid and development programmes operating in unstable and violent contexts can help to fuel the escalation of violence, or reduce it. The following section (to p.72) draws on and adapts the work of Mary B. Anderson in *Do*

No Harm, How Aid Can Support Peace or War (see chapter 10 for details).

TRANSFER OF RESOURCES
When external resources are introduced into an area of conflict, they can change the balance of power. This happens most directly through **theft**, when agencies provide new resources which are then stolen, taxed or diverted by conflicting parties to feed their own troops.

However there are several more **indirect** ways in which harm is done.

• **INCREASING RESOURCES FOR WAR:** When aid agencies meet civilian needs, and specifically those of the supporters of different factions, local resources are freed up to support the fighting forces. This narrowing of responsibility can lead to commanders redefining their roles as exclusively military, with the result that, when the fighting is over, they have little knowledge of, or sense of responsibility for, civilian affairs.

• **ADDING TO THE INFLUENCE OF THE MILITARY:** When warring factions control the passage of aid, it gives them power and legitimacy as providers for the people and enables them to manipulate populations. For example, they can make people move to another area, and weaken opposition groups by keeping resources from them.

• **DISTORTING MARKETS:** The temporary provision of new resources distorts local economies, making it more difficult to a peacetime economy. For example, if high wages are paid to local skilled staff, then existing organisations and wage structures are undermined and expectations raised. Imported resources damage local markets for food and other items, and housing rents become so high as to be beyond the reach of most local people.

• **REINFORCING TENSIONS:** External resources tend to feed into existing suspicion and rivalry, offering a source of greater power to those leaders who gain control over them. Where the poorest groups are targeted, inter-group rivalry can be especially severe (e.g. refugees and host communities).

HIDDEN MESSAGES

While the intended message of aid is one of compassion and solidarity, the unintended messages often reinforce violent conflict.

- **ACCEPTANCE OF THE TERMS OF WAR:** Negotiating access to civilians and hiring armed guards are examples of behaviour that demonstrates an acceptance of weapons, both as a prime and legitimate source of power and as a satisfactory means of deciding who should receive assistance and how.

- **GIVING LEGITIMACY TO WARLORDS:** When agencies negotiate with the leaders of factions, they give them recognition and legitimacy. They demonstrate that they accept these people as having the right to exercise power in an area.

- **UNDERMINING PEACETIME VALUES:** Wide differences in the standard of living of expatriate and local staff and discrimination between them in terms of security (evacuation for whom?) show that contrasting values are placed on the well-being of local and international staff.

- **DEMONSTRATING IMPUNITY:** Expatriates who use scarce resources such as vehicles and fuel for their own private purposes give local people the impression that it is acceptable to use aid intended for others for one's own benefit. This mirrors how local warlords may use resources for themselves or their supporters.

- **PROMOTING INTOLERANCE:** Inter-agency rivalry suggests that there is no need for us to cooperate with those we do not like and that it is acceptable to be intolerant of differences.

- **PUBLICITY CAN INCREASE HOSTILITY:** Pictures and stories of brutality and suffering by one or both sides are used to raise funds internationally. In the conflict itself this can reinforce the demonisation of one side by the other.

HOW CAN AID AND DEVELOPMENT AGENCIES CONTRIBUTE TO PEACE-BUILDING?

It has long been recognised in the case of food aid that if no account is taken of existing local producers, the long-term result of emergency imports is likely to be the elimination of much local capacity and greatly reduced self-reliance in food. It is taking a long time for the parallel situation in relation to peace-building capacity to become clear. So long as agencies – both local and international – ignore existing resources for peace- and justice-related activity, they lose a great opportunity and risk severely worsening the situation.

A further priceless opportunity is lost when agencies are not sensitive to the potential for integrating new peace-building work into their own programmes.

DISCOVERING AND ENHANCING NEW CAPACITIES FOR PEACE

In every intense conflict there are people who have become involved simply because they could see no way out. They remain silent and accept what is done in their name because to resist would demand too high a price. The compelling sense of group identity in, for example, an 'ethnic' conflict, is born primarily of fear, and overwhelms other sentiments such as morality and friendship with members of the 'enemy' group. People in this position constitute a latent source of new capacities for peace.

More evident, possibly, are some existing institutions and systems. For example, those used by the hostile parties, such as health, education and electricity supplies, embody a common interest and may have the potential for engaging parties in informal communication. Traditional conflict-resolving institutions, such as elders and customary courts, could also become involved.

Aid can, when used imaginatively, provide opportunities to strengthen and support both new and existing capacities for peace, without drastic changes being made to the programmes themselves. Among the less obvious ways of doing this are:

- **SPACE:** Aid can provide a place where people can act in 'non-war' ways, and where they can engage with people on the opposing side(s) in joint initiatives. In doing this, agencies can encourage people to keep alive, and perhaps work for, the hope of a shared future.

- **VOICE:** Agencies can provide a forum where peace and cooperation can be discussed, and even take the initiative in making peace or conflict resolution the subject of meetings and workshops.

- **INCENTIVES:** Agencies can use their financial and other resources, and their access to the wider world and to the media, to encourage actions and the expression of views that work towards peace, and to discourage activities that make for more hostility. This can include a clear policy to counter war-related propaganda with information that can motivate people to withdraw their support for and participation in hostilities.

AID AND CONFLICT: An example from Afghanistan[2] – organising and empowering the community to resist pro-war forces

In Kanisk village in Farah province, the village Jirga (similar to a council of elders) was formed in 1997 to organise its contribution to the village irrigation rehabilitation project. The Jirga was able to organise 200 labourers for three to four months. During this time, new branches of a canal were extended in order to irrigate 1000 jeribs of new virgin land. Later, the Jirga had the courage and power to say no to the authorities when they demanded recruits for military service. The Jirga is also in negotiation with the authorities to reopen the village school, which has been closed since

March 1998. In Aral Musazai village, the Jirga managed to obtain an exemption from sending villagers to military service, which the local authorities had made compulsory.

It is important not to overemphasise the significance of aid, and NGOs more generally, either in encouraging or reducing armed conflict. Nobody is suggesting that wars are caused by international aid or by rival NGOs. However, it is worthwhile to ensure that, as far as possible, a specific programme is not making a potentially violent situation worse. And if it contributes to peace, then an opportunity is not lost.

The following section offers a tool built on Mary Anderson's ideas, devised by RTC to explore the impact of an agency's programme on conflict.

Mapping the impact of aid and development programmes on conflict

The activities described here are intended to produce essential information for policy-making in areas of actual and potential armed conflict. They should enable you to answer the question: Who gains and who loses from the way my programme operates? They should also enable you to examine different policy options, to see wheher they risk worsening the conflicts in the area, or, on the other hand, if they have the potential to strengthen local resources for peace and justice.

MAPPING THE IMPACT ON FACTORS SUPPORTING VIOLENT CONFLICT

The first step is to ensure that your programme is not making the situation worse. One way of doing this is described below.

1. Identify the situation you wish to analyse as precisely as you can.
2. Summarise the main aspects of your programme in the three categories of physical resources, capacity-building and advocacy. Put the details of your programme in the middle of a circle.

3. Draw three outer circles surrounding the programme. Each circle represents a different aspect of society: the **Context** (of systems and groups), their **Attitudes** and **Behaviours**. Elements of all three of these aspects could be forces for violence or for peace (remember the ABC Triangle from Chapter 2).

4. Write in what you consider to be the forces for violence, putting them in the appropriate circles.

5. Now consider the links between the different aspects of your programme and the forces supporting violence:
   - In what ways are you unintentionally supporting these forces? Are you contributing to an economic system that allows the war to continue?
   - Are you fuelling tensions by supporting one group of people at the expense of another?
   - Are you unconsciously reinforcing attitudes of superiority, or jealousy?
   - Are you encouraging behaviour that devalues the opinions of others?

   Draw jagged (lightning) lines where your organisation is supporting these forces, either directly or through indirect/hidden connections and messages, explaining this as necessary.

6. In what ways is your programme undermining the forces supporting violence?
   - Are you reducing the power of groups who benefit from the violence?
   - Are you working actively to build trust?
   - Are you promoting alternative forms of behaviour?

   Draw straight lines to show these factors.

On the next page, Figure 4.5 shows the mapping of a programme's impact on the forces for violence while Figure 4.6 shows its impact on the forces for peace.

ANALYSING IMPACT ON FACTORS SUPPORTING PEACE AND JUSTICE

The second step is to identify existing factors that favour peace and then examine the current

and potential impact of your programme on them. In order to do this, the above process is repeated as follows:

1. With the same well-defined situation in mind, create another similar diagram and list the main influences for building peace and justice.
   - Under **Context** include two subheadings: 'Groups' and 'Systems'.
     Systems could include processes that link people and are participatory and empowering, or traditional systems for managing conflicts.
     Groups could include organisations that are broadly contributing to peace-building, including businesses that need peace to operate, NGOs, specific projects, and so on.
   - Under **Attitudes** include, for example, trust, mutual understanding, lack of prejudice (if these exist), specifying who holds these attitudes if necessary.
   - Under **Behaviour** include actions that are inclusive of hostile groups and build co-operation, and those that are explicitly building peace and justice (mediation, media initiatives, projects that reach across the lines of conflict).

2. Describe in the same brief way the main aspects of your programme, and write this in the middle of the diagram.

3. Now consider the links between your programme and the forces for peace and justice. In what ways are you supporting these forces?
   - Draw solid lines to illustrate the connections, as above, in order to delineate both direct and indirect/hidden connections and messages. Write in additional words as necessary.

4. In what ways could you be supporting these links further, through existing or new work?
   - Indicate this with a different colour/style.

5. In what ways might you unintentionally be undermining any of these 'local capacities for peace'? Use a jagged (lightning) line to indicate this. Can you do anything about it?

IMPACT MAPPING

WHAT IS IT?

▶ *A method for identifying opportunities for peace-building.*

▶ *A way to analyse the impact of programmes on conflict situation.*

▶ *A tool for policy-making to reduce unintended negative impact.*

WHEN TO USE IT

▶ *This tool is intended primarily for groups that are working in conflict areas but not yet on conflict itself.*

▶ *Before intervening in conflict.*

▶ *When a programme seems not to be achieving results.*

▶ *When the situation changes.*

HOW TO USE IT

▶ *Carefully consider what are the forces for peace or violence in your specific situation, before moving on to analyse the links with your programmes.*

▶ *Be very concrete and specific in your analysis.*

▶ *Broaden the inquiry by seeking different views, different perspectives.*

▶ *Share the results with partners and others.*

VARIATIONS

▶ *Use pillars or force fields to show what sustains violence and peace.*

▶ *Compare results with other, similar agencies, to notice patterns and possible areas of joint action.*

FIGURE 4.5: POTENTIAL IMPACT ON THE FORCES FOR VIOLENCE*

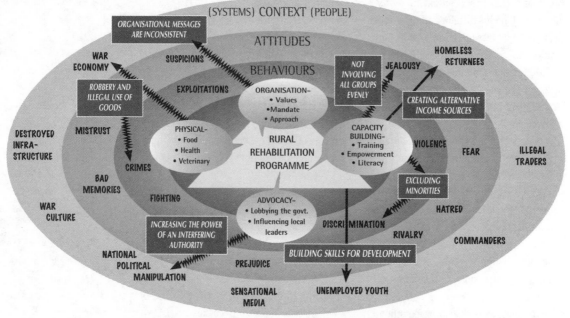

KEY: **CAPACITIES FOR VIOLENCE*/PEACE** POTENTIAL IMPACT ～～～→ NEGATIVE OUTCOME —→ POSITIVE OUTCOME △ THE PROGRAMME AND ITS ASPECTS

FIGURE 4.6: POTENTIAL IMPACT ON THE FORCES FOR PEACE**

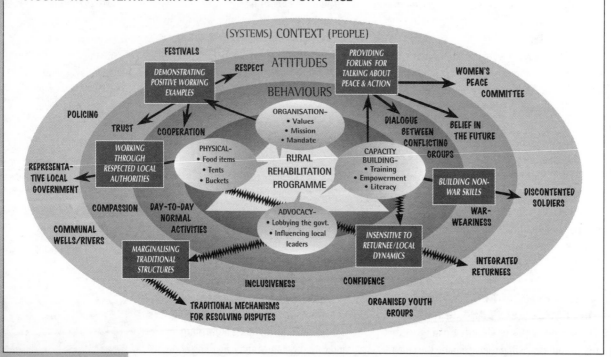

The Strategy Circle

No single action or strategy will achieve peace. It is through collective responsibility and a combination of actions that a real difference will be made.

The Strategy Circle (see Figure 4.7 below) is a way of bringing together all the tools for analysis that we looked at in Chapter 2 as well as this chapter's tools for identifying strategies for action. Working in a group with others from your organisation, you will be able to use the Strategy Circle to bring all of your thinking and analyses together and to plan strategies and specific actions aimed at moving closer to your long-term vision.

AN EFFECTIVE COMBINATION OF STRATEGIES

The numbered activities in Figure 4.7 indicate a series of steps in conflict analysis, which you may want to try. You may have to put aside the main task of strategy-making when you engage in these activities, exercises and bits of research (perhaps with other people), and then bring the results back and incorporate them into the Strategy Circle. You can choose to include any of the steps below:

1. VISION / GOAL
• Re-examine what it is you **really** want to achieve.

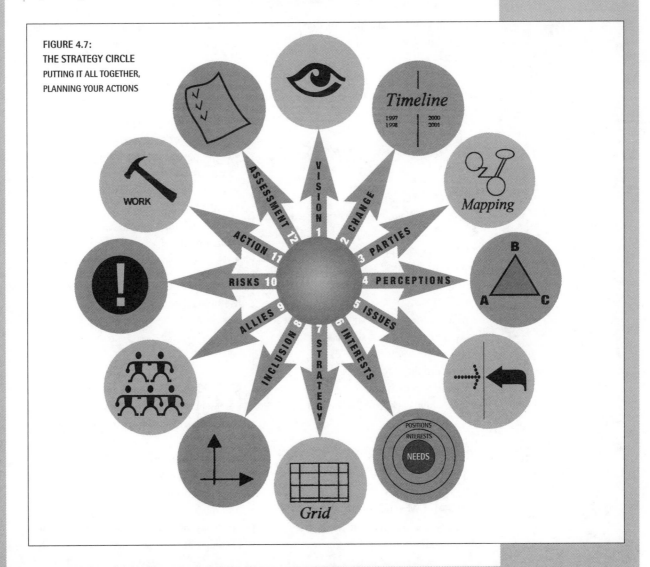

FIGURE 4.7:
THE STRATEGY CIRCLE
PUTTING IT ALL TOGETHER,
PLANNING YOUR ACTIONS

2. CHANGE

• What or who needs to change to make it possible for you to reach your goal?

• How much change has already been achieved?

It may help to draw a **Timeline** (see pp. 20–22) showing both the history of the situation and a possible future.

3. PARTIES

• Who are the major parties in this situation?

It may be useful to **Map** the situation (see pp. 22–5). This will help you to see graphically who the parties are and where they stand in relation to each other. The map may also help you to answer the questions in numbers 5 and 6 below.

4. PERCEPTIONS

• What are the parties' needs and fears?

• How does each party perceive the problem, and the other parties? You may want to use the **ABC Triangle** (pp. 25–7) to analyse the situation.

• What are the attitudes and behaviour of each party, and what part do they play in the situation?

• What are their stereotypes, prejudices and perceptions of each other?

• How would each describe the situation?

5. ISSUES

• What issues, other than the most obvious ones, are there underlying the context?

• What are the particular implications of these issues, and how do they affect each party and their stake in the conflict?

The various issues that are singled out and discussed in Chapter 3 may be relevant in most situations. However, there are also likely to be significant smaller issues in each situation which you may want to consider investigating.

6. INTERESTS

• How does each party relate to your goal?

• Would achieving your goal block other parties in the achievement of theirs?

You may find it useful to look at the layers of each of the other parties' understanding of the situation:

• How does each party define its interests?

• And those of other parties?

• If the parties act according to their own interests, will this actually meet their needs?

• Who has a vested interest in continuing the conflict?

• Are there common interests to which you can appeal?

• Who could block the change you want?

To help with this exercise, you may find it useful to refer to the Onion (pp. 27–9).

7. STRATEGIES

• What strategies can you devise so that everything works towards your goal?

This is an invitation to decide on the way your interventions should take place and the areas you need to address.

A number of tools introduced in this chapter, including the **Grid** (pp.64–7) will be useful in carrying out this task.

8. INCLUSION

• How can you include other parties' interests, needs and fears in your strategy?

• A long-term strategy may consist of many actions. Can your strategy be expanded to include others', without compromising your goals or theirs?

• Your strategy may be more successful if you keep in mind not only your goal but also your relationships with other parties. If you build good links and relationships with other parties, it is likely that they will understand your actions better and fear you less. You may then discover that even though your interests and goals are different, they may yet be compatible.

• If your strategy attempts to address the needs and interests of other parties, they may be prompted to support your efforts as well.

9. ALLIES

• Do you have enough common interest with other parties to form an alliance?

• Could you build wider coalitions, to work together for a limited time or purpose?

• How could you build confidence among the parties?

• Do you share enough objectives, values and ways of working with your potential allies?

• If you work together, can you carry out more kinds of action, at more levels?

• Might you cause problems with your own work or that of your partners by entering a coalition?

10. RISKS

• Are there hazards you have not taken into account?

• Could you make things worse?

• This might be a good time to do a 'Do No Harm' analysis (see Mapping the Impact, p.70: What are the local forces for peace and violence, and how can you support the former instead of the latter?

• How can you test your strategy with minimum risk?

• What do you need to learn in order to decide whether the strategy works? If you can try parts of it, or test it on a small scale, you can then use it later on a larger scale.

11. ACTION

Now is the time to implement the decision that you have arrived at with this method of strategy-making. You may find it helpful here to jump forward to Part 3 (p.91) for guidance on different forms of action. Your actions will be based on the strategy you have just devised, adapted as necessary to your particular situation.

12. ASSESSMENT

• What have you achieved?

• What have you learnt?

• What is your goal now?

This is an opportunity to enter a new strategy circle, having moved on from the one before.

OVERCOMING OBSTACLES

This framework is best developed by a number of people, who may be from the same organisation or may be part of a network with similar goals and values. It can also be used by individuals or groups within an organisation to prepare themselves for introducing changes to a programme. However, implementation of the strategy is likely to be a challenge, as the following example shows:

AFTER THE STRATEGY CIRCLE – AN EXAMPLE

MUSSANZI WA MUSSANGO, AN X-RAY TECHNICIAN, WORKED THROUGH THE STRATEGY CIRCLE WITH A GROUP OF COLLEAGUES DURING THE 'WORKING WITH CONFLICT' COURSE. THIS IS HIS EXPERIENCE ON RETURNING TO NYANKUNDE, A REMOTE HOSPITAL IN THE NORTHEAST OF THE DEMOCRATIC REPUBLIC OF CONGO:

■ We came back, at the end of the course, like Moses from the top of Mount Sinai, with a tablet in our hands – the strategy that I was able to develop during our course. In this project we drew out clearly, using all these tools, what were the problems, the interests and the perceptions of the parties in conflict, the goals, the objectives, the actions and the strategies, the risks and the timeline for the next five years (1997–2002).

■ Unfortunately, exactly as with Moses, it was necessary to 'break the tablet' because of many problems. The first obstacle came from my own organisation, who rejected the project, claiming that it did not tally with their medical objectives.

■ By 'rejection' I mean this: the members of the Annual General Meeting of my mother organisation (Centre Médical Evangélique) are people from so far away that they do not know the reality (tribal conflict) we are struggling against daily in the hospital.

■ Unfortunately they didn't invite me to explain the project I brought from the UK! So they didn't understand why a medical centre could be involved in this new field of 'conflict resolution'. They didn't understand even why the staff of that moment had sent me to the 'Working With Conflict' course. Finally, because of the misunderstanding they decided, as I have already written, that this project 'did not tally with their medical objectives'.

■ The second obstacle came from people who were profiting from the local conflict. Discovering that they were losing their interests, they made an accusation against our team to the new leader – saying that these people are presenting themselves as peacemakers, yet they are instigators of tribal hatred amongst the population!

■ It was an anthropological matter. Indeed, in our area people do believe that if you talk about something, it will surely happen. So the solution, they think, is to avoid talking about something wrong. *Quand on parle du loup, on voit sa queue* [When you talk of the wolf, you see its tail], as they say in French.

■ For example, some tribes in DRC (even my own) do believe that by talking about malnutrition in the presence of children, they'll get this bad disease! This is why it is so hard in these communities, even today, for the medical workers to convince the population that they are wrong.

■ It is in this same sense that I have said that, in the beginning of CRC, people were accusing us, thinking that our team was the instigator of the tribal hatred. Fortunately, today they have discovered that they were wrong.

■ Influential people wrote several letters to the political leaders and to the staff of the hospital (anonymous letters). We had three very bad months (from August to October 1997): these leaders tried vainly to arrest us, to kidnap the leaders of our team, but they couldn't without proof. We have discovered that when you are doing what is right, God himself will be on your side. And the miracle took place!

■ The political leaders decided to invite our team for a one-week seminar to demonstrate their intention (later they announced to us that it was a ruse, because they wanted to know if all these accusations were founded). At the end of that seminar the leaders not only discovered how sweet this training was, but also that we were doing the best job needed by this country, which has been fighting ever since its independence, 40 years ago. This was the end of anonymous letters and the doors were opened.

■ Members of the AGM asked me to organise this project (Centre for Conflict Resolution) as a new and independent organisation, so that it could not destabilise the hospital. We are working now as an independent NGO, not 'under the umbrella' but in collaboration with the mother organisation: Centre Médicale Evangélique. Today we are glad that we are helping this country. We have found some books useful: the Bible, the Koran, *Les Conflits: origines et causes* ['Conflicts: Origins and Causes'], and we are writing our own booklets: *Gestion des conflits d'adolescence* ['Managing Adolescent Conflicts'], *Gestion des conflits conjugaux* ['Managing Marital Conflicts'].

➲ *Sometimes one of the most difficult challenges that faces practitioners, who believe it is important to address conflict in their society, is their organisation itself. Other challenges can include reducing the negative effects of other organisations that are working in the same area but are unable, or refuse, to accept that they are contributing* to violence. *The next chapter suggests ways of meeting these challenges.*

NOTES

1. Adapted from Mari Fitzduff, *Approaches to Community Relations Work*, CRC pamphlet no. 1, Community Relations Council, Belfast, 1993.

2. 'Joining People in their Struggle Against Poverty', Afghan Development Association, Annual Report 1997–8.

5-INFLUENCING POLICY
Bringing your organisation with you

SUMMARY ■ It is vital to bring others with you as you develop your ideas, and to listen to them as well as persuade. Chapter 5 suggests ways of helping your organisation to rethink its role in relation to conflict, and to begin to adjust its policies and practices.

Introduction

An individual working alone, without a group or organisation, is unlikely to make a significant impact on any social or political conflict. Resources of many different kinds are needed to ensure continuity and sustainability. But working alone may often be preferable to being part of an organisation that is incapable of, or opposed to, addressing the conflicts it faces. RTC has considerable experience of instances where highly capable participants in the Working with Conflict course have returned to their organisations motivated and confident, only to become frustrated to the point of leaving. If the management does not want to face these issues then it may use a range of defensive strategies, which often include promoting people to jobs in administration or dismissing them.

The key is to work 'with the grain' in your organisation in order:

• first to sensitise policymakers and other influential people to conflict issues

• then to assist them to rethink and reframe policy in the light of the conflict dimension.

This applies whether you are the director, the main policymaker, or a grass-roots worker. We suggest that, following on from the steps you have taken to develop a strategy to address conflict, you now consider developing a strategy to change the policies of your organisation, using all your strengths. In doing this, in bringing your organisation with you, you will be making a crucial move forward in your work for peace. It is not likely to be an easy task, and

could often seem like trying to walk through a wall. However, an organisation is not an inanimate structure. It is made up of people, and people can and do change.

AN EXAMPLE OF CHANGE

One grass roots worker from an international agency came on a Working with Conflict course and realised that her organisation was ignoring the issue of conflict, though it was working in the midst of it in several countries. She wrote a paper setting out the reasons why the organisation should rethink its policies. She presented it to the staff at headquarters, beginning with those she knew were likely to be sympathetic to the ideas. As a result, field staff in all the organisation's programmes were asked to reassess their work in relation to conflict, actual and potential, and prepare case studies of their experience. A workshop followed where this experience was shared and conclusions drawn about the future policy of the organisation at field and headquarters levels. Since then the organisation has developed a research dimension on conflict in conjunction with other agencies, and has made it a priority for staff at headquarters to systematise the learning on conflict and feed it back to the field.

There is another dimension to policy work which is just as important. It is hard enough to change the way one's own organisation operates, but even more difficult to change the way others do their work. Yet the more analysis you do, the more you realise how crucial it is to influence others. They could be organisations working at the same level as you or those operating at other levels, nationally or

✿ Devagar se vai ao longe. Slowly you get very far.
BRAZIL

▸ *A rapid method to make an organisation's values explicit.*

PURPOSE

▸ *To clarify the basis of an organisation's choices about policies and actions.*

WHEN TO USE

▸ *When re-examining strategy or specific policies.*

▸ *When focusing on the variety of values behind your organisation.*

▸ *Where there are conflicts about priorities.*

HOW TO USE

▸ *It is essentially a group activity. Start with a vision-building exercise (see Chapter 4, p. 59) and draw out key values from these. Explore areas of disagreement openly, without feeling the need to agree on everything.*

internationally for example, who have an effect on what you do or the people you work with. While this is not the main focus of this chapter, it is something to bear in mind as you think about your own organisation's orientation and capacity. There is more about this aspect of policy change in Chapter 6.

How to use this chapter

This chapter introduces a number of tools that can assist you in the process of rethinking and reshaping organisational policy. They provide different perspectives on organisational policy in relation to conflict. The tools can be used independently or in the order given here. They can also be combined with some of the tools introduced in Chapter 4.

- **THE VALUES TREE – WHAT DO WE STAND FOR?** explores organisational and institutional values and invites reflection on these in relation to policy and practice, within the organisation as well as outside.
- **SPECTRUM OF STRATEGIC OPTIONS** offers a range of options for working in a conflict situation and elicits new thinking on

alternative operational roles for organisations within different situations.

- **A CHECKLIST FOR NGOs WORKING IN AREAS OF CONFLICT** offers a means of assessing the relationship of existing work with conflicts in an area and can lead to new thinking on policy.
- **ASSESSING ORGANISATIONAL CAPACITY** provides a means to establish what an organisation needs if it is to develop and sustain serious work on conflicts.
- **HELPING INDIVIDUALS TO CHANGE** offers advice on how to get round people who seem likely to block every move you make.

The Values Tree: what you stand for
EXAMINING AND SHARING VALUES

Like individuals, organisations are often reluctant to examine their values. For them it is easier just to get on with the work. Often there appears to be little time for such activities.

However, because all organisations' actions and strategies are based on value systems – either explicit or implicit – and conflicts have a habit of revealing inconsistencies and divisions at critical moments (just when you want to

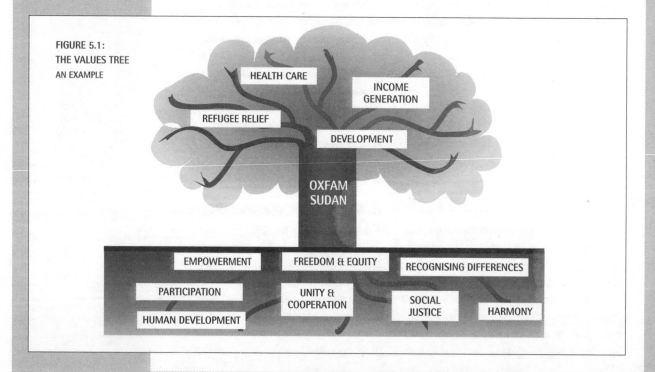

FIGURE 5.1:
THE VALUES TREE
AN EXAMPLE

HEALTH CARE

INCOME GENERATION

REFUGEE RELIEF

DEVELOPMENT

OXFAM SUDAN

EMPOWERMENT　　FREEDOM & EQUITY　　RECOGNISING DIFFERENCES

PARTICIPATION　　UNITY & COOPERATION　　SOCIAL JUSTICE　　HARMONY

HUMAN DEVELOPMENT

'get on with it'), there are advantages to making values explicit, as this helps to clarify an organisation's underlying principles or a policy's justifications.

Values can provide inspiration and underpin commitment, so it is important to remind both individuals and organisations working in areas of conflict of their original aspirations and the values underlying their visions for peace.

The Values Tree is a simple method to help members of a group articulate common values and build a common ethical basis for the group's activities. This tool allows differences to be discussed by members and the richness this diversity offers to be incorporated into a common core.

It was developed when Oxfam GB in Sudan went through the process of examining their core values in a workshop with RTC. Following a visioning exercise, they listed all their key values and agreed what to include – a demanding job in itself. It was then that they devised the idea of a Values Tree (see Figure 5.1).

The trunk of the tree is the organisation itself, the branches represent its programmes, and the roots are the values, which inform and nurture the organisation and its activities. In order to explore the relationship and relative importance of these values, the group spent some time in smaller groups working out how to place the values on the diagram of the roots. They then shared their results. This in turn provided the basis for a broader statement of values for the organisation, which they wrote up at the end of the exercise.

In the drawing of the Values Tree, it is interesting to see that the fruits of the programme fall to the ground and nurture the roots/values.
> **Does this happen in practice?**
> **Do your activities have the effect of reinforcing, or contradicting, your values?**
> **How could you change this if you needed to?**

It is also instructive to ask these questions:
> **Does our organisation actually embody the values identified?**
> **How do we see this embodiment in practice?**
> **What would need to happen for this embodiment to be truer and yet also realistic?**
> **Do others see us this way?**
> **What difference does it make?**

It is crucial that people engaged practically in working for change take time to reflect on their values and try to move closer to a realisation of common values within their groups. Such an exercise was used by Afghan development workers, who were aiming to agree on a set of common values and came up with the statement below:

STATEMENT OF VALUES – COOPERATION FOR PEACE AND UNITY (CPAU)

Cooperation for Peace and Unity was founded in October 1996 by a number of peace-loving Afghans working with various aid agencies in Afghanistan. The CPAU is a movement of Afghans, which promotes peace-building through education and action in Afghanistan. It offers training and advice in conflict management and is striving for the restoration of basic values and the revitalisation of national and traditional values in our country. The CPAU strongly believes that:
- Violence is not the solution to any problem.
- Participation at all levels, practising mutual respect, constructive criticism, and provision of equal opportunities to men and women are the fundamental elements in the affairs of all societies.
- People should have the right to elect their political leadership freely and be allowed to practise differing political and religious beliefs.

The CPAU is working for a world free of discrimination of any nature, in which everyone has the right to social development, including basic health care and education. The CPAU believes that everyone has the right to develop their own identity without fear.

Spectrum of strategic options

Most organisations find it difficult to adapt to the rapid changes that characterise a conflict situation. Often when responses are made they are not based on a deep analysis, or an understanding of what their implications are and what their opportunities might be. Even when an analysis or understanding exists, it is seldom articulated, and many opportunities for learning are lost. Table 5.1 is a list of options available to organisations working in areas of conflict or crisis (see Stages of Conflict, p.19).

Often policymakers assume that there are only two real programme options when faced with violent conflict: either to stay or to leave. When introduced to the spectrum there is often some surprise, followed by a recognition that the options indicated in the spectrum do reflect what agencies are actually doing, even if they are not articulating their strategies in this way.

This spectrum has been drawn up with an external organisation in mind, which is offering services in a situation that is in the stage of confrontation or crisis (see Chapter 2, Stages). It is important to note that there is no 'right' way implied here. There is no best or worst option. Each situation will have its own unique characteristics and will require a unique response. For example: 'Withdraw' can be a deliberate and

publicised act which avoids complicity and makes way for advocacy work to draw attention to an intolerable state of affairs. It can also be a hasty retreat by an organisation that has made no contingency plans and wants to save its expatriate staff at all costs. What remains as important as ever is that the response is based on a thorough analysis and that both its intended and unintended consequences have been considered.

A checklist for NGOs working in areas of conflict
ASSESSMENT OF PROGRAMMES IMPLEMENTED IN AREAS OF CONFLICT

The Checklist in Figure 5.2 represents a tool for assessing the relationship of a programme to conflicts in the area. It was developed in Pakistan for Afghan NGOs, at a workshop in 1994 facilitated by RTC and the Post-War Reconstruction and Development Unit at York University.

The questions can be used together as a checklist for reviewing the orientation, effectiveness and conflict impact of a particular programme. The purpose is to clarify the position of your programme in relation to the conflict you are working in, to raise questions

TABLE 5.1: SPECTRUM OF STRATEGIC OPTIONS IN STAGES OF CONFRONTATION OR CRISIS				
WITHDRAW	REACT	ADAPT	SUPPORT	INTERVENE
The organisation decides to withdraw all or part of its operation, in the awareness that either staying or withdrawing makes a statement and has consequences.	The programme continues with the same objectives, with changes necessary for it to continue, such as negotiating travel permission with armed groups as well as government officials.	The programme is consciously reassessed for balance and differential impact, and adapted to ensure equity and participation of polarised groups.	Local initiatives are sought and suported which actively address the conflict, aimed at preventing escalation or improving communication and relationships between groupings.	The organisation actively intervenes in the conflict, offering links to international mediation, training or resources to 'level the playing field', or other such options.

about programme policy, and to sharpen thinking about specific areas of activity to be addressed. When staff of your organisation are asking questions about how peace-building can be implemented in practice, this exercise can prove helpful. A first step is to decide whether these are the right questions for your situation, and to add or remove questions to fit your particular situation.

If you choose to use the questions as they stand, you can get an overall idea about the status of your programme in relation to the conflict by counting up the number of yes and no answers. An Afghan colleague has offered the following classification. Do you agree with it? Why not improve on it?

a. **CONFLICT UNAWARE:** if your answer is 'no' to all 15 questions
b. **CONFLICT AWARE:** if your answer is 'yes' to 1–5 of the questions

---

FIGURE 5.2: CHECKLIST FOR PROGRAMMING

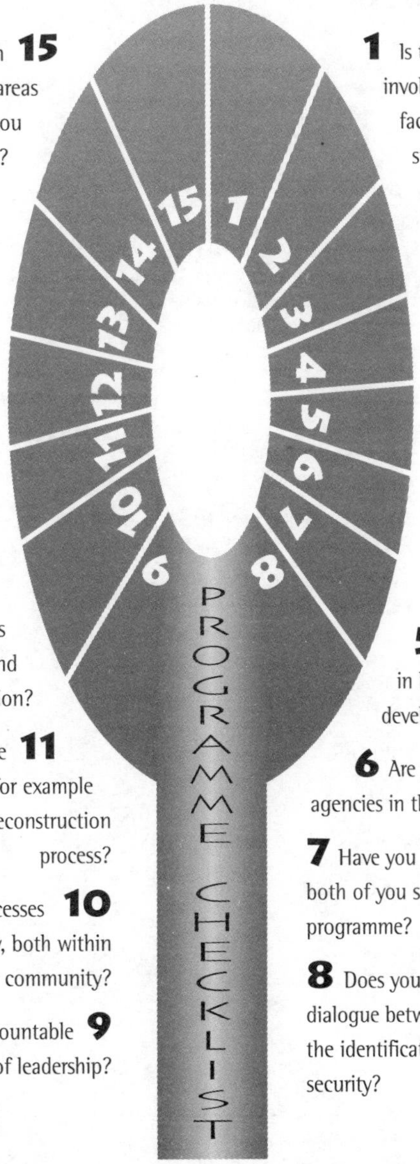

15 Have you made a serious enough long-term commitment to work in such areas to justify the outlay and the hopes you raise?

14 Are you keeping donor agencies fully informed of the progress of the work as well as the continuing needs?

13 Are you doing anything practical to assist the victims of war, in particular widows, children and the disabled?

12 Are you assisting people, as necessary, in coping with the trauma of violence, injury and the psychological damage caused by experiences such as loss of relatives, witnessing atrocities and intimidation?

11 Does your programme foster hope and the vision of a better future, for example through active involvement in the reconstruction process?

10 Do you encourage and make use of processes for handling disagreements peacefully, both within organisations and in the wider community?

9 Does the programme encourage an accountable style of leadership?

PROGRAMME CHECKLIST

1 Is there ongoing consultation and involvement with all affected groups and factions in the area, using indigenous structures wherever possible?

2 Does the programme meet the needs of a range of interests, not just those of one powerful group?

3 Are you monitoring the programme at first hand to avoid the possibility of resources going to support a political faction?

4 Do you take every opportunity to demonstrate your impartiality in the conflict, and your commitment to peace and reconciliation?

5 In any relief work, are you building in longer-term sustainability and development?

6 Are you coordinating your work with other agencies in the area?

7 Have you got an effective policy for the security both of you staff and of others involved in the programme?

8 Does your programme offer opportunities for dialogue between different groups in the area, and the identification of common needs, including security?

WHAT IS IT?
▶ *A quick means to establish
what an organisation needs
if it is to carry out sustained
work on conflicts.*
PURPOSE
▶ *To identify aspects of an
organisation that need to
be strengthened.*
WHEN TO USE
▶ *When you are thinking about
starting a new programme, or
extending an existing one.*
HOW TO USE
▶ *With management, as
a tool to identify future needs
in relation to strategic
planning.*
▶ *With the whole staff, as a
way of gathering information
and identifying different
points of view.*

TABLE 5.2: ASSESSING ORGANISATIONAL CAPACITY

CONTEXT

1. **CONFLICT ANALYSIS**
   Does your organisation have a clear analysis of the conflict? Does this analysis include the history, the current dynamics and thinking about what might happen in the future?

2. **POSITIONING IN CONFLICT**
   Does your organisation have a clear sense of its own position in the conflict and its relationship to the other parties involved?

3. **POLITICAL IMPLICATIONS**
   Is your organisation aware of the possible direct and indirect political implications of its programme(s)?

4. **BALANCE**
   To what extent is your organisation working with people associated with different parties to the conflict–with the various ethnic, religious, clan, gender, age or class groups in the society?

5. **SHARED UNDERSTANDING**
   Are all of the staff in your organisation aware of your position within the conflict? How widely is your position understood by the community, and all the other parties to the conflict?

ORGANISATION

6. **CLEAR VISION**
   Does your organisation have a clear vision, clear values and a clear sense of mission?

7. **SYSTEMS AND PROCEDURES**
   Does your organisation have well-articulated policies and procedures for the programme?

8. **MANAGEMENT STYLE**
   Is your organisation clear about the style and principles of management it desires? Does it assess performance of managers in those terms?

9. **DELEGATION**
   To what degree does your organisation delegate authority? How would you rate the average degree of consultation about key decisions?

10. **HUMAN RESOURCES**
    Does your organisation manage its human resources effectively? Does it have a gender policy? Do staff feel valued and supported?

11. **FINANCE**
    Is your programme funded independently of the conflict? How transparent is your funding policy?

ORGANISATIONAL CAPACITY

PROGRAMME

12. **CONSISTENCY**
    Are the programme's aims and objectives consistent with your vision, values and mission?

13. **LOCAL NEEDS AND CAPACITIES ANALYSIS**
    Does the programme make use of local skills and knowledge? Is it responding to the articulated needs of local groups (and of women in particular)?

14. **STRENGTHENING LOCAL CAPACITIES**
    How effectively does your programme strengthen local capacities for peace?

15. **STAKEHOLDERS' INVOLVEMENT**
    Are all stakeholders involved in planning and implementing your programmes?
    What is the level of participation?

16. **EVALUATION**
    How effective is the monitoring and evaluation of your programme?

17. **SUSTAINABILITY**
    How sustainable is your programme in financial, institutional and knowledge/information terms?

RELATIONSHIPS

18. **ADVOCACY**
    Does your programme have an advocacy component? Is your advocacy work coordinated with that of other organisations?

19. **EQUITY AND DEPENDENCY**
    Does your organisation build equitable partnerships?

20. **INTER-AGENCY COOPERATION**
    Does your organisation have a policy of inter-agency coordination? Is it effective?

FROM AN ORIGINAL MODEL DEVISED BY KOENRAAD VON BRABANT

c. **CONFLICT RESPONSIVE:** if your answer is 'yes' to 6–10 of the questions

d. **PEACE-BUILDING:** if your answer is 'yes' to 11–15 of the questions.

Assessing organisational capacity
WHAT NEW STRENGTHS
DO WE NEED TO DEVELOP?

The questions set out in Table 5.2 are about four different areas of capacity that need to be considered by an organisation working in an area affected by conflict:

• The **CONTEXT**
• The **ORGANISATION** itself
• The **PROGRAMME**
• **RELATIONSHIPS** with other organisations.

In considering these questions, organisations will identify areas of weakness where capacity needs to be built, as well as areas of strength which will provide a solid basis for working on the conflict. It is important that any organisation working in an area affected by conflict considers the effect it is likely to have on the situation. These questions will help to uncover what this effect might be.

For a graphic representation of organisational capacity, this tool can be used in conjunction with the Radar Chart below.

THE RADAR CHART

Answers to questions such as those in Table 5.2 can be illustrated graphically by means of the Radar Chart (Figure 5.3). This chart shows clearly where organisational strengths and weaknesses lie.

✪ A wolf may have sharp teeth, but it will not hunt if it cannot run fast.
ANONYMOUS

THE RADAR CHART
WHAT IS IT?
▶ *A graphic display of organisational strengths and weaknesses.*
PURPOSE
▶ *To identify priority areas for capacity building.*
WHEN TO USE
▶ *During planning and assessment, before taking on conflict-related work.*

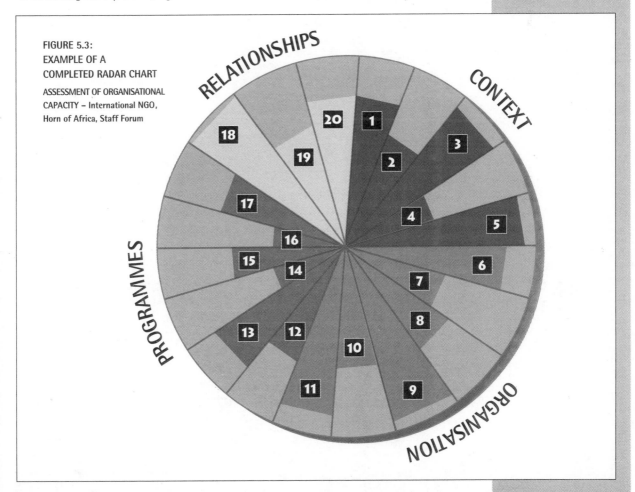

FIGURE 5.3:
EXAMPLE OF A COMPLETED RADAR CHART
ASSESSMENT OF ORGANISATIONAL CAPACITY – International NGO, Horn of Africa, Staff Forum

If this tool is used every few months, it will show what changes have taken place over time. Using it regularly can be a good way of eliciting the views of different levels of staff on where the organisation's strengths and weaknesses lie. It is a participatory tool, making it easy for people to put forward their perceptions of how the organisation is doing in each area of activity.

- **STEP 1:** Check over the questions: are these the areas that apply to you? Rewrite and simplify as necessary.

- **STEP 2:** Ask each question in relation to your organisation. Fill in the relevant section of the Radar Chart on the assessment made by those participating in the exercise. Different colours for the different areas (Context,

Organisation, etc) will make it easier to see significant areas of strength and weakness.

Looking back at the Radar Chart, you can see that the key areas of weakness are 4, 7, 14 and 16. These are the areas of **Balance, Systems and Procedures, Strengthening Local Capacities** and **Evaluation** (taken from the checklist in Table 5.2). This could then be the basis on which plans are made to build capacity in these areas. It is important also to highlight areas of strength and to maintain and enhance them.

CAPACITY-BUILDING AND PARTNERSHIP
RTC has sometimes made the mistake in the past of working with people almost exclusively to enhance their conflict skills, without adequately taking into account the capacity of

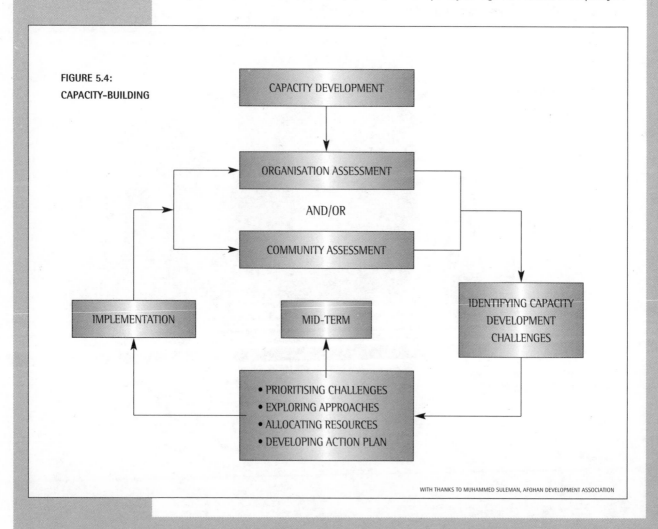

FIGURE 5.4:
CAPACITY-BUILDING

CAPACITY DEVELOPMENT

ORGANISATION ASSESSMENT

AND/OR

COMMUNITY ASSESSMENT

IDENTIFYING CAPACITY DEVELOPMENT CHALLENGES

IMPLEMENTATION

MID-TERM

- PRIORITISING CHALLENGES
- EXPLORING APPROACHES
- ALLOCATING RESOURCES
- DEVELOPING ACTION PLAN

WITH THANKS TO MUHAMMED SULEMAN, AFGHAN DEVELOPMENT ASSOCIATION their organisations to put them into practice over a period of time, and to withstand the stresses that this can bring. Grafting new policies and actions onto an organisation with weak structures and leadership can easily lead to demoralisation and, in the case of smaller organisations, even disintegration.

Capacity-building has become a buzzword and developed a variety of meanings. Broadly, it is about strengthening the qualities, capabilities, skills and resources of both individual members of staff and their organisations. It is therefore a continuous process, responsive to changing conditions in society and within the institution itself. Work on conflict creates new needs for skills and knowledge, while organisations themselves constantly need strengthening and developing.

Figure 5.4 offers one view of the process of implementing capacity-building in an organisation or a community. It illustrates a sequential process, moving clockwise from the first step, assessment of the organisation or community in question, to implementation and a new assessment of needs. In our experience, special attention needs to be paid to setting up effective procedures for decision-making and clear accountability of all those working for the organisation – especially the leadership. Without these procedures, the quality of conflict-related work, and all other forms of work, will be patchy and hard to sustain.

Helping individuals to change
WAYS TO BRING KEY INDIVIDUALS ON BOARD

Introducing change to an organisation can be a frustrating and difficult process. As important as the strategies you develop to bring about a change in a programme are the strategies you employ to encourage people to listen to the

FAHIM HAKIM

TIPS FOR WAYS OF INTRODUCING IDEAS FOR CHANGE

■ Find out what individuals can gain from change: enhanced reputation, for example. How can you make it worth their while to change?

■ Give people time: they need space to question, be confused, argue. They may well be changing their minds, but are unlikely to do this in public until they are sure.

■ People learn and change in different ways: provide different activities and experiences for them. Sometimes a course or workshop can help.

■ Avoid putting too much pressure on people or making them feel defensive or guilty: they may simply become more resistant.

■ Build good relationships: affirm those you are working with and make time to talk to them privately, in a relaxed way.

■ Find other people or organisations where they can encounter a similar message to yours. Do they have peer groups who could give them this?

■ Supply a constant stream of relevant information that supports your argument; let people hear about good practice in this field, even if it is undertaken by 'rival' organisations.

■ Provide sound reasons for change, backed by well-presented evidence.

■ Help people analyse their own experience, and that of the organisation, to see the importance of this dimension in addressing issues that arise.

■ Avoid being the only person trying to bring about this change or you may become a target for peoples' resentment: allow the message to come from a variety of people who are already agreed on the need for this change.

■ Help people believe in a better future: could you develop a common vision for the organisation?

■ Make sure you include others in your lobbying: it would be a mistake to focus only on the one or two people with decision-making power.

changes you are proposing with an open mind and to encourage them to accept that such changes are needed.

This is not about forcing your opinions onto people, but rather it is about finding ways around the problem of individuals who are opposed to change in principle, or who, because of your position within the organisation, do not listen to or respect your ideas. Ultimately, any change will have to reflect the views of all of the people it will affect. However, before these views can be elicited, people have to become open to potentially challenging ideas of change.

Above is a list of ideas on how to introduce people to the prospect of change. It has been adapted from a paper given by Professor Mari Fitzduff to the RTC consultation of international practitioners held in Derry, Northern Ireland in 1998.

OVERCOMING FEARS – AN EXAMPLE FROM CONFLICT AND CHANGE, EAST LONDON

• In a situation of conflict, people often feel powerless and unsupported. We brainstorm ideas for what is needed to support and affirm them, at a structural and an individual level.

• We then ask them to do a simple listening exercise before working in pairs listening to one other person's reactions and feelings about the intended change.

• We identify anonymously (using cards or paper) what fears people have about the proposed change – e.g. will it mean more work, or how will the role of teachers change?

• Having clustered the fears into related groups we then work on one group of fears at a time, identifying what it would need for this fear to be removed.

- Usually this exercise helps people see that there are ways of overcoming their fears and anxieties.
- The important thing is that they have been expressed openly and ideas have been generated for addressing them.

*With thanks to Ruth Musgrove of Conflict and Change –
2A, Streatfield Avenue, London, E6.*

You may want to try this approach to introducing change into an organisation, or develop your own. Be creative!

➲ *So far this book has focused on preparing for action, analysing, planning, being clear about your goals, and involving others in your ideas. Chapter 6 looks at examples of actions that you can take when intervening directly in conflict.*

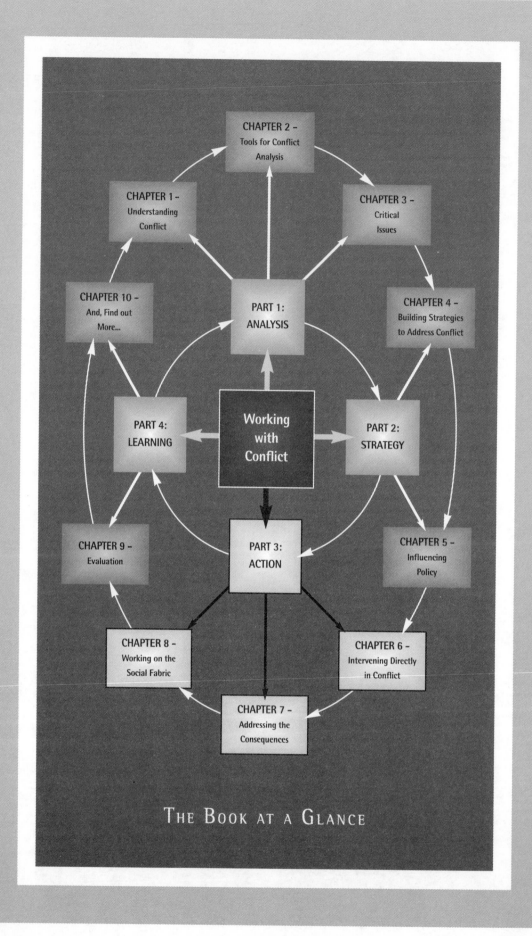

THE BOOK AT A GLANCE

✪ PART 3: ACTION

WHEREVER THERE IS CONFLICT there is the potential for peace-building. Parts 1 and 2 have offered some methods of analysing what is happening and building strategies. Now we come to action. You may well have some experience of active involvement for peace and justice already – in which case you will be familiar with some of what follows here. Or this may be a new area for you, where you may feel a certain nervousness, perhaps because of obstacles you face, or because you feel you need much more preparation.

In either case, we hope you will find much that is helpful in this section. It contains advice on a range of activities that can be undertaken to address a conflict. Our hope is that you will discover some ideas for new initiatives and some encouragement to further develop and strengthen the work you are already doing.

We cover a list of actions that are universally understood and practised, and that can be implemented or adapted for many different contexts. We have divided them into three chapters according to their aims:

CHAPTER 6 INTERVENING DIRECTLY IN CONFLICT This chapter features actions focusing on the conflict itself, including those that aim to change the dynamics and achieve a settlement and peace through managing the conflict and reducing violence.

CHAPTER 7 ADDRESSING THE CONSEQUENCES This chapter features actions focusing on the consequences of conflict, including those that respond to needs arising as a result of violence, both psychological and physical.

CHAPTER 8 WORKING ON THE SOCIAL FABRIC This chapter features actions focusing on the the social fabric of society, including long-term work aimed at transforming injustices in societal structures that could give rise to destructive conflict in the future.

These three categories tend to relate to short, medium and longer-term work. Our experience is that all three dimensions need to be included if real (positive) peace is to be achieved and sustained. It is also important that some actions address different levels: from the individual to the global. Since you cannot expect to do everything, this underlines the importance of finding allies who are working, or can be encouraged to work, on different aspects and different levels of the situation.

We have selected here some of those actions which are within the scope of middle-level practitioners. All of these have been used by our colleagues in various settings. We have included examples from their experience wherever possible. Later in the book, in Chapter 10, we have also provided suggestions of organisations and resources that might help you find out more.

There are, of course, always many entry points into a conflict – and many possible actions to take. The chart on the following page shows how vast the possibilities are, and this list is far from exhaustive. If you are ever tempted to say 'I've tried *everything*', we invite you to spend five minutes looking at this list and see if you still feel the same way.

POLICY TOOLS FOR CONFLICT PREVENTION AND MITIGATION

OFFICIAL DIPLOMACY
Mediation
Negotiations
Conciliation
Good offices
Informal consultations
Peace conferences
Unilateral goodwill gestures
Conflict prevention or
    management centres
Special envoys
Diplomatic sanctions
International appeal/
    condemnation
Crisis and war diplomacy
Coercive diplomacy
Diplomatic recognition
Withdrawal of recognition
Certification/decertification
Hot lines

NON-OFFICIAL CONFLICT MANAGEMENT METHODS
Mediation
Support to indigenous dispute
    resolution and legal institutions
Conflict resolution or prevention
    centres
Peace commissions
Civilian peace monitors
Visits by eminent organisations/
    individuals/witnesses
Friends' groups
Nonviolent campaigns
Non-official facilitation/problem-
    solving workshops
Cultural exchanges
Civilian fact-finding missions
Humanitarian diplomacy

SOURCE: MICHAEL LUND,
*PREVENTING VIOLENT CONFLICT:
A STRATEGY FOR PREVENTIVE
DIPLOMACY*, USIP, 1996.

MILITARY MEASURES
Preventive peacekeeping forces
Restructuring/integration of
    military forces
Professionalisation/reform of
    armed forces
Demobilisation and reintegration
    of armed forces
Military aid
Military-to-military programmes
Alternative defense strategies
Confidence-building and security
    measures
Non-aggression agreements
Collective security or cooperation
    arrangements
Deterrence
Demilitarised zones
Arms embargoes or blockades
Threat or projection of force
Disarmament
Arms control agreements
Arms proliferation control
Crisis management procedures
Limited military intervention
Peace enforcement

ECONOMIC AND SOCIAL MEASURES
Development assistance
Economic reforms
Economic and resource
    cooperation
Inter-communal trade
Joint projects
Private economic investment
Health assistance
Agriculture programmes
Aid conditionality
Economic sanctions
Humanitarian assistance
Repatriation or resettlement of
    refugees and displaced people

POLITICAL DEVELOPMENT AND GOVERNANCE MEASURES
Political party-building
Political institution-building
Election reform, support and
    monitoring
National conferences
Civic society development
Training of public officials
Human rights promotion,
    monitoring and institution
    building
Power-sharing arrangements
Decentralisation of power
Trusteeship
Protectorates
Constitutional commissions and
    reform

JUDICIAL AND LEGAL MEASURES
Commission of inquiry/war
    crimes tribunals
Judicial/legal reforms
Constitutional commissions
Police reform
Arbitration
Adjudication
Support to indigenous legal
    institutions

COMMUNICATION AND EDUCATION MEASURES
Peace radio/TV
Media professionalisation
Journalist training
International broadcasts
Promote alternative information
    and communication sources
Civic education
Formal education projects
Peace education
Exchange visits
Training in conflict management,
    resolution and prevention

INSIDERS AND OUTSIDERS

Most of those working on a conflict are likely to be 'insiders' – that is, people working on their own situation or one they have lived close to for a long time. This may well be true of yourself, reflecting the reality that people more often than not have to solve their own problems. 'Outsiders', those not directly involved but who are concerned about what happens, can be of assistance. But they can also be a hindrance. This is not surprising: arms manufacturers, for example, are outsiders with a particular agenda and thrive on violent conflict. Drug traffickers are another such group.

However, even amongst outsiders who wish to influence the situation in the direction of peace and justice, there are many who have the opposite effect. In our experience the main reason for this is that they act too soon, without listening to people involved in the situation. As a result they act on several assumptions which may be false:

- Nothing significant has been done to address this conflict before.
- There are no local methods of addressing conflict that might be effective.
- There are no local people with the necessary expertise.
- The local culture is much like their own (the outsiders') culture.
- There are no local groups and organisations with the potential to make a difference in this situation – to be capacities for peace.
- The methods they have developed in their home countries can be taught and applied in any other country, with little or no alteration.
- This conflict can be addressed effectively as a local issue.

▶ **However, it is important to say also that outsiders do often play a crucial and highly positive role. In fact, without external individuals and organisations who have and are willing to offer resources and expertise, many initiatives cannot be implemented effectively. Local actors, if not supported morally or materially, not infrequently find themselves too weak to withstand the pressures of the situation, although they may well have the necessary experience and expertise. The key for outsiders is to see their primary role as enhancing the effectiveness of insiders, ensuring at all stages that the insiders are the primary vehicles for change. Revitalising and strengthening local capacities for peace and community structures will be an important achievement to aim for.**

Previously, most outsiders tended to be from the rich, 'democratic' countries. One of the exciting developments RTC has seen over the past few years is the increasing number of practitioners from conflict-affected areas becoming competent and available to assist colleagues in situations in other parts of the world in addition to their regular work. With their hands-on, lifelong experience of conflict and peace-building, such people can be remarkably effective.

▶ **Every society has its own methods for resolving conflicts, and any action to address modern conflicts needs to take these into account. Consider which customary approaches, or elements of them, might be relevant. It is also important to be constructively critical. For example, referring a problem to elders rather than a state institution could seem to be an excellent move. However, if elders in the area, almost by definition, exclude women, one may want to question the wisdom of such an action.**

If you have been invited to help deal with a conflict as an outsider, we suggest that you take time to examine the assumptions you have. Test them by listening to others, and thinking critically. Only in this way can you ensure that your ideas and methods are based on actual needs and are fully orientated to the local situation.

6-INTERVENING DIRECTLY IN CONFLICT

SUMMARY ■ This chapter describes a number of possible actions to influence conflict directly. Chosen from a wide range of possibilities, these actions are practical and within the scope of ordinary people committed to building peace and justice.

Introduction

The categories and suggested actions covered in this chapter are:

PREPARATORY INTERVENTIONS

1. **Identifying and changing approaches to conflict:** framework for understanding how one reacts in conflict and for expanding the range of approaches one can use.
2. **Identifying and reducing prejudice:** steps to help identify and change your own stereotypes and prejudices as well as those held by parties in conflict.

AWARENESS-RAISING AND MOBILISATION FOR CHANGE

3. **Lobbying:** direct approaches to decision-makers and those who have access to them in order to persuade them to make or change specific policies or legislation.
4. **Campaigning:** actions that aim to mobilise the wider public on a particular issue so that decision-makers will be forced to change policies or legislation.

5. **Nonviolent direct action:** actions that aim to change a situation of injustice or oppression through nonviolent force and persuasion.

PREVENTION

6. **Preventing conflict from escalating into violence:** actions dealing with conflict at an early stage to prevent it from becoming violent.

MAINTAINING A PRESENCE

7. **Unarmed protection:** physical accompaniment for the protection of threatened local individuals and groups by unarmed individuals from international organisations.
8. **Monitoring and observing:** actions to collect and report first-hand information on developments in a conflict situation, including verification of agreements.

ENABLING A SETTLEMENT

9. **Confidence-building:** rebuilding and enhancing mutual trust and confidence between the conflicting parties.
10. **Facilitating dialogue:** enabling conflicting parties to have direct communication.
11. **Negotiation:** a process enabling parties to discuss possible options and reach a settlement through face-to-face interaction.
12. **Mediation:** a process guided by a third party that can enable the conflicting parties to find their own agreed settlements.

> ✪ Kupha njoka mkudula mutu. To kill a snake is to cut off its head.
> **MALAWI**

FIGURE 6.1:
INTERVENING IN CONFLICT

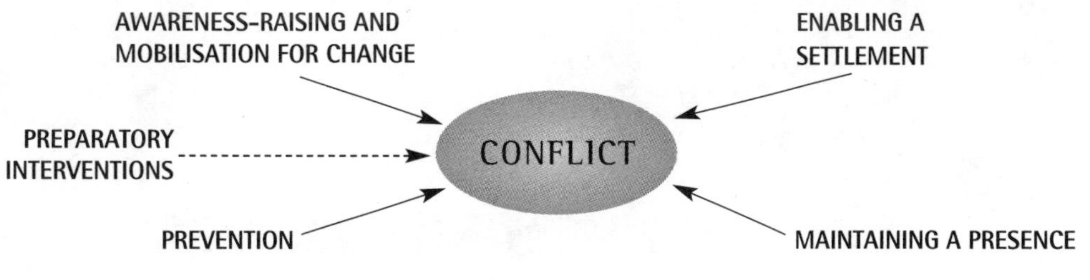

AWARENESS-RAISING AND
MOBILISATION FOR CHANGE

ENABLING A
SETTLEMENT

PREPARATORY
INTERVENTIONS

CONFLICT

PREVENTION

MAINTAINING A PRESENCE

13. **Arbitration:** action by a third party with authority to decide and enforce a settlement.

Nonviolence as an approach to conflict intervention

Conflict, as we have said, is a fact of life. Problems become acute when violence occurs. Therefore our approach to conflict intervention is a nonviolent one, in the sense that we would not want any of our actions to increase the violence or to introduce any new form of violence into the situation. It is important to say something briefly here about our understanding of nonviolence.

Many people who are living and working in situations of instability and intermittent violence have a 'pragmatic' philosophy. This means that they do not use violence because they are unlikely to achieve anything by it, and indeed would be very likely to suffer as a result. Others may be concerned about longer-term damage being caused to the social fabric by adding to the culture of violence.

In addition, almost everywhere it is possible to find individuals, groups and organisations

---

TABLE 6.1: APPROACHES TO CONFLICT

CONTROLLING

'Do it my way.'

Strategies: 'Control', compete, force, coerce, fight.

Character: Impatient with dialogue and information-gathering.

Prefers others to: 'avoid' or 'accommodate'.

(HIGH CONCERN FOR GOALS)

PROBLEM-SOLVING

'Let's resolve this together.'

Strategies: Information-gathering, dialogue, looking for alternatives.

Character: Concerned but committed to resolve.

Prefers others to: 'problem-solve' or 'compromise'.

(LOW CONCERN FOR RELATIONSHIPS)

COMPROMISE

'I'll give a little, if you do the same.'

Strategies: Reduce expectations, bargain, give and take, 'split the difference'.

Character: Cautious but open.

Prefers others to: 'compromise' or 'accommodate'.

(HIGH CONCERN FOR RELATIONSHIPS)

AVOIDING

'Conflict? What conflict?'

Strategies: 'Avoid', flee, deny, ignore, withdraw, delay.

Character: Refuses to enter into dialogue or to gather information.

Prefers others to: 'avoid'.

(LOW CONCERN FOR GOALS)

ACCOMMODATION

'Whatever you say is fine with me.'

Strategies: Agree, appease, smooth over or ignore disagreements, give in.

Character: Interested in others' information and approval.

Prefers others to: 'control'.

HIGH — CONCERN FOR GOALS — LOW

LOW — CONCERN FOR RELATIONSHIPS — HIGH

FRAMEWORK ORIGINALLY DEVELOPED BY KENNETH W. THOMAS AND RALPH H. KILMAN

who are, through belief and conviction, committed to the struggle for peace and justice, and refuse to take up weapons. For them, Gandhi's words are inspirational: '... this is a cause for which I am prepared to die, but there is no cause for which I will be prepared to kill.'

This kind of active nonviolence is more than the refusal to take up weapons. It is positive, creative, imaginative and healing. It seeks to reach out and awaken the common humanity of all involved, while also working actively to stop or prevent destructive behaviour. Constructing a viable alternative to violence and injustice is perhaps the most important power of nonviolence (see 'Active Nonviolence' in Chapter 1).

In practice, the pragmatists and the believers unite in most situations. RTC finds itself in the pragmatist camp.

In general the actions described in this chapter aim at transforming a conflict so as to reduce the extent to which it has become violent or to prevent violence from happening. We encourage you to combine actions in accordance with a longer-term, ongoing strategy. Although we have described each action separately, sometimes one intervention will require a combination of actions. The list here is offered as a starting point to give you some ideas and initial guidance.

Preparing for intervention
1. IDENTIFYING AND CHANGING APPROACHES TO CONFLICT
When intervening in a conflict it is important to be aware of ways in which you and your organisation can influence the process through your own attitudes and behaviour, which tend to reflect your particular approach to conflict. It can be useful to be aware of alternative approaches you could adopt, and to recognise particular approaches in others who are involved in the conflict.

Behaviour in conflict can be represented, at any particular moment, as the outcome of a tension between getting what you want (goals)

and trying to avoid making enemies (relationships). The range of behaviours is vast, and particular styles are defined and valued differently according to culture and context. All can be valid in certain circumstances, all can be disastrous in others. Here we offer you a framework for determining your preferred approach to conflict and some other possible approaches you might like to consider.

Table 6.1 shows five approaches to conflict arranged along two axes related to concern for goals and relationships. For example, 'Controlling' reflects a high concern for goals and a low concern for relationships; 'Accommodation' reflects a high concern for relationships and a low concern for goals; 'Compromise' represents a middle position with respect to concern for both goals and relationships.

▶ **Which of these five approaches do you most often use in conflict, either internally in your organisation or team, or externally in relation to conflicts in the community?**
▶ **Do you and colleagues in your organisation have different approaches?**
▶ **Which approaches have been most successful in dealing with conflicts in your organisation, in your family, in your community, in the wider society? Why?**

❂ If a quarrel gets too hot for you, pretend it's a game. **HAUSA**

FAHIM HAKIM

2. IDENTIFYING AND REDUCING PREJUDICE[1]

Analysis of a conflict will often highlight negative attitudes and images that conflicting parties have about each other. If these are not acknowledged and addressed, they can lead to discriminatory behaviour by each group towards the other and to increased tension and animosity between them. The relevant dimensions of conflict dynamics are:

- **PREJUDICE:** an opinion formed in advance about something, someone, or a group, without good reason or sufficient knowledge or experience.

- **STEREOTYPE:** a generalised image created when prejudice towards a particular group is so simplified that one sees all members of that group as possessing certain traits (usually negative ones).

- **DISCRIMINATION:** behaviour (usually negative) that results from prejudice and stereotypes against a particular group or groups.[1]

Discrimination can be direct, as when a law discriminates against a particular group, or it can be indirect – for example, employment conditions or qualifications that are impossible for certain groups to meet. When prejudices and stereotypes are deeply rooted in a society, discrimination may be reflected in laws and institutions as well as in the behaviour of individuals on each side.

Prejudices, stereotypes, discrimination and the 'isms' (racism, sectarianism, tribalism, sexism, ageism) can be conscious or unconscious. Few of us recognise our own prejudices, and normally we deny them, giving what we deem valid reasons for our feelings and behaviour. Institutions too often refuse to admit their discriminatory practices, claiming that they are unintentional or beyond their control.

In ethnically and politically divided societies, such negative attitudes and behaviour may be passed down from parents to children and be perpetuated by political and cultural leaders. If this is true in your situation, then it will be necessary to undertake work to address not only the actual prejudices, stereotypes and discrimination, but also the deeper aspects of the culture and politics that legitimate them.

Long-standing prejudices tend to become stronger after a violent crisis. Actions aimed at reconciliation and facilitating dialogue between groups therefore need to be included in long-term peace-building work in a post-

---

PREJUDICE: THE STORY OF A FAMILY WHO TOOK A SIMPLE BUT BOLD ACTION

In a deeply divided society, especially one where people are defined by their race, marriage across race lines is a contentious issue. Individuals who take the bold action of asserting their right to marry across the divide face a lot of challenges.

A young girl from a mixed-race marriage had difficulties within her family. These difficulties became more pronounced after her father's death. Her father, who was of European origin, had a son older than her from his first marriage. When she was with her mother's family she was treated as a white outsider, and when she was with her father's family she was treated as inferior because she was black. She was sad and did not like her colour. She always felt out of place. As a young teenager she could not go to social places.

One day her half-brother came to her and told her: 'You are my sister, there is nothing wrong with you. You are a product of love from your parents.'

He started taking her out socially with both black and white people. When the community saw the action of her half-brother they stopped treating the girl badly. This enabled her to relate to people and to appreciate herself.

---

conflict situation, along with efforts to deal with the past experience of hurt and suffering on all sides.

Initiatives aimed at helping both individuals and organisations to identify their prejudices and to find ways of reducing these at an early stage can prevent a conflict from escalating into greater polarisation and possible violence.

Prejudice reduction as an action

In this section we offer, as a starting point, some ways to recognise and explore your own prejudices before they lead you into a confrontation or crisis with other groups.

Begin with yourself and explore the prejudices that affect you without your being aware of them. Answering the following questions can help you do this in a focused way:

1. At what age did you first discover that there were different groups in your society?
2. What did people in your family and your community tell you about these other groups, and about your own group?
3. List the groups – social, political, ethnic, religious and so on – that you instinctively like, and then list those you dislike. What conclusions can you draw?
4. Do you ever feel angry with your own group because of the way it treats another group?
5. Do your responses here give you any insights into prejudices you might have against other groups? How does this make you feel?
6. Would you like to change these attitudes? Have you tried already? How?

Having asked yourself these questions, you may become clearer about your own prejudices and how you could begin to change them. To help others address their prejudices, you could use a similar set of questions (or your own version of the ones listed above) and invite them to answer the questions and discuss their own conclusions, either with you or someone else, to help them reflect on their responses. When you are working with two different groups, you might ask them to do this separately first, and then to share their responses and conclusions with each other.

While awareness of your prejudices is important, giving practical support to victims of discrimination can be helpful at all levels in society, in families, schools, communities or on a national level.

A further step is to examine what underlies the prejudice and discrimination you have observed:

- Are there individuals, organisations, institutions and structures that induce and sustain prejudice?
- What can you and your colleagues do to address these challenges?

You may wish to concentrate on raising awareness, or you may find ways to challenge prejudice more openly. It is important to remember that this can be a very uncomfortable process for people to go through. You can expect to encounter anger and hostility, and should proceed slowly and with great care.

It can be very useful to look for examples of discrimination in the society around you.
For example:

▶ **Do people have the same chances of employment, regardless of their membership of a particular group or their gender?**
▶ **Do they have equal access to justice through the courts?**
▶ **When you identify clear cases of unequal treatment, are there ways in which you can publicise them?**
▶ **Can you find allies to raise questions in places where relevant decisions are made?**

Awareness-raising and mobilisation for change

When dealing with a conflict that arises from structural violence, oppression or injustice, direct intervention may not be the most effective way to bring about the change that you think is needed. You may want to raise awareness about the situation, mobilise allies and build coalitions of individuals, groups and organisations who can join you to bring pressure on those who have decision-making power.

The methods you use will depend on the precise circumstances. Two closely-related categories for this kind of action are lobbying and campaigning. Nonviolent direct action is another type of action to be considered in this section.

3. LOBBYING

Lobbying involves direct approaches to decision-makers and those who have access to them. It is sometimes done privately so as to make it easier for those with decision-making power to change their minds without losing face, and to present the change in their own way. Lobbying is a major world industry, and whole firms are dedicated to undertaking this work on behalf of wealthy clients. The arms manufacturers have strong lobbyists, as do tobacco manufacturers.

Within an organisation lobbying often takes place before a crucial meeting, when staff or members are trying to influence a particular decision. Organisations, networks and coalitions we work with can also lobby decision-makers for changes in laws and behaviour that will promote justice, peace and human rights.

4. CAMPAIGNING

Campaigning is a broader action. It aims primarily at creating a climate amongst the wider public that will encourage or force decision-makers to change their policies. It will often include lobbying, reinforced by public pressure. The long campaign on international debt has used meetings of the G8 industrialised countries to good effect, organising imaginative activities (such as encircling the building in which they were meeting in Birmingham, UK with a vast human chain) to raise media interest. The impact was to put international debt on the summit agenda, where it had not been before, and to compel the British prime minister to meet representatives of the campaign. The International Campaign to Ban Landmines is another well-organised and highly successful initiative. The Anti-Apartheid Movement is an example of a lengthy campaign that has now been wound up after much influential work.

Campaigns can be very focused and practical. There is, for example, a strong international campaign to free Mordecai Vanunu, who 'blew the whistle' on the nuclear weaponry of Israel more than ten years ago and has been in prison there ever since, spending most of that time in solitary confinement.

Both lobbying and campaigning can take place at all levels, in organisations, communities and the wider society. Where there is freedom of expression and a measure of democracy it is an easier process, but there are always means to mobilise others, within or outside one's own situation, in support of issues which concern basic human rights and values such as justice and freedom. Amnesty International uses both techniques. It has groups all over the world that are lobbying for the release of political prisoners, and at the same time it campaigns to change public attitudes on issues such as the abolition of the death penalty.

Normally, a campaign addresses attitudes and opinions, whereas lobbying often aims to change the context (e.g. a law) and thus alter behaviour. Figure 6.2, right, uses the ABC Triangle (see Chapter 2, p.25) to illustrate the likely focus of both of these actions in a conflict situation.

Some basic guidelines for lobbying and campaigning

- Be very clear about what changes you want to take place.
- Build a small group of people committed to this. Individual efforts are likely to be less effective.
- Identify individuals and groups who you think are at least open-minded on this issue, and possibly supportive. Approach these people as potential allies; avoid those whom you know are likely to be strongly opposed.
- Do your research thoroughly, so that the arguments and evidence are strong, and the outcomes of your proposals clear.
- Try to ensure that there are no obvious losers, especially among those taking the relevant decisions.

- Take time to prepare and build a strategy.
- Try to ensure that information favourable to your aims circulates amongst those you want to influence, using the media if appropriate.
- Do not start if you are not prepared for failures along the way.
- Decide the length of time you will work on this issue, and then assess the impact, rather than beginning an indefinite effort which may run down in a demoralising way.

5. NONVIOLENT DIRECT ACTION

If parties in conflict feel that they are not being heard or cannot elicit a response, you may need to find a way of taking the dialogue to the public in order to raise people's awareness and build support. This can be done in a number of ways without resorting to violence. Types of nonviolent direct action include protest, non-cooperation, civil disobedience and fasting.

Protest

The three examples of successful nonviolent protest that follow were all taken collectively by ordinary people suffering under a particular system or process.

■ **In Brazil, a landowner used private police to harass peasants struggling to remain on their land. These police were poor people, like the peasants. One day the peasants, in silent procession, took food to the police. This was much more effective than verbal dialogue and from then on, after months of harassment, the police and army refused to shoot at the peasants.**

■ **In the Larzac area of southern France the peasants were struggling to prevent the army occupying more land for military exercises. Few people were aware of the peasants' predicament, so one day they took their sheep, with tractors and trailers, to Paris and released them under the Eiffel Tower to show in a dramatic way that sheep need land to graze on. They got enormous media coverage and suddenly the whole of France was alerted to their struggle.**

■ **In Colombia, women living in the crowded, squalid barrios of Medellin decided to take action over their lack of clean water. First they went to speak to the mayor, who made**

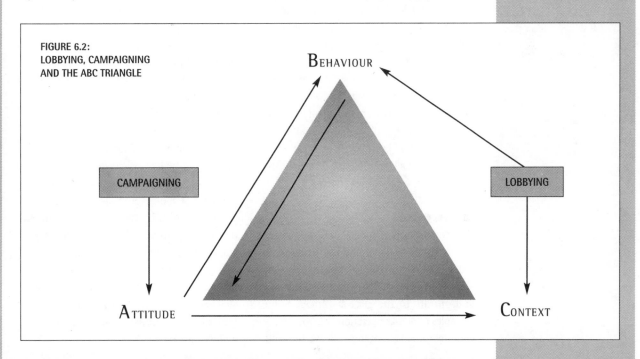

FIGURE 6.2:
LOBBYING, CAMPAIGNING
AND THE ABC TRIANGLE

BEHAVIOUR

CAMPAIGNING

LOBBYING

ATTITUDE

CONTEXT

promises but did nothing. After three months the women decided it was time for further action. They took what they had – their youngest children – and walked with them to the lovely illuminated fountain in the town and washed them in the dirty puddles around the fountain. When the first group of ten women came and did this, the middle-class women who saw them reproached them for what they were doing and this gave the poor women a chance to explain their suffering. Then the police came and pushed them away. Then a second ten women came and did the same. They were beaten by the police, and now the middle-class women defended them, but they were taken away. Then a third ten women came with their children and the reactions were further intensified. As a result, a committee was formed between the middle-class women and the women from the barrio. Together they persuaded the mayor to allow the women to build their own water system in the barrio. A plaque was put up there in honour of the women who had the courage to stand up for water and for life.

Such cases can inspire one to design and implement nonviolent actions in a variety of forms. But every situation is unique: only you and your colleagues can decide what exactly to do. It is important to remember that any non-violent action needs to be planned carefully so that the methods used are consistent with your goals. Try to foresee difficulties that may arise (e.g. intervention by police or onlookers) and make sure that all participants understand and accept the possible consequences.

Non-cooperation

Non-cooperation in this context is a refusal to participate in some process, structure or activity that you perceive to be unjust or violent. Your action can be carried out in any way appropriate to the circumstances. Some examples of non-cooperation are: boycotts of consumer goods, refusing to leave the land,

refusal to work in circumstances of injustice, military tax refusal, conscientious objection to military service, refusal by seamen to dump nuclear waste at sea.

Non-cooperation is about exerting pressure by cutting relationships and refusing to fulfil certain roles in order to achieve an important goal. When people find out that they are part of the problem they are concerned with, and that they can change the situation by taking a stand, they may be willing to stop cooperating with the system. However, analysis is necessary before acting, to see what will be lost in the process and how much of the goal is likely to be achieved. It is also important to be aware of the costs involved, including the possibility of violent repression.

Building alternative institutions

A related type of nonviolent direct action is what Gandhi called a 'constructive programme'. In short, it involves opting out of an unjust or violent system and building alternative institutions. For example, in South Africa during apartheid, people in townships opted out of official local government structures and set up their own civic structures.

Civil disobedience

Through civil disobedience people challenge unjust laws, or use the law to challenge the injustice in the system. In their struggle against racial discrimination black people in the United States persisted in using facilities reserved for the whites; this was a form of civil disobedience. A more common form is public demonstrations in places where free expression is forbidden. In some cases civil disobedience has involved direct interventions, such as putting one's body in the way of a bulldozer that is about to destroy a squatter settlement, or 'disarming' computers that control nuclear missiles.

Non-cooperation and civil disobedience are options for action that require serious moral and strategic preparation. They can undo even dictatorships if the people are united, courageous and well organised.

Fasting

As a means of purification, self-discipline and entering into the suffering of the oppressed, fasting is a very common way of nonviolent resistance. It is sometimes a successful means of drawing attention to the gravity of a situation and conveying the depth of feeling and commitment in those trying to remove the injustice or bring an end to the violence.

Many of the nonviolent actions described here, including fasting, require a high degree of commitment and endurance. They do involve risk and can even be life-threatening.

Spiritual preparation

As a support for nonviolent actions, people often adopt spiritual and inwardly reflective practices, either on an individual basis or with groups. Group prayers, meditation, and other activities of this kind provide not only a level of reassurance but also a way of expressing solidarity in the face of a problem.

Some of the actions described above may lead to unexpected consequences for the participants. It is important to anticipate and prepare for the worst that may happen, while remaining optimistic about the chances of real change.

Prevention

6. PREVENTING CONFLICT FROM ESCALATING INTO VIOLENCE

We intervene in a situation because we want to bring change for the better. What makes a conflict suddenly escalate from hostility or stalemate into violence? Is it possible to predict when this might happen? If such a change seems likely, is there anything that would forestall this escalation? We focus here primarily on the last question: how to avert an escalation into violence.

We have used the phrase 'preventing the conflict from escalating into violence' to make it clear that we do not believe that conflict

FAHIM HAKIM

itself should be prevented. Our expectation and experience is that conflict, if properly handled, can be a positive force for change. It is only when it becomes violent that conflict is automatically destructive.

In the stages of confrontation, outcome and post-conflict, it is more difficult to do preventive work because of the experiences of the people involved. When they find themselves involved in the process of trying to change their ways of relating to each other and deciding whether or not they can trust each other, a simple incident can easily be seen as proof that trust is not possible. Thus, it is especially important at these times to find ways of dealing with each incident, usually in increments, one step at a time, so that small tests of trust can be passed and small gains made in confidence-building.

Prevention of escalation into violence is a useful strategy with limited aims. It is not an end in itself and should happen within the broader context of peace-building.

In order to understand the dynamics of the conflict, preventing the situation from escalating into violence requires:

• Contextual analysis and understanding of the elements of that conflict–parties, actors, forces.
• Identifying the patterns and stages of the particular conflict.
• Identifying indicators of the different stages.
• Identifying available mechanisms, structures, as well as new ones needed to address the particular problems.
• A process of planning and designing actions to suit the situation.
• Creative thinking about new ways to do things.

Identifying and recognising indicators of escalation

People working in a situation of conflict often seem to have a sense of when things are reaching a critical point. Prevention of escalation requires being able to identify clues and signals clearly, and then intervening before the situation becomes more violent.

It is possible to develop indicators that enable you to track how a conflict is intensifying or reducing. There are many specific indicators, which vary according to the situation. They may include:

• Increase in cases of harassment by one group towards another or by police towards a particular community.
• Increase in violent incidents, even minor ones.
• Increase in incidents of public conflict, for example, in the marketplace or bus park.
• Presence of groups who are not in communication with the rest of society, whether the society seems to exclude them or they seem to refuse contact.
• Repeated expressions of grievance by the same group, which seem not to be heard or addressed.
• An apparent lack of confidence in existing structures for justice or security – whether modern or traditional – demonstrated by a reluctance to make use of these structures and a preference for 'private' justice, such as vengeance.
• Social and political tension: distrust and uneasiness among parties in the situation may manifest itself in a variety of behaviours which indicate that one party is feeling ill-at-ease or aggrieved.
• Lack of representation: people want to be represented by those they themselves select. If there is a group that lacks acceptable representation, any attempt to implement decisions affecting that group can easily make the conflict worse.
• Unbalanced development: both government agencies and community groups need to ensure as far as possible that development takes place amongst all sections of the people. Sometimes there is the danger of one ethnic or political group receiving more resources than another. This can fuel conflict, confirming one particular group's sense of injustice or grievance. (See Chapter 4, 'Aid and Conflict', p. 68.)

PREVENTING ESCALATION IN DAGESTAN: BUYING TIME FOR DIALOGUE

■ In Dagestan the Chechen minority is unpopular with many amongst the majority population. For historical reasons they are often unfairly scapegoated for many problems in Dagestan.

■ During 1999, as tension rose, 20 houses belonging to Chechens in one village were burned. At the same time a leaflet was widely circulated in Dagestan urging the population to attack and kill Chechens wherever they could find them.

■ A local NGO saw the signs of a wave of violence against Chechens, with a likely violent response from the Chechens. They tried, without success, to get government action to stop this.

■ The NGO was a member of the UNHCR-sponsored Working Group on Conflict Management and Prevention for the CIS (former Soviet Union) whose members are NGOs from the whole region. The NGO asked representatives of the Working Group to write urgently to the government of Dagestan. In the letter they said, in summary: 'We support the Federal Government of Russia in their actions against Chechens in Russia, in view of recent terrorist activities in Moscow. However, we are also aware of the unjustified violence against Chechens in your country. We have seen a leaflet that threatens the destruction of their whole population. If you allow this to go ahead the whole world will know, and condemn you for allowing it.'

■ Some members of the Working Group refused to sign the letter as they thought it was too favourable to the actions of the Federal Government who were at that moment planning to invade Chechnya.

■ The day after receiving the letter a minister of the Dagestan government appeared on television. He said that the government had not been aware of the leaflet until now, nor of the seriousness of the violence. He condemned the violence against Chechens and said the government was totally opposed to it.

■ As a result the rising tide of violence stopped, at least temporarily.

■ The Dagestan NGO immediately contacted the Committee for Youth Affairs. Together they organised a team of volunteers, consisting of different communities and ethnic groups. The volunteers brought materials to the village where the houses had been burned. They rebuilt the roofs and replaced the shattered windows.

Note: This account represents the viewpoints of several participants in this story. Others will have different views.

Some common mechanisms for preventing escalation

In intervening to prevent conflict from escalating into violence, both traditional and modern mechanisms have a role to play. In many situations there are existing mechanisms that are supposed to deal with conflict.

Good preventive strategies weave these parallel strands together. Successful initiatives use a variety of mechanisms, which might include:

• Forming a group of people from across the lines of division, which could include, for example, representatives of all the ethnic or clan groups, local government, security forces, clergy, and community leaders.

• Sending clan, tribal, or other traditional elders as emissaries.

• Inviting religious figures (e.g. leaders) to intervene, with the aim of providing space for dialogue.

• The use of ritual in order to draw people together by emphasising shared values and visions.

• The use of respected existing structures or groups (e.g. women's groups, school boards, community development committees), either as they are or modified for conflict prevention.

- Careful use of publicity to highlight the need for urgent action.

Some guidelines for preventing escalation into violence

A specific structure, mechanism or action is unlikely to work outside its own context. However, there are patterns which suggest some of the functions that need to be taken into consideration when designing a strategy to fit new circumstances.

Some common examples of the factors to be considered when designing a strategy to prevent a situation from becoming violent are given below. They need not all be done by one actor, but all must be addressed somehow.

- Investigating incidents to clarify who is involved and what actually happened.
- Controlling rumours to correct misunderstandings and malicious reports
- Facilitating dialogue with people on each side and shuttling between opposing sides.
- Demonstrating solidarity, by visiting and listening to people on all sides of the conflict – specifically, visiting those who have suffered and those who are accused or perhaps attending funerals on all sides (preferably done by a comprehensive group, representing all the sub-groups, including the group that may be held responsible for an incident).
- Building confidence and trust between opposing sides.
- Encouraging reconciliation: bringing opponents together with the aim of acknowledging past wrongs and building up long-term relationships.
- Asking sides to make pledges that such incidents will not recur.
- Asking sides to offer reparation, restitution, compensation: as a commitment to behavioural change, as well as repayment of loss.
- Healing: physical, emotional, psychological, spiritual.
- Changing structures and systems, so that the same problem will not recur.

Successful initiatives also invent new processes and structures to address particular problems, such as the development of regional mechanisms through which groups of people might express grievances that they feel are not being dealt with at local or national level. Creativity is important here, in thinking of possible problem areas as well as solutions to prevent escalation.

Maintaining a presence
7. UNARMED PROTECTION

Working for peace and justice in an area of tension and conflict can be very dangerous. One effective contribution that outsiders can sometimes make is to provide a degree of protection for local activists and peace and human rights workers by coming to live alongside them in order to accompany them in their work and other aspects of their lives. In some situations, external actors, both organisations and individuals, are less easy for an oppressor to eliminate without a public outcry that would draw attention to their methods.

In Guatemala, for example, people working for human rights have often been detained, tortured and killed by violent groups in recent decades. In the early 1980s, Peace Brigades International (PBI) began sending trained volunteers from outside the region to Guatemala to escort local activists who were working for nonviolent solutions to the political problems. This kind of **nonviolent escorting** gave protection against imminent threats to a number of leading activists.

Rigoberta Menchu, the Guatemalan human rights activist and Nobel Peace Prize winner, was regularly escorted by unarmed volunteers from PBI. The assumption in this case was, and still is, that when foreigners stay close to the activists or are present at their offices, the activists are less likely to be attacked.

PBI has now started similar 'unarmed bodyguard' work in El Salvador, Colombia, Sri Lanka, Haiti and the former Yugoslavia. Other organisations have also begun doing this.

This is a 'non-interventionist' way of taking action. The outsiders do not attempt to influence the situation directly with their own agenda. By their presence they aim to create some safe space for local activists to do their work. Besides physical protection, the presence of foreigners offers moral support (the world cares about our work!) and can encourage internal actors to speak out for justice and change.

Principal considerations

This is clearly a very sensitive field of work and requires careful planning.

If you are considering adopting a similar type of strategy, either because you feel it is needed in your situation or because you think you may be able to offer this protection to others, it is important to think it through fully in advance.

Some of the principal considerations to bear in mind are:

1. The context is crucial. This work cannot be done anywhere. It is likely to be effective only in places where the governments – or prospective authorities and forces – have a level of international recognition and therefore are wary of damaging their reputation.

   For example, PBI's work in escorting activists in Sri Lanka is limited to the areas controlled by the Sri Lankan government, which values its international reputation. Similar work cannot be carried out in territories that are controlled by the LTTE (the Liberation Tigers of Tamil Elam – an armed movement opposed to the government), which has no legal recognition and thus no image to protect.

   In Croatia, during the early 1990s, PBI effectively accompanied local human rights activists working to prevent the eviction of Serbian families by Croatian soldiers. In Serbia, however, PBI was a lot more cautious. Under economic sanctions and feeling victimised internationally, Serbs had much less reason to respect the lives of outsiders protecting local activists.

2. It is vital to have a detailed and up-to-date knowledge of the area where the escorts will be sent. Foreign volunteers should not be sent to places where they are likely to be targeted for hostage-taking or assassination.

3. Those undertaking this work must be mature people who have shown that they can stay cool in a crisis.

4. Escorts need to receive specially designed training before moving in to the area. The training should include methods to enhance their ability to respond nonviolently to provocation and to violent or potentially violent situations.

5. Escorts need to be provided with a code of conduct tailored to the needs of this particular context. They need to be clear about how to interact with groups such as the police, military, and armed groups. The basic guidelines for their work should include instructions about when and how to take pictures, take notes, write reports.

6. Escorting must be done in the fullest collaboration and consultation with the individual activist who is being escorted. Otherwise, the potential for further endangering the life of the person being protected is great.

7. Back-up mechanisms are vital in case things go wrong. There needs to be a competent base system that can react rapidly, with excellent communication between escorts and base staff, and more widely.

   PBI, for example, has an **emergency response network**. If a local activist, or a volunteer, is either arrested, threatened or attacked, a network of people around the world are quickly informed. They then flood the authorities or the responsible bodies in that area with letters and messages of protest and concern urging that the action be reversed.

> As with all actions, unarmed protection is appropriate only in specific circumstances. If it does not seem a useful strategy for you, you may still want to reflect on your own situation and identify the people who, as far as you are aware, are threatened. How can they be better protected?

8. MONITORING AND OBSERVING

Monitoring and observing are actions taken by people concerned about a conflict in order to keep themselves and others informed about how a situation changes. These 'monitors' keep track of events in a tense situation and report their objective observations to a central body, or possibly to the press. This technique is most often used either in the stage of confrontation, where feelings are running high but it is still possible to express grievances publicly, or after an agreement, as an aid to reducing tension. Monitoring can help prevent the escalation of violence by showing those who might use force that they will be seen and perhaps held accountable for their actions. Further, by exhibiting concern and interest over the situation, monitors can contribute to building a climate in which change can happen.

Informal monitoring

When you are living in a conflict, it is very

MONITORING OF VIOLENCE AGAINST WOMEN AND VIOLATIONS OF HUMAN RIGHTS
BY U.M. HABIBUNNESA, DHAKA, BANGLADESH

■ I am a member and employee of Naripokkho ('For Women'), an organisation established in 1983, which is supported mainly by contributions from its members (all women) and since 1994 has initiated some new projects with funding from donors. From a base in Dhaka, the capital of Bangladesh, we do work all over the country in order to fulfil our objectives, such as recognising women's subordinate position in order to bring changes to women's position and status in the family, in society and the state or in public life.

■ We have a network with about 260 women's and human rights organisations for our different activities around the country. All of these groups take part actively in our movement for women's rights and some work as partners on the basis of particular issues – e.g. for Naripokkho's monitoring project there are about 21 organisations that are monitoring government services locally to prevent Violence Against Women (VAW).

■ We have done 2 weeks' training for 10 people from 6 of these 21 organisations as project interns this year. We plan to train a total of 40 people from 20 organisations as interns within the 3 years of this pilot project, which began in October 1998.

■ For the other 15 organisations we organised a 3-day training workshop to plan strategy for eradicating VAW and, by the end of the project, 45 women's organisations will go through the same process. In this workshop we trained people on advocacy, networking, the Grid (a tool for strategy-building), etc.

■ Naripokkho itself is monitoring concerned services at Dhaka city level. We collect data of VAW incidents and violation of Human Rights from five national newspapers, police stations, hospitals and in the courts. To monitor the government's activity we stay in police stations, hospitals and in the court an average of 3 to 4 hours in a day. Periodically we organise meetings with concerned police, doctors and lawyers to share our findings.

■ The immediate objective of this project is make accountable and sensitise the service providers; however, the goal of Naripokkho is to reduce VAW in Bangladesh through this and some other ongoing activities.

---

likely that you will find yourself monitoring events to try to discern what is likely to happen next. One major difficulty, which can lead to violence, is the power of rumours, and the difficulty of separating fact from fiction. In some areas community leaders are developing systems which aim to assess the value of information and feed the results back to the population.

As development workers or other active members of a community, you can take on a low-profile conflict-monitoring role, as your work naturally brings you into contact with many sectors of society. As practitioners at local and regional level, you can be sensitised to look out for signs that a situation is moving from, say, a stage of latent conflict to one of confrontation. For this to be useful you need to have a clear method for information to be communicated, checked, and, if necessary, acted upon, as locally as possible.

This kind of monitoring already happens with regard to human rights in many places, with information being fed quietly out of the situation to agencies who can use it constructively. Abuse of human rights is one indicator that a conflict may escalate to violence.

Formal monitoring

Observing and monitoring as formal strategies have developed rapidly over the past few years. They are frequently used by governments, the UN, the Commonwealth and other international agencies for purposes including but not limited to validating elections, reducing tensions in the lead-up to elections and verifying that peace agreements are kept. For this purpose international teams are sent in to provide a visible presence. Unarmed observers provide evidence of the conscience of the 'international community'. Their strength lies in the constituency they represent, and the power of objective evidence to deter aggression. They can be and are ignored where these elements are not respected.

In some cases the observer/monitor role includes an option to intervene. This is called active monitoring, or the mediator–observer model, and can include, for example, anticipating potential flashpoints by communicating directly with the relevant decision-makers, facilitating contact between organisers or leaders and mediating in immediate crises.

An example of this more active role is monitoring for specific events such as marches and funerals, which can be greatly strengthened by the presence of stewards, or marshals, who act as monitors. These are people who are assigned by the organisers to help manage an event on the ground. Often highly organised, with a clear command structure, they keep a demonstration or event to its plan, help avoid trouble if it threatens and maintain communication between organisers and participants.

Formal monitoring often works according to guidelines or codes of conduct. On the following pages are two examples – one from EMPSA (Ecumenical Monitoring Programme in South Africa) and one from INNATE (Irish Network for Nonviolent Action, Training and Education) in Northern Ireland.

Verification

Verification[2] is a specialised kind of monitoring. Information acquired from monitoring is used to determine whether the parties to an agreement are complying with what they agreed to do. Monitoring and verification can make the difference between success and failure in implementing agreements, including those intended to resolve conflicts. Monitoring, in this context, is used to refer to the organised collection of information about the implementation of an agreement. The aim of verification is to build confidence between the parties that an agreement is being implemented fairly and effectively. Verification achieves this through three interconnected means:
- by detecting non-compliance (i.e. when a party is not doing what it agreed to do),
- by deterring parties that might be tempted not to comply, and
- by providing compliant parties with the opportunity to demonstrate convincingly their compliance with the agreement.

CODE OF CONDUCT OF THE ECUMENICAL MONITORING PROGRAMME IN SOUTH AFRICA (EMPSA)
NOVEMBER 1992

In commitment to the Christian faith and the gospel imperative of justice for all,
each EMPSA monitor is expected to adopt the following standards of conduct:

1. To be available to all parties being monitored.
2. Not to work for the advancement of a particular political party or state structure.
3. To promote peace and work to end violence.
4. To report truthfully and accurately on situations.
5. To be committed to nonviolent action methods of monitoring.
6. To act confidently, calmly and diplomatically.
7. To display sensitivity and empathy for the particular vulnerability of victims of violence.
8. To respect the need for confidentiality.
9. To display no party preference in words, clothing, badges or songs during monitoring.
10. To respect the role of, and refer to, other structures that exist to deal with conflict resolution/ mediation.
11. To cooperate with other monitors whenever necessary.
12. To refrain from speaking to public media unless in close cooperation with, and under the agreement of, the local or national EMPSA structures.
13. To work closely at all times with the local EMPSA structures and not undertake unilateral action without consultation and agreement.

Transparency of information is an essential element of confidence-building through verification. Verification is particularly useful in cases where, despite an agreement being reached, deep distrust and suspicion remain. (See also 'Confidence-building' on p.112 later in this chapter.)

One of the key attributes that a monitoring and verification arrangement must have is impartiality. One way to achieve this is by having an impartial third party, acceptable to all other parties, carry out the monitoring and verification. This third party may have a strong self-interest in having the conflict resolved by peaceful means, and may even have been partial to one side or other in the past, but it cannot be seen to be partial in reaching conclusions about compliance or non-compliance.

For agreements between governments, this third party monitoring role is often performed by representatives of another government or intergovernmental body. For example, the United States has been in charge of a verification mission, the Multilateral Force and Observers in the Sinai (MFO), which has since 1982 successfully monitored compliance by Egypt and Israel with the ceasefire and withdrawal agreements. And the Chemical Weapons Convention (CWC) is monitored and verified by an international organisation established expressly for this purpose, called the Organization for the Prohibition of Chemical Weapons (OPCW).

Another way of ensuring a fair verification system is to involve all of the parties in its establishment and operation. This ensures that the process is transparent and that any biases will tend to cancel each other out. Such an arrangement applies to the Mission of Military Observers Peru/Ecuador (MOMEP), which is monitoring the Peru/Ecuador frontier. MOMEP includes representatives of these two conflicting

CODE OF CONDUCT FOR INNATE OBSERVERS
AS USED ON THE GARVAGHY ROAD, PORTADOWN, JULY 1990 & 1991

It is assumed that all those acting as observers through INNATE assent to, and will adhere to, this code of conduct.

1. As observers coming through INNATE, a nonviolence network, our prime responsibility is to add to the likelihood that events will take place without violence and with communication between the different people or groups involved.

1A. We hope that our very presence, as outside observers from a variety of different backgrounds, will help to avoid tempers flaring to a level where violence ensues. We feel that part of our strength is in our diversity and in the fact that we have no particular axe to grind.

2. We are observers. We are present to observe what happens and to report back to the different parties involved as appropriate so that all may learn from what happens.

2A. As individuals we are not necessarily neutral but in our observer role we will cast a critical, watchful and respectful eye on all sides and groups. We will therefore, as far as is appropriate or possible, relate and communicate to and with all sides or groups.

3. We will be clearly identifiable as observers by our white armbands.

4. If as concerned individuals we feel we need to intervene to help avoid violence then we will attempt to mediate.

5. However, we state clearly that we are neither stewards nor police and do not seek to perform either of these roles.

Code of conduct agreed at a meeting of observers in Belfast, 5 July 1990; agreed as code of conduct again, July 1991.

---

countries, in addition to those of Argentina, Brazil, Chile and the United States.

Verification and compliance processes should not be viewed as necessarily adversarial. Often non-compliance will be unintentional. A good verification system will detect this and provide an opportunity for the non-compliant party to correct the situation before any further action is taken. Verification is particularly useful in cases where an agreement may be unclear or lacking in detail. The verification system can provide impartial information that can inform attempts to clarify or rectify deficiencies in the original agreement.

A more recent example of monitoring and verification as part of an attempted conflict resolution process was the Kosovo Verification Mission (KVM) deployed by the Organization for Security and Cooperation in Europe (OSCE). The KVM included 1400 unarmed verifiers drawn from OSCE member states. Its role was to monitor implementation of the December 1998 agreement between President Milosevic of Serbia and US negotiator Richard Holbrooke for a ceasefire between the Serbian security forces and the Kosovo Liberation Army. It was also mandated to monitor the withdrawal of limited numbers of Serb troops and police from Kosovo and the return of ethnic Albanian Kosovars to their homes and communities. The mission experienced difficulties from the outset because:

1. the ceasefire it was meant to monitor never happened,

2. the agreement itself was unclear,
3. the Serbian government exhibited increasing hostility towards the mission, and
4. the mission itself was understaffed.

However, the KVM did succeed in providing the outside world with accurate information on the unfolding situation in Kosovo, including giving information regarding human rights abuses and atrocities. They also managed to prevent, simply by their presence, localised outbreaks of fighting. Ultimately the mission was withdrawn just before the NATO bombing in Kosovo.

This case illustrates both the intention of verification and the difficulties often encountered. While verification can fall prey to political manoeuvring and manipulation, it can also be a powerful tool for determining the truth. Without it, agreements are reliant on self-verification by the conflicting parties, which, in the absence of trust, is a recipe for continuing violence.

Enabling a settlement
9. CONFIDENCE-BUILDING

Following a period of intense conflict, during which there may have been a lot of violence and suffering, it is difficult for members of opposing groups to trust each other. Negotiations may have brought hostilities to a close and brought about some kind of agreement, but the opposing sides will have learned to fear and distrust each other. They will, in fact, be more distrustful of each other than of strangers. It will be a very long time before each side can be convinced that the attitude of the other has changed: change in attitude can only be trusted if there is a consistent pattern of changed behaviour.

Some examples

Imagine an armed rebel group and a government army that have been at war for years. A ceasefire is signed and the two groups stop shooting each other, but both remain fearful and wary. Rather than expect each side to change overnight and to trust the change in the other side, it is often advisable to move step by step. While the army stops nighttime patrols, the rebels will stop ambushes. If this goes well, the army will move half its soldiers back to the capital and the rebels will hand in some of their weapons to a trusted party. Next, the army will confine itself to a token monitoring force in this region and the rebels will begin to report to demobilisation centres. At each step, the risk on each side is limited, and a small degree of confidence can be established in the willingness and the ability of each side to change.

Similarly, after prolonged ethnic or religious conflict the groups involved can only build confidence slowly. Imagine that one group has fled in terror – or has been chased away, depending on the viewpoint taken. Perhaps, if the group that has remained begins to repair damaged buildings, some of the displaced will come with an international guarantor to join in the rebuilding. If the area is patrolled by a joint police force, some of the displaced will move back into one neighbourhood. If this goes well, the displaced people who have returned may suggest that their old neighbours from the opposing group should return as well.

Over time, people will test each other's commitment, and confidence will grow, with positive results. It is important that everyone understands what is happening. They need to know what is being risked, and what is being built. Once people understand the process, they can discuss the behaviours and the interpretations; they can also look for ways to protect the process from elements who want to spoil the intentions of both sides.

Confidence-building as action

Neither of the examples given above should be taken as a blueprint for what should happen. But they do illustrate a way of thinking about confidence-building, an approach that can help to move from an impossible position to a workable one. The incremental approach is important in simultaneously limiting risk and allowing something new to be built. If things go wrong, it will be more difficult the next time to build confidence, but it will be possible to try again.

Confidence-building depends largely on parties to the conflict making step-by-step moves towards each other. Outsiders can of course help with this, especially perhaps in the early stages when there is a severe lack of confidence and communication.

It should be clear that building confidence is a longer-term, comprehensive project. It is not only a give-and-take interaction. An important dimension is the education and awareness-raising it entails. Besides closing gaps between rivals, it challenges commonly held stereotypes among the communities and so contributes to strengthening the social fabric behind the conflict.

In planning and carrying out confidence-building work, consider these questions:

- **LEVEL:** At what level of conflict does confidence-building need to take place? Higher political level or community and grass roots level? (You may refer back to 'Multi-level triangles', p. 60 in Chapter 4.)

- **TARGET GROUPS:** Who are the people between whom confidence has to be rebuilt?

- **CHANGE:** What attitudes and behaviour do you hope to change as a result of the action?

- **CHALLENGES:** What are the difficulties you are likely to face? How do the parties (particularly the people you will be engaged with in the process) perceive these? How different (clashing?) are their perceptions? What are their needs? What are their fears?

- **PERCEPTIONS OF YOU:** How are you perceived by the different sides? Are you trusted enough to do this work, or do you need to find others at this stage?

- **ADVANTAGES:** What people and processes are likely to be allies in helping to build mutual confidence?

- **RISKS:** What risks should you be aware of?

- **MAKING A START:** What is the first step? When? How?

10. FACILITATING DIALOGUE

In the process of handling conflicts it is important to be on the lookout for ways of expanding the possibilities for dialogue amongst the parties involved. Dialogue is often abandoned too early as emotions rise, and forceful strategies begin to be employed. But eventually the parties will return to dialogue as they try to work out an agreement to end the conflict.

Facilitation of dialogue is a skill that can be especially useful during the stage of confrontation, before the situation has polarised to the point of crisis. Of course, the application of this skill will need to be adapted to the particular culture and circumstances in which you are working. Facilitating dialogue enables people to share their own views and listen to differing views about a political or social concern, thus gradually moving towards a deeper understanding of their situation. Agreement is not a primary aim of dialogue, but understanding is.

For example, the Afghan Development Association (ADA), as a neutral party working in Trinkot, where there was a serious dispute going on between rival villages and tribes, 'was able to bring conflicting groups together to discuss the common issue of cleaning and rehabilitating the canals owned by various rival tribes. Since ADA's first project commenced in 1992, no single incident between rival tribes has occurred.'[3]

Some possible scenarios

There are various situations in which one might want to encourage and facilitate political and/or social dialogue, including:

- Within an existing group, whose members have been hesitant to share their views on a difficult political or social topic with each other, or have discussed these only in a negative or adversarial way.

- Between different groups, when they meet together, sometimes explicitly to share views on a political or social issue, sometimes for another task or purpose, wherever a difficult issue is likely to arise.

✪ To agree to have a dialogue is the beginning of peaceful resolution.
SOMALIA

- When a political figure or a prominent political critic meets with a group, perhaps expecting that they will not agree with his or her views.
- When political figures with conflicting viewpoints are asked to speak in front of an audience, in a public forum.
- When political figures are brought together to listen to a speaker on a difficult political or social issue and then to discuss their views on this issue.
- In a private meeting between opposing political figures, facilitated by another more neutral person (who may have brought them together).

Skills in facilitating dialogue
Any effort to encourage conflicting groups to enter into dialogue needs to ensure that it does not increase tensions. The following guidelines are aimed at preventing this.

A. BE CLEAR ABOUT YOUR OWN ROLE AND OBJECTIVES
As facilitator, be clear about what is or is not part of your role. Your role is to assist the process of communication without expressing your own views about the issue being discussed. Your objectives are to provide a setting and an atmosphere in which differing views can be exchanged and listened to honestly but without hostility.

As facilitator you are responsible for the process, but not for the content of the discussion. If you are working as a team of facilitators, then it is important that co-facilitators agree in advance about roles and objectives. It is also important that you explain your roles and objectives clearly to the participants and check that they have understood and agree to these.

B. HELP THE PARTICIPANTS TO IDENTIFY THEIR OWN OBJECTIVES
With existing groups, you should try to meet with key people in advance to help them set their objectives. This will make it more likely that

groups will 'own' and support the structure and aims of the process. In any case, there should be a brief statement of agreed objectives at the beginning, to remind everyone why they have come.

For example, they may want to present their side's perceptions, set forth a party position, win votes for an upcoming election, envision the future or give a personal perspective. Is this objective consistent with the aims of other parties to the discussion?

C. ASSIST PARTICIPANTS TO AGREE ON GROUND RULES FOR THIS DIALOGUE
Help them to set guidelines for themselves which they own and follow during the dialogue. Consider in advance, and make clear, the mechanism for dealing with difficulties.
- How will people signal that they wish to speak, and who will give them the floor? Who will decide whether ground rules have been violated?
- Think in advance about what you, as facilitator, will do in given cases. People may test the limits. How will you respond?
- Are you clear who has set the rules, so that you are able to say that the whole group has agreed them, or that a planning committee decided them?
- Are you willing to discuss the possibility of changing the rules? If so, how? By consensus, or by majority vote, or what?

D. ENCOURAGE PARTICIPANTS TO LISTEN TO EACH OTHER
Political talking often seems to include very little listening – it is what someone called 'the dialogue of the deaf'. While one person speaks, the others prepare what they want to say, and they listen only to contradict each other's arguments.

For change to happen, people must really hear each other, and must feel that they have been heard. As facilitator, you need to have ideas for ways to encourage listening. Some ways in which you might help people to listen to each other include:

- Paraphrasing, i.e. checking what people have said, and demonstrating to them that they have been heard – e.g. 'are you saying that...?'.
- Seeking and articulating points in common or differences.
- Asking questions that elicit personal rather than party statements, if the setting permits vulnerability – e.g. 'have you always held that view?' or 'what experience led you to that?'.
- Encouraging responses to feelings and experiences as well as issues – e.g. 'that must have been difficult/painful/inspiring'.
- Listening to each other's feelings; you need to model empathy yourself and encourage empathy in others – e.g. 'do you see how that would feel to the other person?'

Despite the pressure caused by all the things a facilitator should do, try to focus your eyes and your attention on each speaker, and try to imagine how each listener is coping. Encourage the speaker to slow down, speak more loudly, or define terms, if there is any possibility that listeners might be having problems. If possible, have a co-facilitator who can look after time, process and note-taking, freeing you to concentrate on the content of the discussion and the participants.

E. HAVE A STRATEGY FOR COPING WITH STRONG EMOTIONS

The first step in dealing with strong emotions is to notice them. As facilitator, be attentive to signals that indicate strong feelings. Then:
- Try to provide a safe way for emotions to be expressed, by asking open-ended questions that allow space to talk about feelings without forcing (e.g. 'Would you like to tell us how you react to that?'). Or offer a format or structure that would permit people to express their feelings in a structured way (e.g. 'When you do/say _____, I feel _____ because _____.').
- If possible, get people to share the experience that has prompted the feeling, rather than having multiple expressions of the same feeling.

- Try to provide ways for aggressive emotions to be transformed into more vulnerable ones; for example, anger may mask hurt or sadness, while fear may be an expression of helplessness or powerlessness. But don't force people to take more risks than they are ready for. You can only make the opportunity – they must decide whether or not to take it.
- Though it's best for emotions to be expressed by those who feel them, the facilitator can sometimes verbalise emotions that are diffused among a group (e.g. she/he may say 'that makes me uncomfortable, because it may hurt some people here').
- Be prepared for parallel feelings to arise, and give them room to be expressed – but try to deal with one at a time, promising to return and give attention to other feelings later.
- Where possible, let participants respond to each other's emotions in a natural way, without intervening to protect or direct them unless it seems necessary.

Talking about emotions and experiences can free us of our positions, and enable us to concentrate on needs. (See the 'Onion' analysis tool in Chapter 2, p. 27.)

Getting beyond 'party positions' to honesty is more likely to lead to cooperation and non-adversarial discussion that is focused on the problem, rather than on our strategies for winning. Open-ended questions may allow participants to suggest future actions or new possibilities in an attempt to meet everyone's needs.

11. NEGOTIATION

Nearly everyone employs negotiation skills in everyday life – for example, when deciding as a family where to go on holiday, when agreeing a work plan and setting the allocation of tasks with one's colleagues, or when discussing plans with friends and relatives. What we are looking at here is how to apply this everyday skill within conflict situations. In such a context, negotiation is referred to as a structured process of dialogue between conflicting parties about issues on which their opinions differ.

In most cases negotiation takes place without the involvement of a third party. The purpose is to clarify the issues or problems and try to come to an agreement on how to settle differences. Principally, negotiation takes place between parties either in the early stages of the conflict, when lines of communication have not yet become totally broken, or at the later stages, when parties are attempting to reach agreement on the terms and details of a peace settlement.

In situations in which the level of confrontation and violence makes it difficult for parties to agree to meet up to engage in direct negotiations, a third party may intervene to act as a facilitator in assisting indirect communication, which can prepare the ground for later direct negotiations.

As a process, negotiation has several distinct phases, which are described below. For successful negotiation, participants and facilitators may find it useful to follow the guidelines suggested.[4]

▶ **Negotiation processes are heavily influenced by culture and vary from one place to another. It is your task to separate out those pieces of advice which are useful, and to leave those which are not relevant.**

Phases of negotiation
PHASE 1: PREPARATION
- Analyse the conflict situation, perhaps by mapping it (see p. 22).
- Research/gather information, as necessary.
- Identify needs and interests of own side and other side(s). (See the Onion, p. 27.)
- Consider your preferred options for the outcome of negotiations, as well as the Best Alternative To a Negotiated Agreement (BATNA).
- Make contact with other side(s) and agree on a venue and process for the negotiations, including: ground rules, issues to be discussed, how many people can attend or speak for each side, and whether there will be an independent facilitator.

PHASE 2: INTERACTION
- Upon arrival at the venue, greet each other appropriately.
- Share your different perspectives on the situation.
- Agree a definition of the problem or issue(s) involved.
- Generate options for addressing the problem.
- Evaluate and prioritise these different options, according to the needs and interests of all sides.
- Select, and possibly combine, the best options for meeting the needs and interests of all parties involved.

PHASE 3: CLOSE
- Agree on the best option or combination.
- Develop an action plan for each party.
- Set a time frame and deadlines for actions.
- Plan for a review of the agreement.

The aim is for a negotiation process in which all parties are committed to achieving a settlement that can meet the legitimate needs of all sides. This does not mean that they need to 'give in' to demands of the other side(s), but it does require a willingness to consider and combine options creatively in the desire to find a solution. If negotiators are representing a larger group, then they must come with a clear mandate from their respective constituencies and a clear process for reporting back and maintaining accountability.

Guidelines for effective negotiations
LISTENING AND COMMUNICATION
- If you want the other party to listen to you, then listen to them first.
- If you want the other party to acknowledge your point, then acknowledge theirs first.
- Present your views as an addition to, not in opposition to, what the other party is saying.
- Ask 'what if' questions and open questions in order to explore possibilities.

RELATIONSHIP-BUILDING
- Distinguish between the people and their behaviour. Don't attack the person.

- You can influence other people's behaviour by how you behave yourself.
- Build trust slowly, step by step, through dialogue and reciprocal positive actions.
- The best guarantee of a lasting agreement is a good working relationship.

PROBLEM-SOLVING

- The aim of good negotiating is to change from confrontation to problem-solving.
- The prize in good negotiation is satisfying your interests, not obtaining your position.
- If you are feeling stuck against an intransigent opponent, try reframing the question to make it a joint problem-solving. Get the person to help you understand their concerns.
- Look for low-cost, high-benefit trades. What can you offer that will be of low cost to your side, but of great benefit to the other side?
- Help the other party to save face.

SUCCESSFUL OUTCOME

If a successful outcome is to be achieved, then a range of different factors are required to facilitate effective use of the negotiation process:

- An intention by all parties to achieve a settlement.
- A willingness to explore options and move off stated positions.
- Power that is sufficient to persuade or to make it too costly not to change, but insufficient to force total surrender.
- Clear mandates from a coherent constituency.
- Mutual recognition as bargaining partners.
- Adherence to mutually acceptable ground rules.
- Acknowledgement of both the legitimacy of difference and the existence of common ground in the relationship.
- A belief that negotiation is the best option available for resolving the differences between the parties involved.
- Sufficient resources to ensure outcomes that do not discredit either the use of the bargaining process or those who are seeking to use it.

A successful outcome will include an agreement which:

- meets the legitimate interests of all sides as much as possible and resolves conflicting interests fairly
- does not damage the relationships between the parties
- is workable – that is, the parties must be able to live with it and implement it
- is 'owned' by the parties – that is, not imposed or manipulated by outside parties
- is acceptable to all the parties' constituencies and has no adverse political consequences for the leaders
- is unambiguous, complete and sustainable
- is achieved within an acceptable timeframe.

12. MEDIATION

Mediation, like negotiation, is a skill which many of us practise in our everyday lives, but often without calling it mediation. When two individuals have a disagreement and a third person such as a family member or friend intervenes to help them clarify the problem and talk about it rather than fighting over it, this is mediation. We can learn about mediation from real-life experiences as well as through formal training and practice in mediation skills.[5]

When direct negotiations have failed and communication lines between the two sides are broken, there is space for a third party to intervene. The third party may be a volunteer in the process, or a person approached by both parties to take up the role. In some circumstances, mediators may be imposed by laws or systems, e.g. United Nations mediators. The main principle, however, is that the mediator has to be recognised and accepted by all sides.

Some basic principles for an approach to mediation

- Mediation includes a concern for suffering and a desire to bring a human face into the middle of the conflict.
- Mediators become involved with and attached to all sides, rather than being detached and uninterested.

- All sides must voluntarily agree to participate in the process and must accept the particular mediator(s).
- Mediators must be willing to work with all sides.
- Mediation does not aim to find objective truth, but rather to find an agreed solution that acknowledges and is based upon the perceptions and experience of all sides.
- Mediators guide and control the mediation process, but must avoid trying to direct the content of discussions.
- Options for resolving the conflict must come from the parties themselves who must 'own' any agreement.

The mediation process

The role of the mediator is to explain the process and guide the parties through the steps outlined here, or a similar process that you have established for yourself in your own context. Mediation is usually done by pairs or teams of mediators, with the different mediators combining their individual skills and experience, and their differing backgrounds, so that the team is more balanced in relation to the conflicting sides.

Many of the skills and tools already mentioned for Facilitating Dialogue (see p. 113) are useful for the mediator, such as setting ground rules, paraphrasing, empathy and having strategies for coping with strong emotions. Also important is the ability to recognise common ground and possible points of agreement, and to point these out as the parties move into the later steps.

Possible steps in a mediation process

1. PREPARATION BY MEDIATOR(S):
- Meet with partner mediator(s) to plan a strategy and process.
- Meet separately with conflicting parties to introduce yourselves, explain the process, clarify your role, and get their agreement to you as mediator(s) and to the process.

If and when the opposing parties agree to participate, the following are some possible steps to take when they come together face to face with each other and with the mediator(s):

2. OPENING STATEMENT BY MEDIATOR(S), including:
- Welcome, introductions and words of encouragement to conflicting parties.
- Why are we here? What will happen? How long might this process take?

3. CONFLICTING PARTIES COMMITTING THEMSELVES TO THE PROCESS:
- Commitment to participate and to seek a solution.
- Commitment to ground rules, such as no abusive language, no interruptions and so on.
- Commitment of time necessary to complete the process.

4. INITIAL UNINTERRUPTED STATEMENTS (STORIES):
- Each party, in turn, tells their story, including their understanding of the conflict.
- Mediator(s) control the process and time for each speaker according to agreed rules.
- Mediator(s) may repeat or summarise important points, both to clarify accuracy with the speaker and to ensure that the other party has heard the point.

5. IDENTIFYING THE ISSUES AND SETTING THE AGENDA:
- From the statements and stories, clarify issues of disagreement and conflict.
- Agree an agenda listing the issues to be dealt with in the mediation.

6. DIRECT EXCHANGE AND GENERATING OPTIONS:
- Encourage direct exchange between the parties about their needs and fears on each issue.
- Ask parties to suggest options for addressing or resolving their differences.
- Mediator(s) list all options being suggested without judgement.

7. BUILDING ACCEPTABLE ALTERNATIVES:
- Evaluate alternatives in relation to the needs and interests of both (all) sides.
- Encourage creativity in combining options and seeking common ground.

8. FINALISING AN AGREEMENT:
- Test and clarify points of possible agreement, i.e. Who will do what? By when?
- Parties decide on the form of agreement (written or verbal) and set a timetable for monitoring its implementation.

9. CLOSING STATEMENT BY MEDIATOR(S):
- Review what the disputants have accomplished and the agreement made.
- Offer congratulations to disputants for successful problem-solving.
- Clarify the need for any follow-up activity or further meetings.

Shuttle mediation

As in the Wajir example on the following page, there will be times when it is necessary at the outset for the mediator(s) to meet separately with each side. Sometimes they will move back and forth ('shuttle') until the sides are willing to meet each other directly. In separate meetings with each side, the mediator(s) explain the process, and the parties tell their stories to the mediator(s) in order to feel confident of their ability to face their opponent. This gives them a chance to practise, to get the order of events straight, and to work off some of the immediate emotion. It also contributes to a feeling of having been heard (by somebody, even if the opponent turns out to be an unresponsive listener) and may therefore enable them to listen to the other side's story when they do meet.

The need for shuttle mediation may also arise during the middle of the mediation process. When there are internal disputes on one side or there is a danger of the process breaking down, because one side begins to doubt the process or feels at a disadvantage, then the mediator(s) can meet with either (or preferably both) of the sides separately.

Long-term shuttle mediation

When there is a major block in communication, the mediator may need to have repeated contact with the separate sides. This is true in very polarised political conflicts when there is a complete lack of trust and the parties are therefore unwilling to have any contact with the other side(s). The mediator(s) may guide the separate sides through the mediation process, allowing them to try it out in safety and confidentiality, before attempting it with the opponent. In this type of situation, the process of 'shuttling' between the sides may go on for a very long time before they are willing to meet directly.

The steps taken by the mediator(s) in this extended process might include any or all of the following:

- Establishing the mediator's credibility through reputation, experience, concern.
- Demonstrating a balanced approach and a willingness to listen on all sides.
- Analysing and mapping the conflict and identifying possible entry points.
- Building relationships of trust with key people on each side, including groups that seem to be excluded and marginalised, as well as the recognised major parties.
- Interpreting the fears, hopes and intentions of each side to all the others.
- Clarifying misunderstandings of public statements and positions on each side.
- Maintaining a level of confidentiality according to the wishes of individuals on each side.
- Carrying specific messages between sides, when they request it.
- Testing possibilities: collecting and distributing ideas around a broken circle of participants who are not willing to meet directly.
- Helping each side to assess the responses or to predict the reactions from other sides.
- Representing the views of an opponent well enough for an individual to 'practise' negotiating through the mediator.
- Encouraging direct contacts and arranging for these to happen.
- Getting out of the way and allowing the sides to negotiate directly.

MIRAA–MAENDELEO MEDIATION IN WAJIR, KENYA, 1999

■ Two women's groups in Wajir – the Miraa and Maendeleo – were in conflict over access to and control of the miraa business ('miraa' is a kind of leaf that is chewed as a stimulant). The Miraa group had a monopoly for bringing and selling this commodity. The Maendeleo group felt excluded and that only a few women had access to this market. They tried to start a dialogue with the Miraa group, but the Miraa group refused to allow others to join in. So, the Maendeleo women secured a court injunction barring the Miraa women from proceeding with the business. This action and the lack of dialogue escalated the conflict as the groups exchanged verbal and physical violence.

■ The provincial administration intervened and each time the two groups were called together they became violent and did not listen to each other. The Maendeleo group decided that the matter could not be resolved at the district level, so they got the support of a politician at the national level. This made the matter worse and the Miraa women refused dialogue or any initiative to solve the problem. The politician asked the provincial administration to sort out the matter. The provincial commissioner referred the matter back to the Wajir District level. The issue was then discussed at the Wajir Peace and Development Committee. The chairman suggested, after exhaustive discussion, that this case be handled by Women for Peace and the Council of Elders for Peace and not the Government security committee, and this was accepted. The chairman of the Council of Elders suggested that Women for Peace take the lead in this mediation and that he would back them up.

■ With that understanding, four women from Women for Peace were given the task of mediating in the conflict. They met and discussed their course of action, and identified the leaders of the two groups. The mediators first decided to visit the leader of the Miraa group, Mama Zeinab, who is a powerful character by nature. They visited her in her home, which could have been be risky, but they decided this was best because traditionally she couldn't chase a guest out of her home. Mama Zeinab received the mediators well and they explained the purpose of the visit. She was happy about their initiative and said that she was sick and tired of men younger than her son calling her to their offices and she was now glad that the government had shown some sense in asking their daughters to mediate. She then stated that just because she was old it did not mean that she was always right, and she agreed to come to a meeting if the conveners were the women mediators. The mediators then went immediately to the leader of the other group.

Time was crucial because any delay in reaching the other group would put the whole process at risk.

■ When the mediators visited the leader of the Maendeleo group, Mama Khali, they told her of the initiative and the fact that they had already visited Mama Zeinab. Mama Khali wanted to know the response of Mama Zeinab and they told her that Mama Zeinab was positive and ready to come for dialogue. With that information Mama Khali agreed and said that she would contact her members and give their feedback to the mediators. The mediator gave each group time to consult with their members. Three things came up as issues to be agreed before each group would come for face-to-face mediation: (1) venue, (2) who would be the main mediator, and (3) the process of the face-to-face mediation. The mediators agreed with both groups on these issues and then both agreed to come for the face-to-face mediation. The mediator and the groups also agreed on some basic ground rules for the mediation.

■ When they came together, the mediators gave the background to the initiative and opened the session to both groups. Each group was given time to express their feelings and issues. They talked and listened to each other. There were moments when tempers flared and each group apologised to the other and the dialogue continued. After listening to each others' stories, one of the leaders of the Miraa group said that, having listened to the views, issues and feelings of the Maendeleo group: 'I apologise for the pain and suffering you have endured, I am sorry.' That apology changed the mood in the room and the leader of the Maendeleo group stood up and hugged her counterpart. With that, both groups discussed the way forward. The following points were agreed:

1. Both groups must cease both verbal and physical violence.

2. Any issues were to be discussed and not taken to court or the police.

3. The timetable for miraa trading was to be reviewed to include more women and other interested parties.

4. A committee was to be formed that would consult widely and sensitise the Miraa women on the plight of poor women and youth.

■ The mediation ended with prayer and both groups greeting and hugging each other.

- Being prepared and willing to be the 'scape-goat' if negotiations break down.
- Allowing the sides to claim any credit for successful negotiations.

Negotiation, mediation and power

Figure 6.3[6] was developed by Diana Francis and Guus Meyer to set the methods of conflict intervention in the context of the stages of conflict, and of power relationships. The movement is from a situation of unbalanced power, which reveals itself as oppression, injustice and latent conflict, to one of balanced power, in which relationships can be established in a mutually acceptable way.

The box highlights negotiation and mediation, which, at the right point, can lead to new relationships and to the changed attitudes that are essential to long-term peace. Where the power of the main parties is unbalanced, however, mediation can sometimes prolong a conflict by encouraging concessions from the weaker party.

▶ **Does this sequence correspond with your experience? Have you experience of what can happen if mediation takes place when the power balance is unequal?**

13. ARBITRATION

Arbitrators listen to all sides of an argument and then decide what the solution should be. Sometimes arbitrators fulfil this role by virtue of their position of authority in the community. For example, in many cultures there are traditional leaders or elders who have the authority to intervene in a conflict, listening to witnesses from both sides and then deciding who is right or wrong and what they should each do. In a growing number of countries, organisations have been set up specially to arbitrate, particularly in industrial disputes. In Britain the Advisory, Conciliation and Arbitration Service (ACAS) fulfils this role (among others) at the request of the parties involved, who usually commit themselves in advance to accepting the outcome.

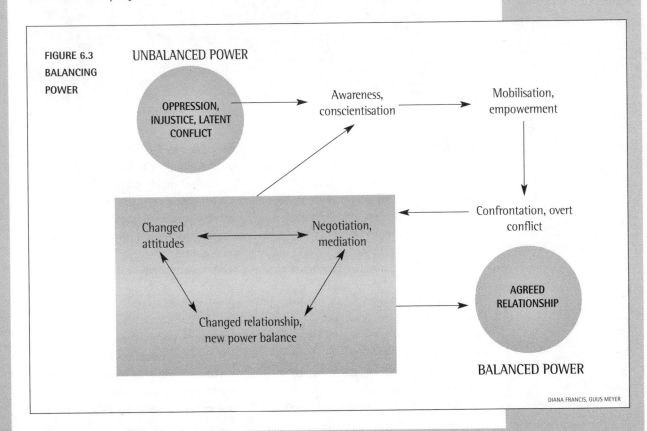

FIGURE 6.3 BALANCING POWER

UNBALANCED POWER

OPPRESSION, INJUSTICE, LATENT CONFLICT

Awareness, conscientisation

Mobilisation, empowerment

Confrontation, overt conflict

Changed attitudes

Negotiation, mediation

Changed relationship, new power balance

AGREED RELATIONSHIP

BALANCED POWER

DIANA FRANCIS, GUUS MEYER

Finding new ways of viewing a 'conflict' as a 'problem to solve between us' – England (top) and Afghanistan.

Medi-arbitration

In our experience, there are many situations where the distinction between mediation and arbitration has become blurred as people have tried to combine the best of both methods in their own cultural context.

For example, a traditional Nigerian ruler who participated in a course we facilitated has incorporated some of the principles and steps from the mediation process into his traditional role as an arbitrator of conflicts. He uses people trained in mediation skills, who meet with each side separately and help them to clarify the issues before they come together in his presence.

When they do come face to face in his 'court', he will ask them each to tell their story and also request that they suggest options for resolving a particular conflict, before he fulfils his traditional role of deciding who is right or wrong and what each of them should do. His decision takes into account the suggestions made by the conflicting parties and his sense of what is a 'fair' outcome.

This is just one example of an area of intervention that combines both traditional and 'modern' methods.

▶ What are the traditional ways of intervening in and resolving conflicts in your context? Do you see how elements of these methods can be combined with processes such as mediation, negotiation and facilitating dialogue?

⊃ Chapter 6 is by no means a comprehensive or final list of all the actions that can be taken when intervening in a conflict. It does, however, offer a variety of examples that should help you formulate further ideas on specific actions, which you can adopt and apply to your own situation. Moving on to Chapter 7 now, we look at actions that can be taken once the violence has ended and people find themselves having to face its legacy and its consequences.

NOTES

1. *Community Conflict Skills* by Mari Fitzduff (Belfast, 1988) has proved very useful on this topic.

2. Adapted from a paper by Trevor Findlay, Executive Director, The Verification Research, Training and Information Centre (VERTIC), Baird House, 15/17 Cross Street, London EC1N 8VW, UK.

3. Afghan Development Association, Annual Report, 1997–8, p. 25.

4. The sources drawn upon for this section include *Conflict Resolution Trainers' Manual: 12 Skills*, published by the Conflict Resolution Network, Australia; *Negotiating Conflict: insights and skills for negotiators and peacemakers* by Mark Anstey (see Chapter 10 for details); and exercises and materials prepared by Paul Clifford.

5. Sources drawn upon for mediation include *Being in the Middle by Being at the Edge*, by Sue & Steve Williams; *Mediation Across Cultures* by Daniel Augsburger (see Chapter 10 for details of both); and *Conflict Resolution Manual*, published by the Conflict for Resolution Network, Australia.

6. D. Francis, 'Power and conflict resolution', in *International Alert: Conflict resolution training in the north Caucasus*, 1994.

7-ADDRESSING THE CONSEQUENCES

SUMMARY ■ This chapter explores possible actions for addressing the consequences of violent conflict and includes physical, psychological and social factors. The chapter covers post-war reconstruction, helping individuals to deal with the past, and reconciliation, exploring the concepts of truth, justice, mercy and peace.

Introduction

In the aftermath of any intense violence it is easy to see the physical damage that has been done: the destruction of buildings, the displacement of individuals and communities, the absence of public services, and in some cases the death or disappearance of thousands of people.

However, it is often below the surface, in the hearts and minds of the population, most of them civilian bystanders, that the real damage has been done.

Economic and political interests dictate that, after a war, most of the attention is focused on the physical reconstruction of infrastructures and service delivery systems. Of course, this physical reconstruction is crucial to the process of building a new society, but all too often the human consequences of violence – the memories and experiences of the people involved – are left unattended, allowing them to fester and intensify.

Violence is not part of the social make-up of a society in real peace. It is an abnormal pattern that wreaks havoc with the traditional systems of human behaviour and interaction. Values break down and are replaced with the ethics of war, relationships crumble, and often communities and even entire nations are divided or shattered. People are left feeling traumatised and damaged, many of them having lost friends and family members, or having been witness to intense violence.

Ironically, though, the period immediately following experiences of crisis or long-term violence can also be times of intense reflection and an affirmation of commitment to a vision of an alternative future.

This commitment can serve as a catalyst for building unity and embarking on a process of reconstruction. Through people's involvement, and by tapping into the desire for something different, processes can begin that turn the past on its head and start to build a future that goes beyond what existed before the war. This is a future that enshrines the beliefs and values of those who share in its vision and are prepared to commit themselves to developing new ways of interacting and behaving.

> **What are the beliefs and values of your vision? How would you like to see people interacting and behaving?**

The challenge that faces all of us is to find the processes and methods that can bring about this kind of change. This chapter focuses on the social and psychological damage of violence and is an attempt to begin to meet the challenge. It begins by addressing **post-war reconstruction,** focusing on the physical needs, then it looks at **psychological reconstruction,** helping individuals to deal with the past, and finally it explores what is meant by **social reconstruction:** reconciliation, truth, mercy, justice, peace.

It is important to emphasise two principles that run like a thread through this book and apply here as much as at any other stage, if not more so:

- **Ownership of actions taken to address the consequences of conflict needs to rest with local actors working for a peaceful future.** The goal in any post-conflict situation must be the establishment of conditions which can meet the basic needs and aspirations of

❂ When the elephants fight, the grass gets trampled.
KISWAHILI – AFRICA

people beyond the involvement of outside assistance. If one keeps this long-term goal of building the social fabric in mind, then the second principle becomes self-evident.

- **Capacity-building, based on existing knowledge and expertise, needs to be an integral part of every intervention.** Outside experts can destroy as much as they create if they disregard or devalue those with ability and good will already in the situation. Even technical know-how can never be separated from the context in which it occurs; if it is, problems rapidly arise. Dilemmas of this kind occur every day for development organisations, and it is by focusing on the empowerment and active participation of local people that solutions can be found.

Any action taken to address violence and its consequences can either contribute to building peace or unintentionally deepen the crisis. This should not stop you from doing anything at all, but emphasises the need to reflect and analyse, and to be as clear as you can on both the intended and possible unintended outcomes of what you do before you act (see Aid and Conflict, p. 68).

Another aspect that often restricts our ability to act is the sheer enormity of the task. In situations of sustained violence it is difficult to find ways of acting that appear substantial enough to make any real difference. The nature of most conflicts ensures that there are no quick-fix solutions once the violence has subsided.

However, if one accepts that at the roots of most violence is the breakdown of just relationships between people and groups, then by implication it is in the rebuilding of these relationships that the seeds of peace will grow. This can and should take place between individuals, between members of our communities and between communities themselves. It will be up to you to take the initiative, to encourage others to do the same and to link your initiatives to those of others.

Post-war reconstruction: combining physical and social aspects

The word 'reconstruction', although so widely used, can be highly misleading when the damage it is addressing has been caused by violent conflict. In many cases, to attempt to put things back as they were before is to invite a further outbreak of violence. It may also stifle any new initiatives that have been created out of the crisis.

What the affected communities and societies need is to move forward, to build something new which contributes to healing. Often they are not given the chance, as big business moves in, often disguised as aid programmes. Materials are dumped in the area, and outside experts provided to supervise the process. Resources are eaten up by the high costs of international personnel, and by corruption.

The experience of agencies working in this field is that re-creating order out of destruction is potentially a form of peace-building. If it is to work, the process of rebuilding needs to unite architects, planners, development workers, private enterprise, national and local leadership – both formal and traditional – and the affected communities themselves. The task is both physical and social: the creation of just and durable structures for the future, which will be based on the elicited needs of the affected population.

The principles that underpin the recovery process should acknowledge the local cultures and way of life as basic to all planning. People, with their different groupings and representatives, need to be involved at all stages, and their expertise and labour should be the first resource. Any intervention should be based on full consideration of the realities on the ground. There will be disagreements and conflicts, so the intervention should be prepared to address these constructively, seeing them as opportunities for capacity-building within conflict transformation. A constructive process of recovery will create opportunities for new forms of interaction and avoid reinforcing the divisions of the past.

Inevitably this takes time and resources, which must be built into budgets and proposals, probably with some essential education of donors. Any extra cost is amply repaid by the much greater likelihood of avoiding future violence and achieving genuine development.

The aim of the extract below, drafted by the Post-war Reconstruction and Development Unit of the University of York, is to assist war-stricken communities, NGOs and International Organisations in the development and application of sound reconstruction policies.

THE YORK CHARTER FOR RECONSTRUCTION AFTER WAR
Post-War Reconstruction and Development Unit, University of York

The regional and national roles of settlements have to be kept in mind while planning for reconstruction. Settlement reconstruction should be an integral part of a comprehensive nationwide development and unlike the war itself reconstruction should be an incremental learning process by local people, who have to learn to grow with it.

The social and economic nature of rural communities often enables them to engage in rebuilding their way of life, while urban communities and NGOs are more able to participate in the 'management' task of reconstruction.

Rebuilding that takes the form of centralised housing policies and public service projects is unlikely to be efficient or culturally sensitive.

This Charter promotes the notion that gradual, harmonised and participatory restoration and improvement of infrastructure, services and housing stands a better chance of succeeding. The following are 'good government' practices:

- *APPROPRIATE TEMPORARY SHELTERS FOR REFUGEES* who are often the unfortunate consequences of war. As the period of war is unpredictable, the 'temporary' refugee camps may easily become permanent settlements. The longer people seek refuge the less the likelihood of their return. Rural refugees, dependent on agricultural land, are more likely to return than urban refugees. They have shown themselves to be more easily adapted to the camp environment than urban refugees. The latter tend to be more dependent on external help.

- *CAREFUL RELOCATION OF SETTLEMENTS* may become necessary for security considerations, or because of total devastation. Still, relocation imposes long-term economic, social, cultural and psychological burdens on the people, and should be avoided as much as possible.

- *DAMAGE AND NEEDS ASSESSMENTS* are essential and need to be carried out prior to the planning and implementation of any reconstruction programme. The employment of qualitative assessment methods, besides the conventional quantitative ones, is necessary to fully cater for the social and cultural needs of communities.

- *MITIGATING WAR DAMAGE* may prove impossible. Still, there are a number of well-tried regional and national planning measures that can help to reduce the damage of future possible conflict. Attention needs to be drawn to the 'social and cultural vulnerability'.

- *TIMING THE ACTION* is crucial. Do not wait for the signing of an 'everlasting' peace treaty, neither should you wait for political and economic reform. Wherever and whenever security is achieved, the process of maintaining life-lines and rehabilitation should start, to avoid the accumulation of damage and destruction.

- *THE USE OF LOCAL RESOURCES*, both human and material, is essential for an exhausted post-war economy to recover. Furthermore, sections of the war economy should be adapted to the reconstruction effort.

- *CONSERVING CULTURAL IDENTITY* becomes a critical issue after war. There should be a balance between restoration and reform. Settlements restored in this way will greatly help the returning population to adjust to their new post-war environment.

- *ASSSESSMENT OF ENVIRONMENTAL SUSTAINABILITY* needs to be made at every stage of reconstruction work. Long-term planning on national, regional and international levels should be taken into account.

> ▶ What do you think about this Charter?
> ▶ How would you change it?
> ▶ Do you think the needs of women are adequately taken into account? And the needs of children?
> ▶ Do you have experiences of a situation where the existence of a Charter such as this one might have helped?

Post-war reconstruction and rehabilitation, including aid-based interventions, can, if well implemented, alter the social character of a war-affected society and effectively minimise the possibility of reverting to violence by devising an infrastructure for peace. To do this, those in leadership roles need a high degree of coordination, learning from each other. For example, in Mozambique after the 1994 elections, some aid agencies and local NGOs worked with communities on local peace-building initiatives that combined physical and social programmes to address the consequences of the war.

TABLE 7.1: PEACE–BUILDING INITIATIVES

	INTERIM/SHORT-TERM MEASURES	MEDIUM-TERM MEASURES	LONG-TERM MEASURES
MILITARY/ SECURITY	Disarmament, demobilisation of factions, separation of army/police	Consolidation of new national army, integration of national police	Demilitarisation of politics, transformation of cultures of violence
POLITICAL/ CONSTITUTIONAL	Manage problems of transitional government, constitutional reform	Overcome the challenge of the second election	Establish tradition of good governance, including respect for democracy, human rights, rule of law, development of civil society with genuine political community
ECONOMIC/ SOCIAL	Humanitarian relief, essential services, communications	Rehabilitation of resettled population and demobilised soldiers, progress in rebuilding infrastructure and de-mining	Stable long-term macro-economic policies and economic management, locally sustainable community development, distributional justice
PSYCHO-SOCIAL	Overcoming initial distrust		Healing psychological wounds, long-term reconciliation
INTERNATIONAL	Direct, culturally sensitive support for the peace process	Managing conflicting priorities of peace and justice	Integration into cooperative and equitable regional and global structures

SOURCE: H. MIALL, O. RAMSBOTHAM & T. WOODHOUSE, *CONTEMPORARY CONFLICT RESOLUTION*, POLITY PRESS, 1999

Table 7.1 sets out the types of work possible, and the levels on which this work takes place, in the move towards peace following an experience of intense violence.

Local organisations may find it useful to draw up guidelines that set out the way in which they would like to see outside agencies taking up work in their areas.

For example, in 1995 the guidelines shown below were developed by a group of Afghan aid workers for the aid agencies working for the rehabilitation of Afghanistan.

▶ Physical reconstruction, no matter how sensitively handled, will never adequately address all the aspects of reconstruction that are required following violent conflict. In the following sections of this chapter we go on to look at psychological and social reconstruction.

Psychological reconstruction: helping individuals to deal with the past

Where people have suffered a great deal, the process of helping them come to terms with what has happened can be extremely difficult and thus require highly skilled help. However, often such help is not available, or is offered only in a culturally inappropriate way. The process we offer here is intended to be used, flexibly and sensitively, where there is no alternative, and where a quick remedy is needed, perhaps as a prelude to a deeper and longer process.

When memories of the past are retrieved, complex and violent emotions can boil up. In some cultures, elders or women who are taking a leading role for reconciliation and forgiveness talk expressly to sufferers about their past, deliberately stirring up their emotions. In Afghanistan, women mourn with the victims over their losses, but at the same time ask them to forgive others.

✪ Entre los individuos como entre las naciones, el respeto al derecho ajeno es la paz. Between individuals as between nations, respect for each other brings peace.
SPANISH, MEXICO

TEN GUIDELINES FOR GOOD RECOVERY PRACTICE IN KABUL
NGOs and Peacebuilding in Afghanistan, November 1995

1. Any rehabilitation action should reflect the complexity of the actual rather than the perceived situation.

2. Investing in rehabilitation can be a means of investing in peace, no matter how far off peace might seem. The only way to assess whether it is suitable to initiate rehabilitation projects or not is actually by starting something.

3. One of the most viable ways of encouraging more suitable recovery is by stimulating livelihoods and economic activities and thus stimulating market and commerce.

4. Recovery action should be based on working with local structures, at both the community and institutional levels.

5. Maximum use should be made of local resources, both human and material.

6. Sustainable recovery is dependent on the development of local institutions.

7. The difficult working circumstances in a war emergency should be seized on as an opportunity to maintain high professional standards and avoid quick fixes and the 'dump and run' syndrome.

8. Commitment by implementers is vital to ensure effective recovery. Partner institutions should, where appropriate, be encouraged to adopt a constructively critical approach in their demand for high standards.

9. The design of recovery programmes should take into account the need for flexibility in response to circumstances that may change rapidly.

10. There is no such thing as a neutral emergency programme; it either supports the future development of the affected population or prejudices it.

FAHIM HAKIM

Their experience is that people are freed to see things differently when their emotions have been expressed. In Eritrea, following the independence war, the government declared a month of mourning to enable everyone to grieve for their lost ones.

However, addressing this area is very culture- and context-specific. It is therefore, like most other areas of conflict-related work, not desirable or possible to give any recipes for methods to be used. Helping people rehabilitate themselves from past abuses may take the form of trauma relief or responding to other effects of war, or it may include organising social and cultural events to replace the grey memories of the past with something positive.

For example, as part of the collection of stories from people who had suffered human rights abuses, the South African Truth and Reconciliation Commission offered trauma counselling to groups and individuals, and encouraged communities to set up forums where they could meet and discuss their feelings about the past. In Russia the post-Soviet Union authorities, in accordance with the public mood, replaced the names of many places and buildings with those used before the communist era.

TRAUMA RELIEF

Psychological restoration and healing can only occur through providing the space for survivors of violence to feel heard and for the details of the traumatic event to be re-experienced in a safe environment. There are times when you need to give immediate support, until more help becomes available. This can only be done effectively if it takes into account the cultural and social needs of the people concerned, and builds on the support that is available locally.

PSYCHOLOGICAL DEBRIEFING

The following process offers a way in which people who have experienced traumatic events can be helped to speak about their experiences and recover. It can be part of a quick and urgent intervention until time and resources permit something more thorough, or it may be enough as it is.

▶ Again it must be emphasised that cultural circumstances can make even this limited form of intervention inappropriate. In some cultures, following an incident of rape or sexual assault, women may feel endangered by talking about their experience, or fear social stigma. In other cultures people may prefer to speak only to community members traditionally assigned a counselling role.

The steps of psychological debriefing could roughly follow the line of Figure 7.1 below. Readers will notice some similarities with the 'loss cycle' used widely in counselling.

Following a particular incident, focus attention first on the facts – then the thoughts, decisions taken, sensory impressions, and finally the emotions and reactions. At each stage it is good to let others know what you intend to do. You can ask these questions at each step:
• FACTS: What happened? Where were you?
• THOUGHTS: What did you think was happening? What was your first thought?
• DECISIONS: What did you decide to do? What else could you have done?
• SENSORY IMPRESSIONS: What did you see, hear, smell, taste?
• EMOTIONS/REACTIONS: What did you feel or feel like doing? What was your worst moment?

▶ This is not a blueprint for psychological debriefing but may help you in developing ideas of your own that suit the context in which you are working.

Social reconstruction: building relationships

THE DIFFICULTIES OF RECONSTRUCTION – A BALANCING ACT (from *Out of the Shadows of the Night: The struggle for international human rights*, by M. Frankel)

A nation divided during a repressive regime does not emerge suddenly united when the time of repression has passed. The human rights criminals are fellow citizens, living alongside everyone else, and they may be very powerful and dangerous.

If the army and police have been the agencies of terror, the soldiers and the cops aren't going to turn overnight into paragons of respect for human rights. Their numbers and their expert management of deadly weapons remain significant facts of life… The soldiers and police may be biding their time, waiting and conspiring to return to power. They may be seeking to keep or win sympathisers in the population at large.

If they are treated too harshly, or if the net of punishment is cast too widely, there may be a backlash that plays into their hands. But their victims cannot simply forgive and forget.

These problems are not abstract generalities. They describe tough realities in more than a dozen countries. If, as we hope, more nations are freed from regimes of terror, similar problems will continue to arise.

✪The bitter heart eats its owner.
XHOSA - SOUTH AFRICA

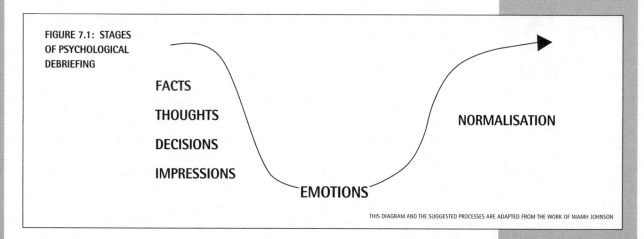

FIGURE 7.1: STAGES OF PSYCHOLOGICAL DEBRIEFING

FACTS
THOUGHTS
DECISIONS
IMPRESSIONS
EMOTIONS
NORMALISATION

THIS DIAGRAM AND THE SUGGESTED PROCESSES ARE ADAPTED FROM THE WORK OF NIAMH JOHNSON

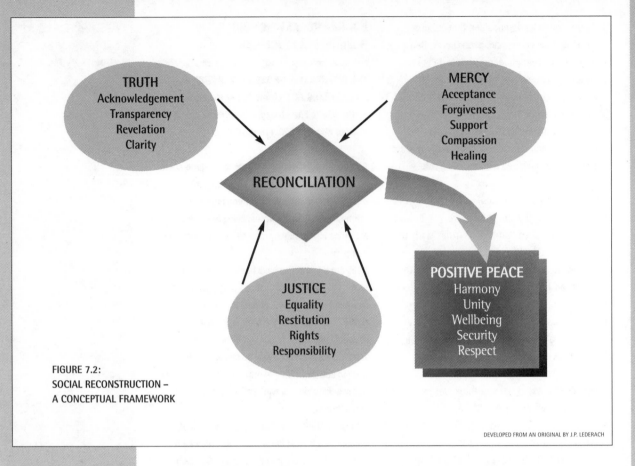

FIGURE 7.2:
SOCIAL RECONSTRUCTION –
A CONCEPTUAL FRAMEWORK

DEVELOPED FROM AN ORIGINAL BY J.P. LEDERACH

SOCIAL RECONSTRUCTION – A CONCEPTUAL FRAMEWORK

There are three key elements that require focus when thinking about the rebuilding of a society that has been affected by violence. As you can see from Figure 7.2, it is within the concepts of truth, mercy and justice that the bridge from violence to peace can be found. We believe that, by finding a balance between these three, reconciliation can be fostered, and that it is reconciliation that provides the foundation stone for building positive peace.

Reconciliation is a process as well as a goal. It is the way in which each society chooses to bring together the concepts of truth, mercy and justice in the aftermath of violence. This does not happen overnight, or simply because legislation is passed. The full and active participation of the people who have been affected by the violence is crucial to the process of reconciliation and the establishment of peace.

SOUTH AFRICAN MINISTER OF JUSTICE DULLAH OMAR –
SPOKEN TO THE SOUTH AFRICAN PARLIAMENT IN HIS INTRODUCTION TO THE PROMOTION OF NATIONAL UNITY AND RECONCILIATION LEGISLATION IN 1995

[This is] a Bill which provides a pathway, a stepping stone, towards the historic bridge of which the Constitution speaks, whereby our society can leave behind the past of a deeply divided society characterised by strife, conflict, untold suffering and injustice, and commence the journey towards a future founded on the recognition of human rights, democracy and peaceful co-existence, and development opportunities for all South Africans irrespective of colour, race, class, belief or sex.

It is because all situations of violence and war are unique, each with their own complexities, that the journey towards reconciliation and peace will also need to be unique – each with its own complexities. Often the concepts of Truth, Mercy and Justice are understood differently. It is in the unique way in which each society, or each community, chooses to interpret and pursue them that reconciliation will become meaningful and peace will become more than just a vision. We encourage you to discuss with others how best these processes can be initiated and taken forward within your own context.

Truth

What do we mean by truth, and whose truth are we talking about? There is no final answer to these questions but it is useful to explore some of the work that has been done around the world.

Following the process of deliberations before and during the life of the Truth and Reconciliation Commission in South Africa, participants broke the concept of truth down into four notions, as set out below.

The commission went further to emphasise that establishing the truth cannot be divorced from the affirmation of the dignity of human

✪ Meeta ormorwo ingonyek edolisho. An old man sees without eyes.
MAASAI, TANZANIA

FOUR NOTIONS OF TRUTH – TRUTH AND RECONCILIATION COMMISSION IN SOUTH AFRICA

FACTUAL OR FORENSIC TRUTH

The familiar legal or scientific notion of bringing to light factual, corroborated evidence, of obtaining accurate information through reliable (impartial, objective) procedures.

PERSONAL AND NARRATIVE TRUTH

By telling their stories, both victims and perpetrators gave meaning to the multi-layered experiences of the South African story. These personal truths were communicated to the broader public by the media. In the [South] African context, where value continues to be attached to oral tradition, the process of storytelling was particularly important.

SOCIAL TRUTH

While narrative truth was central to the work of the Commission, especially to the hearings of the Human Rights Violations Committee, it was in its search for social truth that the closest connection between the Commission's process and its goal was to be found.

Judge Albie Sachs, a prominent participant in the debates preceding the establishment of the Commission and now a Constitutional Court judge, made a useful distinction between what he called 'microscope truth' and 'dialogue truth'. 'The first,' he said, 'is factual, verifiable and can be documented and proved. "Dialogue truth", on the other hand, is social truth, the truth of experience that is established through interaction, discussion and debate.' [Albie Sachs in Alex Boraine & Janet Levy (eds), *Healing of a Nation*, Cape Town: Justice in Transition, 1995, p. 105.]

HEALING AND RESTORATIVE TRUTH

The preceding discussion rejects the popular assumption that there are only two options to be considered when talking about truth – namely factual, objective information or subjective opinions. There is also 'healing' truth, the kind of truth that places facts and what they mean within the context of human relationships – both amongst citizens and between the state and its citizens. This kind of truth was central to the Commission.

From the Final Report of the Truth and Reconciliation Commission, 1998

☼ The one who forgives gains the victory.
YORUBA, NIGERIA

beings. The process whereby the truth is reached is itself of great importance, because it is through this process that people learn again how to relate to each other. The process thus becomes a way of establishing a new set of norms and a new way of relating, which can move the society beyond the horrors of violence, and replace the old order with values that reflect a vision of the future.

A remembering process should be a chance for the victims to confront and defeat their fears, for the perpetrators to acknowledge and understand their actions and for all members of a community or society to embark on a deep process of social awareness that examines the causes and consequences of violence. Lessons need to be drawn that enable people to avoid a repetition of history.

THE IMPORTANCE OF REMEMBERING

■ All that a truth commission can achieve is to reduce the number of lies that can be circulated unchallenged in public discourse. In Argentina, its work has made it impossible to claim, for example, that the military did not throw half-dead victims in the sea from helicopters. In Chile, it is no longer permissible to assert in public that the Pinochet regime did not dispatch thousands of entirely innocent people.
From 'Articles of Faith', Index on Censorship, 5, 1996, p. 113.

■ Those who forget the past are doomed to repeat it.
Emblazoned at the entrance to the museum in the former Nazi concentration camp in Dachau, Germany.

Some people argue that it is damaging to try to open up old wounds, and that it is better to simply 'forgive and forget'. However, Roberto Cabrera argues against this in the context of Guatemala, following 36 years of internal war:

NOT REMEMBERING IS *NOT* FORGETTING

■ Most of the excuses not to remember say that we should not reopen the wounds of the past, but denying the past will never lead to the closing of wounds. People have to remember because they have not forgotten. The wounds are there, fresh and painful. The society must do something to heal them.
From 'Guatemala's Search for Truth', produced by Bob Carty Rabinal, Guatemala: http://radio.cbc.ca/programsthismorning/archives/1998/guatemal.html

Drawing on the experience of Latin American efforts to recover from decades of military dictatorship, Human Rights Watch concludes that 'if any country is to come to terms with its past and successfully turn its attention to the future, it is essential that the truth of the past be officially established. It is impossible to expect "reconciliation" if part of the population refuses to accept that anything was ever wrong, and the other part has never received any acknowledgement of the suffering it has undergone or of the ultimate responsibility for that suffering.'[1]

But remembering in and of itself is only a part of the process, knowing the truth about the past, without knowing how to proceed towards the vision of the future, can lead to bitterness and resentment. This is where the concepts of mercy and justice begin to play a key role in the process of reconciliation.

Mercy

Mercy includes the concept of forgiveness, but is more than that. It is the ability of people who have been affected by violence to cultivate a respect for their common humanity and agree that it is possible for them to co-exist. It is important for people to recognise that it is possible for them to share responsibility for what has happened and to agree on a shared vision of the future – despite the anger, fear,

A WITNESS AT THE PORT ELIZABETH HUMAN RIGHTS VIOLATION HEARINGS IN SOUTH AFRICA

■ Thank you, Bishop, but I am sorry, there is something else that I would like to ask. Do not take me wrong, my Bishop, you cannot make peace with somebody who does not come to you and tell you what he has done. We will have peace only when somebody comes to you and says: 'This is what I did.' I did this and this and that and that. If they do not come, if we do not know who they are, we will not be able to. But now I will forgive somebody who has. That is the whole truth, sir. We take it that the people who are listening and the people who are coming to the Commission will be touched as well. Their conscience will tell them that if they want forgiveness they should come and expose themselves so that they can also get the healing that the victims are getting.
(From the full report of the Truth and Reconciliation Commission, 1998.)

guilt and suspicion engendered by the past. Above all, it is a realisation that the process towards this vision can be healing for everyone.

Of course each situation will again be different, and each will demand a unique approach. But mercy is something that needs to take place at all levels of society – not only between leaders but on a community level and between individuals.

In many cultures and societies recovering from violence there will be opposition to the showing of mercy, or it will not be possible to overcome the hate and the anger. Often the lead will have to be taken with some form of court or hearing that considers the past actions of groups or individuals and then agrees either to set the normal sentence aside or to grant amnesty for past actions. This can be a contentious process that evokes tremendous emotion. It is another process that needs to involve as many people as possible in discussions and

action; it is also another way of beginning to define the normal social relations of the future.

Mercy depends upon the willingness of people to show compassion, to overcome their anger, to support a new post-violence concept of justice, without vengeance.

Justice

It is important not to equate forgiveness with reconciliation. The road to reconciliation requires more than a collective memory of the past and the ability to forgive. Reconciliation requires not only individual justice but also social justice. But what do we mean by justice?

If justice is seen as retribution, revenge for what has been done, then it becomes difficult to see how the pursuit of justice is not contradicted by the concept of mercy, and of amnesty in particular. Revenge, though, is a human response, and the suppression of the anger behind the desire for revenge may well be damaging.

Thus there is a need to challenge the behaviours that have become accepted within the culture of violence. Individual acts of revenge need to be exchanged for support for Restorative Justice – justice that focuses on the healing of social relationships and attempts to build the type of society that reflects the values of those who suffered.

ARCHBISHOP DESMOND TUTU – AFTER A VISIT TO RWANDA

■ We must break the spiral of reprisal and counter-reprisal… I said to them in Kigali: 'Unless you move beyond justice in the form of a tribunal, there is no hope for Rwanda.' Confession, forgiveness and reconciliation in the lives of nations are not just airy-fairy religious and spiritual things, nebulous and unrealistic. They are the stuff of practical politics.
From the final report of the Truth and Reconciliation Commission, 1998.

✪ Em casa de pobre sempre cabe mais um.
In a poor man's house there is always room for one more. **BRAZIL**

✪ The heart knows
its bitterness as
the owner knows
his body. HAUSA

Social justice also requires a deep look at the injustices of the past, not only those committed during the times of violence, but also those that lie at the root, those that contributed in the first place to the outbreak of violence. This will often require extensive physical and social reconstruction and may involve a more equitable redistribution of resources. Many people will have benefited materially from the past and ways will have to be found to compensate those who have suffered. Concerted efforts need to be made by everybody to work against these injustices and to lay the foundation upon which peace and reconciliation will be built.

Reconciliation

Through the exploration of these three notions – truth, mercy and justice – a community can embark on a process of reconciliation.

The South African Truth and Reconciliation Commission identified the following lessons from its own process of grappling with these issues:[2]

- Reconciliation does not come easily. It requires persistence. It takes time.
- Reconciliation is based on respect for our common humanity.
- Reconciliation involves a form of restorative justice which does not seek revenge, nor does it seek impunity. In restoring the perpetrator to society, a milieu needs to emerge within which he or she may contribute to the building of democracy, a culture of human rights and political stability.
- The full disclosure of truth and an understanding of why violations took place encourage forgiveness.
- Equally important is the readiness to accept responsibility for past human rights violations.
- Reconciliation does not wipe away the memories of the past: it is motivated by a form of memory that stresses the need to remember without debilitating pain, bitterness, revenge, fear or guilt. It understands the vital importance of learning from and redressing past violations for the sake of our shared present and our children's future.

- Reconciliation does not necessarily involve forgiveness. It does involve a minimum willingness to co-exist and work for the peaceful handling of continuing differences.
- Reconciliation requires that all South Africans accept moral and political responsibility for nurturing a culture of human rights and democracy within which political and socio-economic conflicts are addressed, both seriously and in a nonviolent manner.
- Reconciliation requires a commitment, especially by those who have benefited and continue to benefit from past discrimination, to the transformation of unjust inequalities and dehumanising poverty.

Through the full and active participation of as many people as possible in this process, peace can begin to be built – a peace that moves beyond the absence of violence, to establish new ways of living and of thinking about each other and how we relate.

DULLAH OMAR, IN HIS INTRODUCTION OF THE RECONCILIATION BILL TO PARLIAMENT

Having looked the beast of the past in the eye, having asked and received forgiveness and having made amends, let us shut the door on the past – not in order to forget it, but in order not to allow it to imprison us. Let us move into the glorious future of a new kind of society where people count, not because of biological irrelevancies or other extraneous attributes, but because they are persons of infinite worth created in the image of God. Let that society be a new society – more compassionate, more caring, more gentle, more given to sharing – because we have left 'the past of a deeply divided society characterised by strife, conflict, untold suffering and injustice' and are moving to a future 'founded on the recognition of human rights, democracy and peaceful co-existence and development opportunities for all South Africans, irrespective of colour, race, class, belief or sex.'

Peace

'A culture of peace consists of values, attitudes, behaviours and ways of life based on non-violence and respect for the fundamental rights and freedoms of every person. In a culture of peace, power grows not from the barrel of a gun but from participation, dialogue and cooperation.

It rejects violence in all its forms, including war and the culture of war. In place of domination and exploitation by the strong over the weak, the culture of peace respects the rights of everyone, economic as well as political.

It represents a caring society which protects the rights of those who are weak, such as children, the handicapped, the elderly and

> ✪ They have healed the wound of my people lightly, saying 'Peace, peace' when there is no peace.
> **THE BIBLE** (AUTHORISED VERSION)

COMMUNITIES OF PEACE – 'WE MADE NEW WAYS WHERE THERE WERE NONE'

Hundreds of thousands of peasants in Colombia were forced from their homes during the mid-1990s as a result of civil war. Oxfam supported them. Irma Garcia, a former Oxfam staff member and Working with Conflict participant, writes:

Some ten thousand peasants from the north and north-west established three new settlements on the basis of neutrality towards the perpetrators of violence. Their intention was to rebuild their communities and prepare themselves to return. In this process, the peasants emphasised three key values:

■ **RECONSTRUCTION OF HISTORICAL MEMORY:** Where did we come from? Why did we leave? Who evicted us? What are our values and customs? In a word, what is our history?

With these questions as a guide, the women, the men, the old people and children began to think again about their life, their families, their friends, their cultural values and the need to plan for a possible return home. As they did this, the use of mapping was fundamental in establishing the causes of displacement, identifying the relationships between the different armed groups and, very importantly, what it meant for them, in their lives and social and family relationships, to co-exist as civilians alongside armed fighters. In addition, mapping and the story of 'The Collector of Dreams' who 'brings messages from the sacred spirits' were essential tools in helping rebuild the collective memory.

■ **PLANNING THEIR RETURN:** The opportunity to be together and to reconstruct their families and communities fostered their hopes of returning. Together, with a notable contribution from the women, the people designed a proposal to return, which they presented, discussed and negotiated with the authorities.

In doing this, they developed new skills of leadership and the ability both to interpret the law and to understand the state, which previously they had been unaware of, because they had been forgotten communities in the hands of the armed groups. An important part of this proposal was the project of life, which they began to put into practice in the shanty towns and which they planned to apply on their return, on the basis of truth, liberty, justice and solidarity and fraternity.

■ **CULTURE:** Far from their lands in their sanctuary, they started to revive their cultural values. Music was a fountain of creativity. Young people told of their exile, their sorrows and their lives before bursting into song. The old people recalled the songs of their youth and they all danced, although still grieving. Very important was the revival of social institutions – in particular the committees of elders, both men and women, who, with their moral authority, their knowledge and experience, fulfilled functions such as solving everyday conflicts and dealing with marital problems, violation of community norms and petty crime.

'We made new ways where there were none… As a result of all this we shall return stronger in the face of the armed groups, and if we are displaced again, it will not be as difficult as it was this time.'
– Jeronimo, a member of the Turbo community.

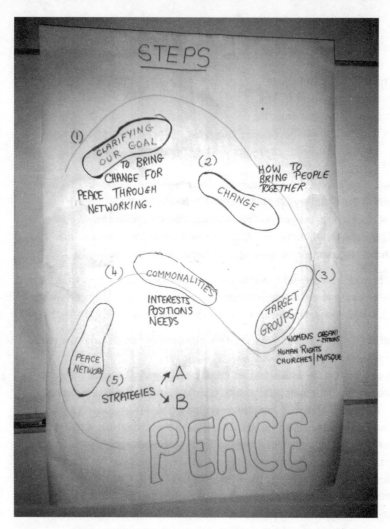

Pathways to peace – flow chart created by participants in a Working with Conflict course, Birmingham, 1998.

the socially disadvantaged.'[3]

The movement for a culture of peace is like a great river, fed from diverse streams – from every tradition, culture, language, religion, and political perspective; its goal is a world in which this rich diversity lives together in an atmosphere marked by intercultural understanding, tolerance and solidarity.

Village elder in Mozambique

You can bring us the culture of war in a plane and humanitarian aid in a truck, but you can't bring us the culture of peace, because it is a tree with its roots deep in our land.

In a culture of peace, people assume a global human identity that does not replace, but is built upon other identities, such as gender, family, community, ethnic group or nationality. Where there are contradictions among these identities, there is a commitment to their nonviolent resolution. It rejects all hatred, xenophobia, racism and the designation of others as enemies.

The full participation and empowerment of women is essential to the development of a culture of peace. In fact, it is essential that all groups that are marginalised from the traditional power structures are involved in these processes.

A culture of peace cannot be imposed from outside. It is a process that grows out of the beliefs and actions of the people themselves and develops differently in each country and region, depending upon its history, culture and traditions.

Conclusion

Dealing with the consequences of violence requires reflection, analysis and time. There are no magic answers or quick-fix solutions. Each of us must find the the tools and processes most suitable to our particular contexts and involve others in refining and pursuing them.

➲ *By providing the energy and commitment to keeping these processes going, and by linking our efforts to those of others, we can begin the journey along the road that will take us beyond the violence. Chapter 8 will look further at steps we can take along this road.*

NOTES

1. From Brandon Hamber (ed.), *Past Imperfect: Dealing with the past in Northern Ireland and societies in transition*, Human Rights Watch.

2. From the final report of the Truth and Reconciliation Commission, 1998.

3. Extracted from David Adams (ed.), *UNESCO and a Culture of Peace: Promoting a global movement*, Paris, 1995.

8-WORKING ON THE SOCIAL FABRIC

SUMMARY ■ From the infinite range of possible activities to transform the context and attitudes underlying a conflict, we include three themes that have universal application. They are:

1. Education for peace and justice
2. Promoting participation in decision-making
3. Developing good governance.

Given the unique make-up of each society, to give specific advice under these themes would be inappropriate. Instead, as in all previous chapters, we will set out some of the core issues in each area, share some insights that we and our colleagues have had, and, where possible, give examples of how people have done this work. This will hopefully add to, and enhance, your own experiences.

Introduction

In Chapters 6 and 7 we looked first at actions that address conflicts directly and then at the long-term consequences of violence. It is also crucially important to look at ways of addressing the many factors that can underlie conflict.

There is much more to serious social and political conflict than the behaviour you see on the surface. In Chapter 1 we showed how, below the surface, lie the roots – or deep structure – embedded in the social fabric: the history and systems of a society, supported by the beliefs, values and attitudes of those involved. It is these deep structures that need to be addressed, determinedly and over the long term, if there are not to be recurring phases of open conflict of varying intensity and violence.

The term 'social fabric' is used here to cover the structures, processes and relationships between people in a society. It spans elements such as religion, gender, culture, traditions, civil society, the political system, and the balance of power and influence wielded by different sectors.

Working on the social fabric will require commitment over the long term, and much

✪ Gaba si sansa ng'uta sumgda. Everybody feels pain when the spear stabs.
BARABAIG, TANZANIA

FAHIM HAKIM

patience, as things will happen slowly, with inevitable setbacks along the way. However, the rewards for yourself and your organisation on the one hand, and for the wider society on the other, may be great and lasting. You will be working to reduce or avoid the future suffering of many people and to enable them to live their lives in peace.

Education for peace and justice

The United Nations Charter states that, since wars originate in the 'minds of men', it is in the minds of men that the defences of peace must be constructed. Much of the education that women and men receive assumes that violence and injustice are a fact of life. Most history books emphasise battles and victories over other nations, and many glorify the armed forces of the country concerned.

The mass media regularly bombard people with information about wars and crime, so that they become deadened to the fact that things can be different. The power of the media has been shown in many recent conflicts. In Rwanda in 1994, for example, Radio Mille Collines urged the Hutu population to murder their Tutsi neighbours, with horrendous results.

Education for peace sets out to redress the balance. It aims to help people see that we do have choices – it is possible for us all to live in harmony with each other, and with the planet.

It is unique in that it looks to the future, and asks: 'What will happen if we go on as we are?' and 'How can we build a better world?' It puts a priority on developing attitudes of self-respect, tolerance, empathy, justice and fairness. It invites people to become active participants in their world, not just passive bystanders.

There are two principal ways of viewing education for peace:
• As a long-term, broad-based programme focusing on important problems and trends of a society and promoting, mostly through

schools and colleges, what we have called, in Chapter 1, positive peace.
• As a more focused activity aimed at addressing or preventing a specific conflict.

Education for peace is an activity suitable for both children and adults, in formal and informal settings, wherever people gather to do things together and learn. In terms of content and the specific activities to be carried out, the two types of work described above often appear distinct from each other, but in reality they are closely linked.

There are other programmes of conflict-related education which tend to be more focused on a specific dimension of peace: for example, education for human rights or education for democracy. These are often carried out with specific groups, such as soldiers, police or prison officers, or are linked to specific events such as educating people about their democratic rights and responsibilities prior to an election.

FORMAL PEACE EDUCATION
Peace as a topic can be taught within many school subject areas, including:
• **RELIGIOUS EDUCATION** (e.g. looking at the peace messages from each religion)
• **HISTORY** (e.g. studying significant examples of nonviolence and peace-building)
• **GEOGRAPHY** (e.g. tackling prejudice and showing the inter-relatedness of peoples)
• **SCIENCE** (e.g. raising questions about human needs and scientific responsibility)
• **LITERATURE** (e.g. reading and analysing literature written about peace and conflict).

Some universities have specialist departments for peace and conflict studies, which analyse the common features of conflict at different levels, from the personal to the international, and where modes of intervention are studied as well. As peace educators from these departments develop their understanding of these issues, in collaboration with practitioners, they will begin to incorporate their insights into their teaching practice and dialogue, thus contributing to a more peaceful world.

Education for peace aims to change attitudes and behaviour in order to achieve greater cooperation and peaceful problem-solving. It can be implemented both in violent societies and in those where widespread violence is as yet only a threat, as illustrated in the first example below.

There are many forms of peace education in action in different parts of the world, in the formal sector and the informal, with children and adults. It is most successful when content and methods are developed locally, in response to commonly identified problems, as in the second example shown below.

Figure 8.1, on the following page, illustrates the framework of a British project carried out in the 1980s, called 'World Studies', which has since been taken up widely elsewhere and which drew on many traditions worldwide. What follows is an elaboration of the World Studies objectives listed in the diagram, which could also be understood as a general outline

---

PEACE EDUCATION IN PRACTICE – TWO EXAMPLES

A PROJECT IN ULSTER

■ The Ulster Quaker Peace Project was asked to go to Uganda to meet teachers worried that after twenty years of brutal violence children there knew no other methods of solving problems. The project team showed them peace education methods they had developed in Northern Ireland. The teachers took up the methods with enthusiasm and founded Jamii ya Kupatanisha (the Ugandan Fellowship of Reconciliation), which, twelve years later, is still running regular training courses. The project also went to Belarus, a former Soviet republic, which has no overt problem of political violence. Yet teachers there adopted the same ideas with great enthusiasm. When asked why they found them so valuable, the teachers said:

> 'For seventy years we were all educated to conform to a system. To every question there was one right answer and it was in a book somewhere. Now we know that those answers have failed, but we don't know how to teach our children to think for themselves. When we see you [the project] getting eight- and nine-year-olds to cooperate and solve problems together, we know this is something we need to teach.'

From John Lampen's paper, 'Peace education: an introduction', UK, 1994.

AN ORGANISATION IN PALESTINE

■ A Palestine-based organisation, Pathways Into Reconciliation (PIR), developed a peace education programme which included constructing a formal curriculum. Three curriculum development teams – Israeli, Palestinian and Jordanian – met to develop a common peace education curriculum. Their goal was to incorporate agreed values (human rights, democracy, pluralism), content (multiple perspectives on the conflict's history) and skills (deferring judgement, listening empathetically). They studied the existing curriculum used by each country's ministry of education, and developed ways of introducing these values, content and skills in culturally sensitive ways.

The teams focused on literature, history and civics/sociology. After a two-year introductory period, sixteen Israeli-Jewish, Israeli-Arab and Palestinian schools were using the peace education curricula, which reached 2,000 students (half Palestinians and half Israelis).

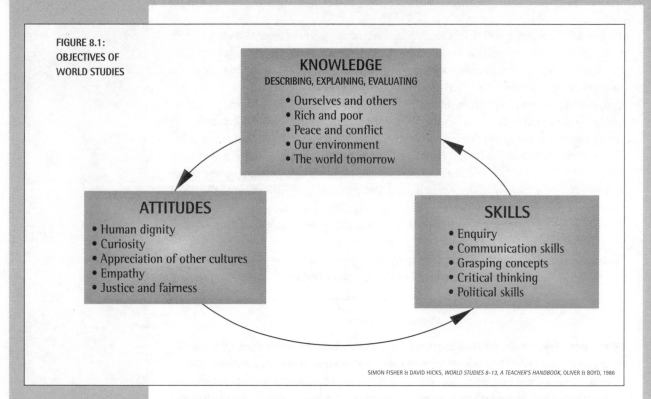

SIMON FISHER & DAVID HICKS, *WORLD STUDIES 8-13, A TEACHER'S HANDBOOK,* OLIVER & BOYD, 1986

FIGURE 8.1:
OBJECTIVES OF
WORLD STUDIES

KNOWLEDGE
DESCRIBING, EXPLAINING, EVALUATING

- Ourselves and others
- Rich and poor
- Peace and conflict
- Our environment
- The world tomorrow

ATTITUDES

- Human dignity
- Curiosity
- Appreciation of other cultures
- Empathy
- Justice and fairness

SKILLS

- Enquiry
- Communication skills
- Grasping concepts
- Critical thinking
- Political skills

of what a widely focused formal peace education programme might include:

KNOWLEDGE

- **Ourselves and others**: Students should know about their own society and culture and their place within it. They should also know about societies and cultures other than their own, including minority cultures within their own society. They should understand the nature of interdependence, and the economic and cultural influences – both helpful and harmful – of other people on their own way of life.
- **Rich and poor**: Students should know about major inequalities of wealth and power in the world, both between and within other countries as well as in their own country. They should understand why such inequalities persist and know about efforts being made to reduce them.
- **Peace and conflict**: Students should know about the main conflicts – both currently in the news and in the recent past – as well as attempts to resolve such conflicts. They should also know about the different ways

of resolving conflicts in everyday life.
- **Our environment**: Students should know about the basic geography, history and ecology of the earth. They should understand the interdependence of people and planet and should know about measures being taken to protect the environment, both locally and globally.
- **The world tomorrow**: Students should know how to investigate and reflect on a variety of possible futures, not only personal, local and national but also for the world as a whole. They should also be aware of ways in which they can act to influence the future.

ATTITUDES

- **Human dignity**: Students should have a sense of their own worth as individuals, and that of others, and of the worth of their particular social, cultural and family background.
- **Curiosity**: Students should be interested in finding out more about issues related to living in a multicultural society and an interdependent world.

- **Appreciation of other cultures:** Students should be ready to find aspects of other cultures that are of value to themselves and to learn from them.
- **Empathy:** Students should be willing to imagine the feelings and viewpoints of other people, particularly people in cultures and situations different from their own.
- **Justice and fairness:** Students should value genuinely democratic principles and processes at both local, national and international levels and should be ready to work for a more just world.

SKILLS

- **Enquiry:** Students should be able to find out and record information about world issues from a variety of sources, including printed and audio-visual, and through interviews with people.
- **Communication skills:** Students should be able to describe and explain their ideas about the world in a variety of ways: in writing, in discussion and within various art forms; and with a variety of other people, including members of other groups and cultures.
- **Grasping concepts:** Students should be able to understand certain basic concepts relating to world society, to use these concepts to make generalisations and to support and test them.
- **Critical thinking:** Students should be able to approach issues with an open and critical mind and to change their ideas as they learn more.
- **Political skills:** Students should be developing the ability to influence decision-making at local, national and international levels.

This World Studies framework indicates how broadly a peace education programme can be designed. It aims to promote positive peace as we have described it. An interesting and rare feature is its orientation towards the future, asking questions that invite students to think about likely future scenarios, and about their preferred futures.

The World Studies project was also cross-curricular; it aimed for these themes and topics to be integrated into all subjects within the curriculum. It was, and still is, relatively rare for schools to find room to teach peace education as a specific subject.

It is worth noting why this project was called World Studies, rather than Peace Education. Often it is inadvisable to use the term 'peace education', as it can stir up unwanted political interest. In this case the UK Government was attacking peace education as unpatriotic and attempting to close down such activity.

INFORMAL PEACE EDUCATION

Schools and colleges are only two of the places where people learn. A disadvantage is that they often emphasise acquiring knowledge in order to permit success in examinations, rather than for practical purposes.

Much peace education takes place in informal settings, wherever people gather for work or leisure. Just as in schools, informal peace education addresses primarily attitudes and aims to have a direct impact on personal behaviour. For peace education in both formal and informal settings, a more relaxed atmosphere than the standard lecturer/pupil relationship needs to be created – a more open and inviting arrangement, whereby people can feel encouraged to embark on the difficult task of looking at issues that are important to them, reflecting on their own behaviour and attitudes and generating alternatives for the future.

Peace education can help people to become aware of bias and prejudice in themselves and their society. For example, in many cultures if a group is asked to 'brainstorm' famous people, it quickly becomes apparent how few of the names suggested are those of women or black people. Or, if the members of the group are asked to react quickly, without censoring their thoughts, as the names of undervalued minorities (e.g. 'homosexuals', 'disabled' or 'gypsies') are repeated, negative responses tend to be expressed, including ideas the group would normally say they did not hold or believe in.

○ Hate has no medicine. **GHANA**

The reason for these underlying attitudes within societies is that we have all been conditioned by the information we receive from the culture around us. The first step toward counteracting these 'recordings' is to become aware of them.

A second step can be to listen to people who have been labelled in this way describing how such attitudes have hurt them. Almost all of us have been hurt at one time or another by someone else's prejudice, whether it was against our gender, our class, our racial identity, our physical appearance, our profession, or even our positive personal qualities (like the prejudice often displayed against bright pupils in schools).

A criticism of much current peace education, both formal and informal, is that it relies on making people be nicer to each other. Many practitioners are realising that peace education needs to focus on building a 'culture of resistance' – against negative propaganda from the media and governments, against the overt presence of violence in society, and against being manipulated by more powerful groups. When members of different groups list the things they never want to hear said, or done, against the group they belong to, they may well discover so many similarities between their respective groups that it will create a powerful feeling of understanding and solidarity between them.

Peace education can tackle important issues such as this, and be designed in an almost infinite number of ways. It can take the form of a workshop, for example, or a training course, or an awareness campaign. But the possibilities are much wider.

For example, in Afghanistan a network of individuals who were planning to devise a peace education programme decided not to limit the programme to a formal school-based activity. They explored areas such as publishing storybooks for children, designing posters, distributing peace badges and printing T-shirts with peace messages.

One suggested activity was to undertake research into the contemporary folk language and identify all the proverbs, old poems and anecdotes that promote peace or war. This way they were able to raise people's awareness of how language can shape attitudes and behaviour, and even come up with proposals to make the language more peace-sensitive.

WHAT YOU CAN DO

Peace education is a possible area of action for many people. Actions small or large can have a surprising impact in raising awareness. Whether you are working individually or as part of an organisation, you will need to decide what time and resources you can make available. This is an area in which everyone can do

TABLE 8.1: PEACE EDUCATION – RESOURCES		
	HIGH LEVELS OF RESOURCES	**LOW LEVELS OF RESOURCES**
LONG-TERM	Long-term formal peace education programme aimed at sustainable peace-building (e.g. a curriculum-based programme for schools and colleges, radio/TV programmes on justice and peace issues, peace and conflict studies website/database on the Internet)	Long-term formal/informal peace education activities aimed at sustainable peace-building (e.g. speaking to local groups about peace and justice issues, simple peace and justice publications for schools, awareness-raising events/ festivals, public seminars on peace)
SHORT-TERM	Short-term formal/informal peace education programme aimed at immediate peace and justice issues (e.g. mediation training for teachers and students, courses on conflict-handling skills for peace and justice workers, international awareness campaign, training of peace monitors, programme of public education about how to protect human rights)	Short-term informal peace education activities aimed at an immediate concern for peace and justice (e.g. holding public meetings or public vigils about a peace/ justice issue, publishing posters on peace/justice issues, writing letters to decision-makers about a human rights abuse, negotiation skills training for community leaders in a conflict situation)

something. Table 8.1 may help you to see some of the options.

The examples given in Table 8.1 are intended to stimulate your thinking about possibilities. A good piece of advice is to start small, with the resources and energy that you and your colleagues have. A point to note is that when you are considering what kind of action to take, it is vital to make an assessment of the needs of the situation right at the beginning. The action you decide to take should aim to address those needs. At the same time, it is important to acknowledge that you and your organisation have needs and interests (see 'The Onion', p. 27) and that these may be a motivating factor for you in taking this action. However, you must still be careful to put the interests of the situation ahead of your own.

Promoting the participation of people in decision-making

Participation is a widely accepted principle of development: people should be involved in decisions that affect them. Why? Because it leads to better decisions, because it motivates people, and, ultimately, because it is just.

Arguments in favour of participation become clearer when it is absent – in humanitarian programmes, for example. Where emergency provision is made without consultation with the people affected, damage can easily be inflicted unintentionally.

A purely technical approach to meeting the emergency needs of a community may well miss the fact that women are likely to have the greatest needs, bearing the responsibility – as they usually do – for the management of shelter, food, health care and child care. It may also give additional power to the men and take away traditional authority from the women.

It is not uncommon, in an emergency situation, for the only health care available to be for pregnant and breast-feeding mothers, although all women and men (and children) may need medical attention for physical injury and other damage to their health. Women on their own may be vulnerable to rape and sexual harassment, especially if shelter is ill-advised and sanitation facilities are too far from safe/lighted areas. Men will have their own problems relating to loss of role and power over their own lives.

Discussion with all concerned is essential to get the most appropriate programme and not further disempower men and women who have already lost much. People affected by an adverse situation need to be involved in how that situation is addressed: to own the actions being taken.They will have to do so very shortly anyway, when the emergency resources are withdrawn.

PEACE AND PEOPLE'S PARTICIPATION
One of the reasons why well-managed groups and organisations succeed over the long term is that all the individuals feel themselves to be part and parcel of the whole system: there is a sense of belonging and ownership. People feel a shared responsibility for their colleagues, and believe themselves to be working for a shared future.

When we speak about a society where positive peace prevails, we assume that people in the society are empowered enough to take an active part in decision-making. Conversely, where negative peace and oppression prevail, people tend to be passive with little interest in fulfilling social or political roles.

Conflicts are most likely to be handled creatively, and to end constructively, where levels of participation are high, and where channels exist for the expression of disagreement and mechanisms are available for handling disagreement and reaching consensus. All sections of the community have a voice, both women and men, young and old, disabled and able-bodied, employed and unemployed, rich and poor.

Violent conflicts seriously undermine people's ability to participate in the positive processes of decision-making, while post-conflict situations create huge opportunities for expanding

✪ Nsamva za anzake anamva nkhwangwa ili mmutu.
If you do not listen to others' advice, you will face the consequences.
MALAWI

the base for decision-making. For example, a government that comes to power through war is unlikely to be comprehensively representative. Even more importantly, besides the systems at macro (or national) level, community-level institutions and mechanisms tend to be eroded or destroyed. As a result, people who have already suffered through war are further disempowered, as they find themselves unable to participate in the process of rebuilding. Therefore, strengthening the participation of people in conflict-affected areas is a crucial challenge, if a truly sustainable peace is to be built.

Figure 8.2 was drawn to illustrate a change in relationships between government and the local community in Wajir, Northern Kenya, which took place over a period of several years in response to community pressure.

FIGURE 8.2: GOVERNMENT AND LOCAL COMMUNITY RELATIONSHIPS – WAJIR, NORTHERN KENYA

5. GOOD GOVERNANCE
There is a high level of trust and communication between the people and the representative government. So, decisions can be made without direct dialogue every time.

4. DIALOGUE
Direct participation of people in decision-making. The government and the people meet and make decisions through dialogue.

3. CONSULTING
Direct participation is still low. However, the government authorities meet with people and take their views through their representatives.

2. MEETING
Participation of people is very low, but government authorities meet people face to face and inform them about the decisions.

1. INFORMING
There is no participation by people. At most their representatives are informed of decisions made by the government.

The stages (which begin at the bottom and move upwards) illustrate how the government position moved from distant and autocratic to responsive to local needs and structures. At the end of this process, each side realised how much it needed the other and could assist it in being effective.

More widely, this series of diagrams can be seen to illustrate the different types of relationship that are possible between communities and the authorities. If participation and empowerment proceed to their fullest extent, the outcome is not total independence of a community from the government, but real cooperation; the state is an essential part of modern life. People can find a role in strengthening its institutions and its mandate to work for the good of the people rather than for its own benefit.

WHAT YOU CAN DO

It is encouraging that there is a growing acceptance of the value of 'people-based development'. Though this does not necessarily mean that development principles are being successfully applied internationally, the universal recognition that no development can be brought about without direct involvement of the people themselves is of significant value and could have a revolutionary effect, if it could be turned into reality on the ground. Thus, by adopting development principles, projects of the World Bank and other international institutions could be adapted to serve the real needs of people worldwide.

It is clear that genuine development can bring empowerment to people. So, if you are part of the aid and development system in an area that is affected by conflict, you may have many opportunities to help people recover and to help institutions develop, which will allow the people themselves to make some of the important decisions affecting their livelihoods.

There is no prescription for promoting participation. It can be done through any type of work and project, by recognising the potential that exists in both men and women, and by promoting structures that allow people to find answers to their own problems. **Peace needs to be built 'with' people, not 'for' people.** This is a major factor in peace becoming sustainable in the long term.

Developing good governance

Governance here refers to a number of levels of power. There is the level of international governance by organisations such as NATO and the UN, the national level consisting of state governments around the world, and the community level, which includes provincial and local governments.

Societies with high levels of agreement on structures and processes, and that govern legitimately, are societies with mechanisms for dealing with conflicts as they arise and with a social fabric strong enough to encourage disagreement and withstand dispute. Societies in which people disagree about the structures

---

GOOD GOVERNANCE

The combination of institutions, laws, procedures and norms that allow people to express their concerns and fight for their interests within a predictable and relatively equitable context forms the basis of good governance. Efficient administration of public resources is an additional element. The entire edifice of good governance ultimately rests upon a legitimate use of power: public authority must be sanctioned by the consent of the governed.

D. Ghai & C. Hewitt de Alcantara, 'Globalisation and social integration: patterns and processes', Occasional Paper no. 2, Geneva, UNRISD, 1994, p.15.

---

and processes of decision-making also tend to have a high level of conflict, often expressed through violence (in part because disagreement is feared and repressed). In other words, well-governed societies need to be able to deal constructively with conflict so that its underlying causes are addressed without recourse to violence.

There are no set rules about the order in which to attack these problems. If your society is unstable – if it is one that has elections whose results are disputed, sees frequent attempts to overthrow the state and constant incidents of violent conflict at all levels, is rife with contested laws or competing systems of law, or fosters deep social divisions that are reflected in political polarisation – it may be difficult to choose and defend a single priority. A public campaign to enhance the legitimacy of government may be premature before the post-holders appear to take responsibility and are legitimately elected. Improving the legal system may seem pointless until levels of violence can be reduced.

How can one group be persuaded to accept the state, when it is excluded from any possibility of power or access to resources? Our experience is that it is important to tackle all the issues, in whatever order possible, because all of them will need to be addressed in order for the situation to improve. And if you are fortunate to have fairly good government and levels of acceptance, it is still vital to work to improve these in order to avoid a future crisis of governance.

GOOD GOVERNANCE, SOCIAL FABRIC AND CONFLICT

We have said already that conflict, if in any sense it is more than a surface disagreement, is generally not the outcome of an isolated action or event. The main causes are inherent in the social, cultural and political composition of the society involved, and in the processes pertaining to it. This may be true even in apparently insignificant instances, which may seem trivial to an observer.

MORE THAN MEETS THE EYE

An eighteen-year-old youth is trying to get onto a bus that is already overcrowded.
He is already feeling irritated after seeing that one of his parents in hospital is not receiving proper treatment. He finds himself being pushed aside by a middle-aged man who leaves the bus in a careless manner and seems too disturbed and mentally absent even to notice.
The boy curses and pushes the man back.
The man is angered by the way the boy is looking at him. He sees him as belonging to an age range in which people do not respect their elders.
The two begin to trade insults. There begins to be enough heat for them to come to blows. Other bystanders start to become involved on each side…

The above example may appear to be an everyday incident, with no cause other than coincidence. However, further investigation may suggest that this is not so. The inadequacy of transport facilities, the poor conditions of hospitals, the low salary of the man, the lack of employment possibilities for the youth – all these factors could have a bearing on the incident. In addition, a lack of self-awareness or poor communication skills could lead to the incident becoming violent, and involving more people.

So, the way a society is run and the predominant system of social governance are very important factors in determining individual behaviour and attitudes. Individual attitudes impact in turn on social institutions and behaviour generally, and influence the way in which decisions are made and policies drawn up and implemented. There is, in effect, a cycle of influence, in all directions.

Figure 8.3, opposite, shows conflict as a constant reality that is influenced by three social components: the **INDIVIDUAL**, the **SOCIETY** and the **SYSTEM** that prevails in that

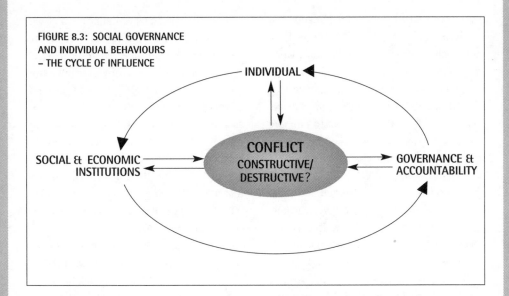

FIGURE 8.3: SOCIAL GOVERNANCE
AND INDIVIDUAL BEHAVIOURS
– THE CYCLE OF INFLUENCE

society and characterises the relationships of the individuals operating within it.

Conflict can be either constructive or destructive, depending on the way it is dealt with. If there are effective and widely accepted mechanisms for the expression and exchange of views and aspirations, change can take place peacefully, taking all interests into account. Where the channels of expression are blocked, and people see their own group as being in conflict with others, there is much more likelihood of frustration and violence.

▶ **What aspects of governance in your own situation do you see that are currently causing frustration and perhaps violence?**
▶ **Is work being done to address this?**

The work of improving governance within a society is one that extends across all levels and sectors. While it certainly includes initiatives to promote effective political structures, it has a social focus also. The aim is no less than to upgrade the capacities of political, economic, social and community structures so that the basic needs and rights of the population are met. Part of this process is to enable these institutions to be managed and structured in such a way that conflict can be dealt with effectively within them, and in the communities in which they operate.

CONSULTATIVE STRUCTURES

When there is no violent conflict and the situation is relatively stable, there is a great deal that can be done to avert future violence.

This stage, whether pre- or post-conflict, is conducive to a vital aspect of peace-building work: establishing or renewing the major structures and institutions that direct and underpin the life of the society. At national level this includes government itself, economic structures, the military and police forces, and the judiciary. At a more local level, schools and other educational and administrative institutions may be crucial.

In a post-conflict society, where consensus may well have been destroyed (if it ever existed), renewal cannot come by means of a simple decision from the top, if it is to last. It has to be forged in a painful process that involves the different social groups in seeking common ground again, and, wherever possible, building the new together.

In South Africa, for example, protracted negotiations (the CODESA talks) began in 1991, involving the full range of political parties, from the Freedom Front to the Pan-African Congress and Azanian People's Organisation. The aim was to devise an interim constitution acceptable to all. Each stage of the negotiations was punctuated by breaks in which the parties liaised with their membership and educated them on developments. This smoothed the potentially destructive re-entry stage, when negotiators have to sell the painstakingly negotiated outcome to their constituencies.

Further, a nationwide structure, the National Peace Accord (NPA), was set up to promote dialogue between communities and interest groups at all levels in preparation for the first national elections in 1994. While a national secretariat coordinated regional and local structures, the strength of the NPA lay mainly in the local peace committees, which included representatives from the business communities, residents' and civic associations, trade unions, political parties, local relief organisations, development and rights activists, churches and mosques.

While the police and the military were outside these committees, they were frequent attenders in unstable areas, such as Kwazulu-Natal and the Vaal Triangle. These committees met regularly and helped to anticipate crisis points and prevent potentially violent incidents. The peace committees were renamed reconstruction and development committees in the months leading up to the general election and often tried to coordinate projects in their areas. Although funded by the apartheid state, the NPA was inclusive enough in its membership to be accepted as relatively impartial – no small achievement in such a polarised context.

Another model has been followed in Somaliland, where the emphasis has been on re-inventing traditional structures rather than creating entirely new ones. Here, elders have been centrally involved in building peace from the grass roots upwards through a mixture of workshops, lengthy sessions of dialogue, and conferences.

THE ROLE OF CIVIL SOCIETY
Civil society is a catch-all term to describe the social institutions, both customary and modern, which operate within a society. It is distinct from government, but is seen as essential for the good functioning of any society.

It tends to be an agreed principle that the level of social and political stability in any society depends on the strength of its civic structures. Where civic organisations and groups are active and effective, the likelihood of social disintegration and public violence as a response to conflict is lower than where there is not a thriving civil society. Unfortunately, one of the effects of violent conflict is to disrupt and destroy those parts of civil society that are functioning well, and to undermine the values that underpin social initiatives and development work in general.

In Afghanistan, for example, the role of community elders has historically been instrumental in developing and maintaining community-based governance structures. For generations, individual communities lived in peaceful coexistence – not because the central governments were effective, but because the local mechanisms were. However, as a result of the war the role of elders and respect for fundamental values has been weakened, and local structures have repeatedly failed to forge solutions.

A crucial point, when it comes to the role of civil society, is the question of leadership. Many groups, communities and societies fall into destructive conflict because their fate is in incompetent or corrupt hands – and they allow this state of affairs to continue.

In societies that are governed by dictatorships, social institutions such as churches, schools, development projects and so on tend to develop the same style of authoritarian leadership; as a result, mini-dictatorships are spawned across the whole social spectrum. In this situation the problems for communities trying to assert their genuine needs and promote their own actions for development and peace are great.

WHAT YOU CAN DO
People wanting to take action for peace and justice can often feel disoriented when they encounter the real size of the challenges facing them – particularly so in the area of governance.

It is important, however, to begin where you are, with the resources that you have, and encourage others to do the same.

If you belong to an organisation, take a look at its leadership:
▶ **Does it reflect in itself the values it claims to uphold?**
▶ **If your organisation believes in empowerment, does it empower its own employees?**
▶ **What kind of leadership do you want and need?**
▶ **What kind of followers do good leaders need?**
▶ **Can you begin some discussions on this which can lead to improvement?**

If your organisation is working on development, rights, peace or related issues, you will already be involved in this work, perhaps without thinking of it in this way. For example, a programme to enable women in a community to have employment opportunities equal to those of men is almost certainly contributing to building better, more inclusive governance, from the domestic level upwards. If you are campaigning for increased legal assistance to political asylum-seekers, you are also working to improve governance within your society. There are many others who are working on this area and will share your objectives.

You may, however, want to address this question at a higher level that includes major institutions and the government itself. You may want to do so quietly, without creating unnecessary enemies. There are many who may feel threatened by your action. You will be the best judge as to how to proceed. An initial decision may be whether to approach this issue as an insider, part of the institution you are trying to change, or as an outsider. Another is whether to do this work publicly, and mobilise public opinion, or to do it confidentially, without attracting attention.

➲ *Whatever you decide, remember that your actions need to be based on good analysis of the situation and a strategy that is designed to address the identified issues and needs. This will take you back to the tools and frameworks we offered you earlier in this book, in a cycle of analysis, strategy, action and evaluation. We now move on to Part 4, which focuses on evaluation of and learning from action.*

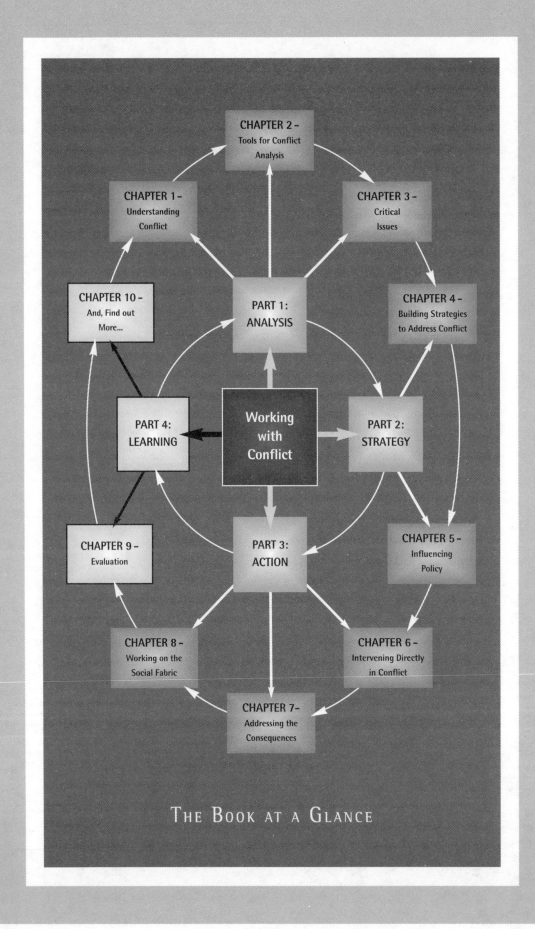

THE BOOK AT A GLANCE

✪ PART 4: LEARNING

IF WE SIMPLY ACT, and continue acting on a situation without a pause, we very soon realise that we are becoming less effective, to the point where it is impossible to go on. Our work, we begin to understand, depends on feedback from those we are working with and trying to influence. Often this feedback is intuitive. People do not set up special procedures to make sure that education takes place in everyday life. But in conflict our experience is that you do need to make special arrangements for it, or the learning does not happen adequately.

CHAPTER 9   Chapter 9 sets out some of the questions to consider in evaluating work, either formally or informally. It is based on the assumption that evaluation is crucial in helping us understand the results of our intervention. It provides a moment for standing back and reflecting on what we have done and what the consequences have been, whether intended or unintended, so that we can act more wisely and effectively in the future.

There is as yet no agreed and effective methodology for the evaluation of work for development, peace and justice in general; programmes of conflict transformation and peace-building in particular present specific challenges. In this chapter we examine practical issues you will face when evaluating this area of work, and look at some of the methodologies available.

CHAPTER 10   We hope this book has helped you to reflect on conflicts taking place at different levels of the community, society, country or region in which you work. Having used the tools we have discussed for analysis and strategy-building, you may be left with further questions about particular issues or processes that are important in your particular context. In Chapter 10 we offer some suggestions on where to find more information or assistance, as you plan practical actions to address the problems and challenges ahead of you.

Finally, as you near the end of the book, we hope you will have been inspired to find new and creative ways to build peace with justice – and new partners for reaching these goals.

9-EVALUATION

Introduction

Evaluating an activity or programme is an important step in the cycle we have introduced as the framework for this book. In formal settings, evaluation is part of a defined procedure aimed at comparing the achievements of a project with its intended objectives, as well as determining how effective the process of implementation has been. However, evaluation can also be an informal procedure to inform you of the result of an activity you have undertaken, and to help you learn and make use of that learning to improve your practice.

Whether formal or informal, evaluation is crucial in helping you to understand the results of your intervention. It provides a moment for standing back and reflecting on what you have done and what the consequences have been, whether intended or unintended.

Evaluation addresses fundamental questions, such as:

- What is the overall vision behind this project or action? Is it a shared vision?
- What are the goals? Whose goals are they? Are they being achieved?
- Are these the goals that ought to be promoted? Are they appropriate to the situation?
- Are there structures in place to support the work? Do structures at different levels work well together?
- What are the objectives of the specific project or action?
- How is this project or action contributing to the overall peace process?
- Is this intervention making any difference? What difference is it making?
- Are the changes that have so far been made positive or negative, or are there some of each?
- Would these changes have occurred without this intervention?

- Are there other factors, or other stakeholders, contributing to the changes?
- What is the impact of this project on the community as a whole and on the different individuals within it?
- Are there unanticipated impacts? What are these? Are they positive or negative?
- Is the programme cost-effective? Is it worth the investment of funds, resources and time?
- What does success mean for the different stakeholders or constituencies?

Each constituency will have its own perception or interpretation of the questions:

- **THE COMMUNITY** wants to know: Are these programmes or activities helping us, or are they making things worse? Are all sections of our community benefiting? How can we support and encourage the good work, and help to change what is not right?

- **FUNDERS AND SPONSORS** want to know: Are the funds and resources that we have contributed helping to improve the situation, or are they making it worse? Are we supporting the most effective ways of working and is the work being carried out in the most productive way? Do the benefits justify the costs?

- **WORKERS AND INTERVENORS** want to know: Do our efforts bring good results? Is this the most effective way to use our time and energy? Are the risks we are taking worth it? Do our efforts combine with and strengthen those of others, or are we actually in competition with them? Are we addressing all the problems at all levels?

- **GOVERNMENTS (THE AUTHORITIES)** want to know: Is the programme making the situation more stable or less? Does it support or undermine the authority of government?

> ✪ O gură numai are omul si urechi două, dar dimpotrivă mai mult grăieste decât ascultă.
> Nature has given us two ears, two eyes and but one tongue: to the end we should hear and see more than we speak.
> **ROMANIA**

How can we encourage the best efforts, and reform or curb those we regard as destructive?

All these stakeholders have their own aims and their own style of evaluation, and each of them needs to be included in the process. A key question is: Who? Who conducts the evaluation, directs the process and decides on its shape? Who funds it and on what basis? Who holds power? Another question is: How? The process of evaluation is as important as its outcome. These questions raise dilemmas that should be dealt with at an early stage.

However, it is easier to pose the questions than to find the answers. There is, as yet, no agreed methodology for the evaluation of work for development, peace and justice in general, and programmes of conflict transformation and peace-building, in particular, present specific challenges.

Programmes that are intended to address conflict have distinctive characteristics that may require special approaches for their evaluation. Conflict is caused by many factors at different levels and requires a corresponding variety of interlinking interventions in response. No single activity, person or group can build peace alone. So, just as the work of conflict transformation has to be built on a comprehensive understanding of the context, so evaluation needs to

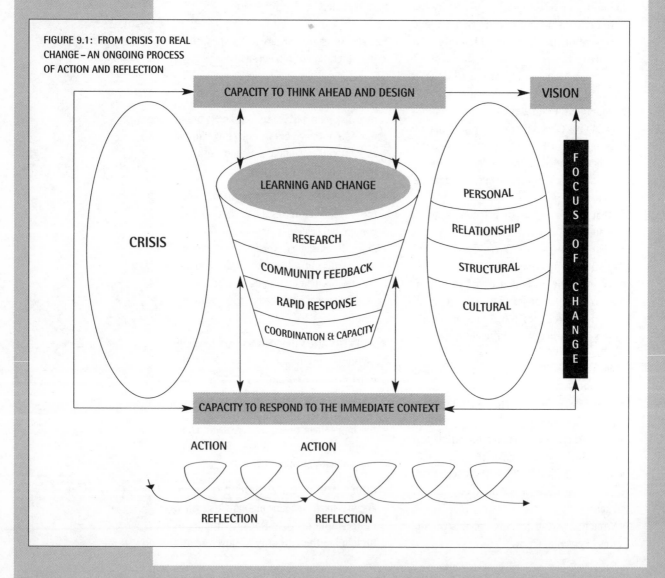

FIGURE 9.1: FROM CRISIS TO REAL CHANGE – AN ONGOING PROCESS OF ACTION AND REFLECTION

CAPACITY TO THINK AHEAD AND DESIGN

VISION

LEARNING AND CHANGE

CRISIS

RESEARCH

COMMUNITY FEEDBACK

RAPID RESPONSE

COORDINATION & CAPACITY

PERSONAL

RELATIONSHIP

STRUCTURAL

CULTURAL

FOCUS OF CHANGE

CAPACITY TO RESPOND TO THE IMMEDIATE CONTEXT

ACTION   ACTION

REFLECTION   REFLECTION

be equally broad in its examination of the levels of activity, the range of actors involved and the interconnections between them.

COMPLEXITY AND CONTEXT –
SOUTH AFRICA, 1990s

Rupert Taylor's attempts to evaluate the impact of particular interventions in the South Africa conflict led him to the conclusion that the programmes could not sensibly be evaluated individually, in competition with each other. On the contrary, he found that the actual impact was cumulative: one web of organisations influenced other webs of organisations, all of them interconnected, with shared founders and memberships. The interconnectedness of conflict transformation organisations themselves, and their close relationships with, yet distinctiveness from, development and welfare agencies on the one hand and political organisations on the other, led to their having an enormous impact on the situation itself.

(See South Africa: The Role of Peace and Conflict Resolution Organizations in the Struggle against Apartheid, by Rupert Taylor – a forthcoming publication from the International Study of Peace and Conflict Resolution Organisations, funded by the Aspen institute.)

Assessing the impact of a particular piece of work on conflict is made all the more difficult by the assumptions underlying any approach that aims to be both long-term and sustainable.

WORKING ASSUMPTIONS [1]
• Peace-building is about seeking and sustaining processes of change; it is not exclusively, or even primarily, about sustaining outcomes. Rebuilding societies torn by violence and war involves rebuilding relationships and finding new ways of relating. What you are trying to measure is therefore not a static outcome but a dynamic process.

• Peace-building requires changes across multiple levels and perspectives. You must understand, create and sustain the space for change along a continuum that includes personal, relational, structural and cultural dimensions.

• Pursuing such a range of changes in a society torn by war requires vision and a design for attaining that long-term goal. The design of any process of change is built on some understanding of how change works and what produces it. A concern for evaluation suggests that you need, therefore, to be explicit about your own often implicit theories of change, which are inherent in the designs and proposals you carry forward.

• Social conflict is based in relationships. Societal change within a framework of strategic peace-building can only be accomplished through sustained initiatives that promote vertical and horizontal integration of people and processes.

• When you approach evaluation, you need to think about the longer-term context as well as the immediate conflict episode and its dynamics.

• Responsive evaluation needs a continuous cycle of action and reflection.

In a conflict situation you are often working in a context of permanent emerging crisis and constant intervention. Work on conflict should have the capacity to be responsive and intensive in the short term, and at the same time to have a long-term vision. This means that, as you act on the immediate crisis, you should build in time for reflection that helps your learning and informs you about change, as necessary. Figure 9.1, left, attempts to capture and clarify this understanding.

Evaluating 'Working with Conflict'
By its nature this work takes place in situations that are unstable, where changes happen fast and violence is never very far away. These changes take place in settings where emotions

✪ A fall into a ditch makes you wiser. CHINA

are highly charged and violence has been experienced by many.

Building peace is itself a change process and one that is often highly political. Evaluation is not a neutral activity, but takes place in an environment that is rife with power dynamics. It may easily be perceived as an overtly political exercise by actors who are otherwise trying to appear impartial. There may be negative consequences not only for the process, but also for the wider community.

It is essential, therefore, for those who are evaluating interventions in conflict to understand both the forces at work in the present context and the previous history of the conflict, including the differing interpretations of that history. The causes of a conflict are multi-faceted and complex. There are many issues involved and different stakeholders may have widely differing perceptions.

Many agencies still see evaluation as a one-off exercise – a snapshot of how things are going at a specific moment, although awareness is growing of the need to link evaluation with ongoing monitoring and to involve the people affected by the programme in these processes.[2]

In our experience evaluation needs to be a continuous process. Conflict situations are dynamic; changes happen, often quite rapidly.

EVALUATION OF RTC

RTC commissioned its own evaluation in 1998, from an external consultant, to address the central question: Have we made any difference after six years? The methodology aimed to identify the explicit links between RTC's actions and the intended outcomes, and to search for the implicit links – specifically, consequences that were not planned. As this was a genuine attempt to discover what was happening, rather than an exercise to satisfy funders, the process of learning amongst RTC staff and trustees was seen as being as important as the final evaluation document.

In terms of wider impact, the report highlighted three main areas for development:

■ It identified a gap that had emerged between individual change (which RTC courses and consultancies often promote) and change at organisational level, where, amongst policy-makers especially, incomprehension and even suspicion about work on conflict can create obstacles. This has led RTC to look for ways to strengthen partnerships with particular organisations in order to complement the relationships we have with individuals, and to work more deliberately with policy-related staff.

■ It said that RTC risks being preoccupied with action at the expense of reflection and learning. While this may have been necessary in the early stages, any organisation has to strike a balance between these two poles if the work is to prosper in the longer term, and contribute to the development of the field as a whole. A new post has since been established which incorporates organisational learning as a major activity. It is still proving difficult, however, to ensure that time is allocated for the reflection to take place.

■ Also the report recommended that a strategic process is needed to give shape and coherence to the many activities RTC undertakes, both those it initiates, such as international courses and the programme of video case studies, and those where it is responding to others' requests. We have now developed a strategic framework, and are seeking to marry up the sense of purpose it gives with the messy reality of everyday demands and urgent requests.

A full report of this evaluation is available from RTC.

It may be difficult to establish a moment for evaluation. Because of this, evaluation should be regarded as engagement in a process of continuous self-reflection. It is an opportunity for learning rather than an examination or a judgement, and the learning from evaluation needs to be fed back into the programme, as well as to those with managerial or funding responsibilities.

A programme that is working on conflict is **process-oriented**, addressing both people and their relationships as well as what they aspire to achieve. An evaluation should therefore be **people-centred**, and involve all the stakeholders from the original conception of the project to the setting of indicators, monitoring, managing, and evaluating. All of these factors present a challenge to the more traditional forms of evaluation.

The evaluation web

The impact of any specific activity in terms of peace and conflict can be evaluated in isolation: Does this initiative work, or not work? Is this programme of peace education changing the attitudes of pupils? However, this may not tell you very much unless you set your evaluation in the wider context of the situation.

If a peace education programme has been implemented in local schools in response to gang warfare in the neighbourhood, and after five years the number of violent incidents has not reduced, it would still be possible to evaluate the programme as a success in terms of popularity, perhaps, and change of behaviour within the school. However, the wider context remains apparently unaffected.

The Web, shown in Figure 9.2 below, is designed to show the different levels of a programme and the relationships between all of the elements. Ideally, these will come together to create a focus for change. An assessment of the effectiveness of these linkages will build a picture of what is happening in the broader context and may identify issues that need to be resolved to achieve positive impact and real change.

The following questions may help you to conceptualise how to set your evaluation in the wider context:
• What is the vision of the project?
• What are the values that guide and inform the vision?

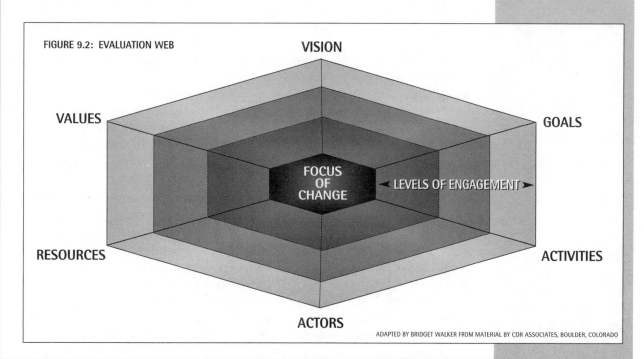

FIGURE 9.2: EVALUATION WEB

VISION

VALUES

GOALS

FOCUS OF CHANGE ◄ LEVELS OF ENGAGEMENT ►

RESOURCES

ACTIVITIES

ACTORS

ADAPTED BY BRIDGET WALKER FROM MATERIAL BY CDR ASSOCIATES, BOULDER, COLORADO

⊘ Sinek kucuktur,
ama mide bulandirir.
The fly is small,
but it is big enough
to make one sick.
TURKEY

- Are the vision and values known to / shared by all stakeholders?
- Do the goals reflect the vision and values?
- What are the activities undertaken?
- At which levels are the activities undertaken?
- Are the values and vision reflected in activities at all levels?
- Are the activities helping to achieve the goals?
- What are the indicators to assess progress towards goals?
- Are the goals and indicators known to/shared by the actors at all levels?
- Who has set the indicators, and at which levels?
- Are the resources (human/material) appropriate /adequate for the activities?
- What is the focus of change and is it taking place? If not, what needs to happen now?

PARTICIPATION

People's participation forms the foundation of sustainable work to build peace, and the evaluation of these processes needs to acknowledge that fully.

There are many techniques that can be applied to evaluation, such as Participatory Rural Appraisal, which will increase the level of community participation. One project paying particular attention to the evaluation of peace and conflict activities is the Action-Evaluation Project.[3]

A number of other initiatives are under way as well, with the aim of testing different approaches and methodologies for evaluating conflict resolution/transformation activities and programmes. As their results become known, more and better choices should become available. The methodologies, however, should not obscure the importance of involvement and ownership by those who have most to gain or lose in action to address conflicts.

Impact assessment

When assessing the effect of a project to, for example, rebuild a bridge, it is clear at the end whether or not the planned physical impact has been achieved. With work on peace and conflict, however, the question of assessing impact is more complex, but equally vital.

Our understanding of impact assessment includes two components: the impact on peace and the impact on violence.[4]

- **PEACE IMPACT** The term 'peace impact' includes those effects that foster and support the sustainable structures and processes which strengthen the prospects of peaceful coexistence and decrease the likelihood of the outbreak, occurrence/recurrence or continuation of violent conflict.
- **VIOLENCE IMPACT** The term 'violence impact' includes all social, economic, and political effects that increase the likelihood that conflict will be dealt with through violent means.

The aims of peace and violence impact assessment are:

1. To assess, over a period of time, the positive and negative impact of different kinds of intervention (or the lack thereof) on the dynamics of the violence.
2. To contribute to the development of a more coherent violence prevention and peace-building policy.
3. To serve as a sensitising tool for policy-shapers and policy-makers, helping them to identify weaknesses in their approach (such as: blind spots, incoherence, bad timing, inadequate priority setting).

Peace and violence impact assessment is a useful tool to assist development and humanitarian organisations in analysing situations of actual or potential conflict, identifying strategic opportunities for violence prevention, and monitoring the impact of their activities.[5]

An impact assessment exercise will capture the essence of a situation at a particular moment in time. However, as conflict is highly dynamic and there may be rapid change, it is important to have a means of ongoing observation, monitoring and analysis of that change, both for programme planning and implementation, and also so that the moment of evaluation can be set in context.

Indicators

An important component of assessing impact is indicators that can suggest whether the project is leading towards the intended goal or not. Indicators are helpful in setting standards against which achievements will be judged.

Particularly in this field of work, it may never be clear that objectives have been fully attained. Have we reached perfect peace? Even if there is not perfect peace or we are not quite near it, the indicators are a way to check whether things are heading in the right direction.

For sustainability of the project, the indicators should be set, wherever possible, by the beneficiaries, so that their standards are used to judge impact and so that they understand and own the results. This will also enhance community participation in both the activity and the evaluation, and make it possible for the community to monitor its own situation, celebrating improvements and acting quickly if the situation worsens.

What constitutes peace and violence is complex and variable. To assess the impact using peace indicators or violence early warning indicators, you need to consider various aspects both of the situation and of the programme.

In Table 9.1 on p.164 (which is adapted from a table devised at a community workshop in Wajir, north-east Kenya) we set out an example that includes indicators of peace and violence, divided into different subcategories. Be aware that the list shown is neither prescriptive nor exhaustive. But it may give you a starting point for identifying possible indicators in your own situation, upon which you can expand.

The area of impact assessment is constantly being developed and updated. It is another key policy area where the experiences of practitioners, working on the ground, need to be captured so that they can influence and inform the direction of research and methodology.

AN EXAMPLE FROM THE INTERNATIONAL DEVELOPMENT RESEARCH CENTRE IN CANADA

In Canada, Dr Kenneth Bush has been leading work on Peace and Conflict Impact Assessment (PCIA). He suggests some specific questions that need to be asked when beginning a programme of peace-building activities.

At the planning stage:
- Are the minimal political, legal, security and infrastructural conditions in place?
- Is there enough political support for the activity, on the ground and at other key levels?
- Is the window of opportunity opening or closing?
- Is the timing right?
- Does the proposed activity have the right mix of resources?
- Does the lead organisation have experience on the ground?
- Are the expected positive impacts achievable?
- How will these be assessed?
- Might the activity aggravate violent conflicts?
- What precautions are proposed?
- Will the activity be sustainable?

At the monitoring and evaluating stages:
- Has the activity created or exacerbated violent conflict?
- Has it reduced the level of violence and fostered reconciliation?
- Has it led to sustainable processes, which enhance prospects of peaceful coexistence?
- Has it led to substantial changes on issues underlying the conflict?

IDRC Workshop Report, 'A Measure of Peace: Peace and Conflict Impact Assessment (PCIA) of development projects in conflict zones', Ottawa, 1–2 June, 1998

Key issues in evaluations
RECORDING

It is important to record the proceedings. This can be done using tape recorders and other

TABLE 9.1: INDICATORS OF PEACE AND VIOLENCE – DEVELOPED IN WAJIR, KENYA

PEACE INDICATORS	VIOLENCE EARLY WARNING INDICATORS
PHYSICAL AND PSYCHOLOGICAL HEALTH INDICATORS • Low population mortality • Few injuries/death caused by weapons • High nutritional status • Rejection of acts of violence • Participation in society's affairs	**PHYSICAL AND PSYCHOLOGICAL HEALTH INDICATORS** • Population mortality • Injuries and death caused by weapons of war • Desire for vengeance • Prevalence of depression
ENVIRONMENTAL INDICATORS • Inter-communal management of natural resources • Inter-communal sharing of natural resources • Normal patterns of cultivation and livestock-tending	**ENVIRONMENTAL INDICATORS** • Refusal of access to natural resources • Burning of grass
SECURITY INDICATORS • Refusal of incitement to violence • Free assembly of people • Creation of community peace structures	**SECURITY INDICATORS** • Presence of army • Riots and demonstrations • Disappearances • Political detainees
SOCIAL INDICATORS • Freedom of thought, belief, religion, speech, and media • High-level and varied types of social interaction • Intermarriage	**SOCIAL INDICATORS** • Censorship, spying, religious persecution, self-censorship, silence • Low level of social interaction • Sectarian organisation, polarisation
POLITICAL INDICATORS • Cross-communal political parties • Fair and free elections • Freedom of movement	**POLITICAL INDICATORS** • Sectarian political parties • Emergency rule or martial law • Deprived of one's nationality, exiled, or internally displaced
JUDICIAL INDICATORS • Human rights legislation • Equality under the law • Repeal of discriminatory laws	**JUDICIAL INDICATORS** • Political interference in the judicial process • Use of discriminatory laws • Use of mechanisms of informal justice
ECONOMIC INDICATORS • Progress in addressing economic grievances • Reduction in levels of poverty and unemployment	**ECONOMIC INDICATORS** • High level of poverty • Unfair distribution of land, goods and services

electronic means, provided that all the people involved understand and accept this form of recording. While it is important to try to record everything, sometimes the evaluator's reliance on equipment can be counterproductive.

AN EXAMPLE FROM A RURAL KENYAN VILLAGE

Mr Elias, an Education Officer, was given the task of evaluating the effectiveness of a school management committee. He went to interview the various stakeholders, including the school management committee itself. Mr Elias held a series of focused discussions with a group of elders. He obtained permission to use audiotape to record the proceedings and started the dialogue. Everyone participated and told him everything, and Mr Elias felt very satisfied with the meeting. He then checked his tape and realised the battery had run flat and he had no spare, but he told the committee to proceed with the meeting anyway.
One of the committee members was happy that Elias was not recording anything: 'Well,' he said, 'now that you are not recording on tape, we can tell you the real story.'

People may give more candid answers if the proceedings are being recorded by them, for their own benefit, and using methods they are familiar with. This may include not only written records, but the designation of one person to act as the oral memory of the event. Community involvement in documentation also makes it more likely that records can be retrieved later. All of this simply emphasises that the evaluation is done, primarily, not for the purposes of the evaluator, but for the stakeholders and the community.

REPORTING

One of the problems in this type of work is lack of data. A lot of successful peace initiatives are conducted off the record, with no minutes or reports kept. This can pose a difficulty for the evaluator. But we must remember that peace-building represents sensitive, delicate and highly confidential work, where lives may be on the line. The work itself is more important than its assessment. While reporting is important to the donor for the purposes of accountability and transparency, it should be done in a way that enhances the work and is not counter-productive.

Questions to consider include the following:
• Who writes reports? Who sees them before they are widely distributed?
• Who receives reports, and in what order? How is this decision made?
• How/when are results fed back to:
  a. the community?
  b. beneficiaries and other stakeholders of the programme?
  c. the staff of organisations involved?
  d. those actually interviewed as part of the evaluation process?

AN EXAMPLE FROM CENTRAL AMERICA

During the years of repression in Guatemala and Nicaragua in the 1980s, the keeping of written records had the potential to be life-threatening if the records fell into the wrong hands. One agency carried out all its activities according to an oral tradition. Verbal reports were made to the relevant committees, and nothing was committed to paper that could have been dangerous for those concerned. When the danger receded, the agency funded a major study to record and evaluate the programmes that had been supported. A wide range of individuals, groups and organisations were consulted and interviewed, and the results analysed, shared, recorded and published.

TEAM COMPOSITION

Just as an approach to conflict is best undertaken by multidisciplinary teams, so too is an

Evaluation takes many forms – including workshops and informal discussions.

approach to evaluation. In a contested situation it is an advantage to have a team with diverse perceptions, experiences and regional/gender/ethnic/linguistic identifications, as this may make more people comfortable when called upon to give their views.

Since evaluation is itself an intervention in an ongoing process, the team should be equipped with conflict-handling skills, such as mediation, facilitation, listening and negotiation. These are especially important because sometimes an evaluation can trigger painful memories that need to be handled with care and sensitivity, or it can provoke new, unpredictable tensions.

CONTESTED RESULTS

Because these are situations of conflict, there can be no single interpretation of events. An evaluation, including its objectives, process and results, is more than likely to be contested. For this reason, the evaluation of work dealing with conflict, like the direct work on the conflict itself, should exhibit the characteristics mentioned so often in this book.

Evaluation should always aim to be:
- **INCLUSIVE**
- **PARTICIPATORY**
- **BALANCED**
- **HONEST**
- **TRANSPARENT**

MARK TWAIN (1835–1910)

When I was a boy of fourteen, my father was so ignorant I could hardly stand to have the old man around. But when I got to be twenty-one, I was astonished at how much he had learned in seven years.

⊃ *Evaluation and learning are both crucial to a dynamic and sustainable process of change. A thorough and ongoing process of evaluation, analysis and reflection, which captures the learning from our actions and informs the direction we take, will make us* *increasingly effective as we struggle on towards our vision. Chapter 10 gives information on resources that we hope will support you in all your activities.*

NOTES

1. Adapted from John Paul Lederach, *Building Peace: Sustainable Reconciliation in a Divided Society*, United States Institute of Peace, Washington, 1997.

2. See *ONTRAC*, newsletter of the International NGO Training and Research Centre (INTRAC), no. 13, September 1999.

3. The Action-Evaluation Project is located at the McGregor School, Antioch University, Yellow Springs, Ohio, USA, and directed by Dr Jay Rothman. Its website – www.aepro.org – includes an online sample evaluation process.

4. See Luc Reychler, 'Conflict Impact Assessment (CIAS) at the policy and project level', 1998: 3, CPRS, University of Leuven.

5. From 'Peace and conflict impact assessment project', a paper by Manuela Leonhardt for International Alert, 1999.

10-AND FIND OUT MORE...

Introduction

This book has, we hope, helped you to reflect on conflicts at different levels of the community, society, country or region where you work. Having used the tools for analysis and strategy-building, you may be left with further questions about particular issues or processes that are important in your context. In this final chapter we give you some suggestions of where and how to find more information or assistance, as you plan practical actions to address conflicts and violence.

What we offer here is only a small selection from a wide range of organisations and resources that might be useful. In general, we have selected those organisations with which we have had some contact and positive experience and those resources we have used and found to be relevant. There are, no doubt, many other active organisations and useful resources not mentioned. You may find or be directed towards more of these, after beginning with the ones suggested here.

Chapter 10 is divided into these categories:

ORGANISATIONS: A listing of selected international organisations that are actively engaged in conflict transformation and peacebuilding, giving a brief description of each, together with relevant contact details and our suggestions of how the organisation might be useful to you. We have included only organisations that work internationally, while recognising that there are many other organisations that are undertaking effective conflict transformation and peace-building activities on a national or local level in particular countries. The development organisations mentioned are those with which we have worked, which clearly recognise the importance of conflict analysis and intervention and are acting on this within their own mandates.

RESOURCES, including:
- **SELECTED BOOKS** (60), listed according to their relevance to the chapters of this book, with a brief description of the contents of each.
- **SELECTED JOURNALS,** with a brief description of the types of article the journal normally publishes, and information about how to subscribe.
- **SELECTED VIDEOS,** with information about how to obtain copies.
- **SELECTED WEBSITES,** with a short description of each, including links to other websites.

Organisations

The description of each organisation listed below is based on our own experience and knowledge of it, combined with information and contact details from the organisation's printed literature and/or website.

ACCORD is a South African-based organisation involved in conflict resolution, peacekeeping and preventive diplomacy throughout the continent of Africa. Its programmes include various regional consultations and seminars related to conflict transformation, peacekeeping and the transition to peace. It publishes a magazine, *Conflict Trends*, and some occasional papers, available online via the organisation's website as well as in hard copy format.
- **POSTAL ADDRESS:** ACCORD, Private Bag X018, Umhlanga Rocks, 4320, Durban, South Africa
  TEL: +27 31 502 3908 **FAX:** +27 31 502 4160
  EMAIL: info@accord.org.za
  WEBSITE: www.accord.org.za

AGENCY FOR COOPERATION AND RESEARCH IN DEVELOPMENT (ACORD) is an international consortium of 155 non-governmental organisations from Europe and North America working with partners in Africa. Helping people to cope with conflict and build peace is one of ACORD's top priorities, along with reducing poverty and vulnerability, and helping people to secure their basic rights.

- **POSTAL ADDRESS:** ACORD, Dean Bradley House, 52 Horseferry Road, London SW1P 2AF, UK TEL: +44 20 7227 8600 FAX: +44 20 7799 1868 EMAIL: acord@acord.org.uk

ACTIONAID is a UK-based agency that specialises in long-term integrated development programmes. Working in over 20 countries, the agency has vigorously developed its approach to conflict as a crucial element in its work worldwide.

- **POSTAL ADDRESS:** ACTIONAID, Hamlyn House, MacDonald Road, Archway, London N19 5PG, UK TEL: +44 20 7281 4101 FAX: +44 20 7281 5146 EMAIL: mail@actionaid.org.uk

BERGHOF CENTRE FOR CONSTRUCTIVE CONFLICT MANAGEMENT combines research into methods of addressing ethnopolitical and socio-cultural conflicts with applying them in a practical way. Its area of interest is Europe and the European successor states of the Soviet Union, including the Caucasus.

- **POSTAL ADDRESS:** Berghof Centre, Altensteinstrasse 48a, 14195 Berlin, Germany TEL: +49 30 831 8090 FAX: +49 30 831 5985 EMAIL: n.n@ berghof.b.shuttle.de WEBSITE: www.b.shuttle.de/berghof/

INTERNATIONAL COOPERATION FOR DEVELOPMENT (CIIR/ICD) is the overseas programme of the Catholic Institute for International Relations. It sends experienced professionals to share their skills in small-scale development projects overseas. CIIR lends advocacy support to civil organisations and to countries affected by internal conflict. It is currently running a three-year advocacy and research project on the role of civil organisations in peace and democratisation processes in Colombia, Guatemala, South Africa, Angola and East Timor.

- **POSTAL ADDRESS:** CIIR/ICD, Unit 3, Canonbury Yard, 1900 New North Road, London N1 7BJ, UK

TEL: +44 20 7354 0883 FAX: +44 20 7359 0017 EMAIL: ciirlon@gn.apc.org

CENTRE FOR CONFLICT MANAGEMENT (CCM) is a Kazakhstan-based international organisation working in Central Asian countries. CCM is dedicated to the prevention and management of social and ethnic conflicts in the region. Its activities include conducting research, organising seminars and training workshops on human rights and on conflict management and prevention, and the dissemination of information.

- **POSTAL ADDRESS:** CCM, 57 'V' Timiryazev Street, Apt. 23, Almaty 480 070, Kazakhstan TEL: +7 3272 437417 FAX: +7 3272 479449 EMAIL: ccm@online.ru

CENTRE FOR CONFLICT RESOLUTION, Cape Town, associated with the University of Cape Town, works both within South Africa and elsewhere in Africa to promote creative and cooperative approaches to the resolution of conflict and the reduction of violence. Mediation, facilitation, training, education and research comprise the centre's main activities, with the emphasis on capacity-building. The centre publishes a quarterly journal entitled *Track Two*, details of which can be found under 'Resources: Selected Journals' later in this section.)

- **POSTAL ADDRESS:** Centre for Conflict Resolution at UCT, Private Bag, Rondebosch, 7701, South Africa TEL: +27 21 422 2512 FAX: +27 21 422 2622 EMAIL: mailbox@ ccr.uct.ac.za WEBSITE: ccrweb.ccr.uct.ac.za

CHRISTIAN AID works for development through partnership with local communities. Working worldwide, as well as in the UK, the agency has been prominent in campaigning on global issues such as international debt and trade.

- **POSTAL ADDRESS:** Christian Aid, Interchurch House, 35 Lower Marsh, London SE1 7RL, UK TEL: +44 20 7620 4444 FAX: +44 20 7620 0719 EMAIL: caid@gn.apc.org

THE COLLABORATIVE FOR DEVELOPMENT ACTION (CDA) is a small consultancy firm, based near Boston, Massachusetts, USA, which specialises in issues of economic development. CDA has completed a project widely known as 'Do No Harm' (see recommended book by Mary Anderson under the listing for Chapter 4 in 'Resources: Books' later in this section) and is currently working on another, 'Reflecting on Peace Practice', which involves gathering experiences from conflict-focused programmes and trying to identify good practice.

- **POSTAL ADDRESS:** Collaborative for Development Action, 26 Walker St., Cambridge, MA 02138, USA
  TEL: +1 617 661 6310 **FAX:** +1 617 661 3805
  EMAIL: mail@ cdainc.com
  WEBSITE: www.cdainc.com

CONCILIATION RESOURCES (CR) is a UK-based agency that serves as an international resource for local or national organisations pursuing peace or conflict prevention initiatives. Its principal objective is to support sustained practical activities by those working at the community and national levels to prevent violent conflict or transform it into opportunities for social, political and economic development. CR has programme partnerships in Sierra Leone, Fiji, Somaliland, the Gambia and Liberia. CR publishes a journal, *Accord*, three times a year (see 'Resources: Journals' later in this section).

- **POSTAL ADDRESS:** Conciliation Resources, PO Box 21067, London N1 9WT, UK
  TEL: +44 20 7359 7728 **FAX:** +44 20 7359 4081
  EMAIL: conres@c-r.org
  WEBSITE: www.c-r.org

CONFLICT RESEARCH, EDUCATION AND TRAINING (CREATE) offers both short- and long-term consultancies and training programmes for local and international agencies working in situations of protracted violent conflict. Its particular areas of interest are situation analysis, strategic planning, participative design for effective response, and impact assessment. CREATE's current work includes projects in central Europe/the Balkans, Indonesia and Papua New Guinea.

- **POSTAL ADDRESS:** CREATE, Hawthorn House, 1 Landsdown Lane, Stroud, Glos. GL5 1BJ, UK
  TEL: +44 1453 757040 **FAX:** +44 1453 751138
  EMAIL: mhclarge@aol.com or jwl4@gn.apc.org

DEUTSCHE ENTWICKLUNGSDIENST is a German development agency that recruits volunteers to work worldwide on practical projects. The agency plays a lead role in implementing the German Government's policy on Friedens-dienst ('Peace Service'), whereby volunteers are sent to work specifically on peace-building projects.

- **POSTAL ADDRESS:** Deutsche Entwicklungsdienst, Kladower Damm 299, 14089 Berlin, Germany
  TEL: +49 30 36881 244/246 **FAX:** +49 30 36881 271
  EMAIL: ALV@ded.de

EASTERN MENNONITE UNIVERSITY'S CONFLICT TRANSFORMATION PROGRAMME (CTP) comprises an MA degree in conflict transformation at the Institute for Peacebuilding, held for several weeks each year. The institute promotes the transformation of conflict through integrated and culturally appropriate approaches to practice and learning.

- **POSTAL ADDRESS:** CTP, Harrisonburg, Virginia 22802-2464, USA
  TEL: +1 540 432 4490 **FAX:** +1 540 432 4449
  EMAIL: ctprogram@emu.edu
  WEBSITE: www. emu.edu/units/ctp/ctp

EUROPEAN PLATFORM FOR CONFLICT PREVENTION AND TRANSFORMATION is an open network of European NGOs involved in the prevention and resolution of violent conflicts in the international arena. Its aim is to exchange information and experience among the participating organisations, as well as to stimulate cooperation and synergy.

- **POSTAL ADDRESS:** EPCPT, Secretariat, PO Box 14069, 3508 SC Utrecht, The Netherlands
  TEL: +31 30 253 7528 **FAX:** +31 30 253 7529
  EMAIL: euconflict@antenna.nl
  WEBSITE: www.euconflict.org

GERNIKA GOGORATUZ (PEACE RESEARCH CENTRE) aims to contribute to the creation of peace, both in the Basque Country and internationally. It works in the field of reconciliation, conducting research and organising meetings and conferences on this subject. The organisation also teaches and trains people in conflict resolution, staging both seminars and workshops.

- **TEL:** +34 4 625 3558 **FAX:** +34 4 625 6765
  EMAIL: gernikag@sarenet.es

INTERNATIONAL ALERT (IA) is a UK-based non-governmental organisation with a multinational staff team, including volunteers and interns. IA seeks to strengthen the ability of people in conflict situations to make peace by facilitating dialogue at different levels, helping to develop and enhance local capacities, facilitating peace-oriented development and local peace-building initiatives and encouraging the international community to address the structural causes of conflict.

- **POSTAL ADDRESS:** International Alert,
  1 Glyn Street, London SE11 5HT, UK
  TEL: +44 20 7793 8383 **FAX:** +44 20 7793 7975
  EMAIL: general@international-alert.org
  WEBSITE: www.international-alert.org

INTERNATIONAL COOPERATION FOR DEVELOPMENT (ICD), the technical assistance programme of the Catholic Institute for International Relations (CIIR), is active in eleven countries: four in Africa and the Middle East and seven in Latin America and the Caribbean. ICD seeks concrete ways of strengthening the efforts of people as they work towards socially just development. Post-conflict social reconstruction as well as human rights and civic education are included in its programme work. CIIR produces numerous publications that explore key issues raised in this book.

- **POSTAL ADDRESS:** ICD, Unit 3 Canonbury Yard,
  190a New North Road, London N1 7BJ, UK
  TEL: +44 20 7354 0883 **FAX:** +44 20 7359 0017
  EMAIL: ciir@ciir.org
  WEBSITE: www.ciir.org

THE INTERNATIONAL FELLOWSHIP OF RECONCILIATION (IFOR) is an international, spiritually based movement composed of people who commit themselves to active nonviolence as a way of life and as a means of transformation – both personal, social, economic and political. Through its worldwide network of branches, groups and affiliates in more than 40 countries, IFOR acts to promote a global culture of nonviolence through various programmes of education, training and action. IFOR publishes a bi-monthly magazine called *RI* (*Reconciliation International*) – see 'Resources: Journals' later in this section.

- **POSTAL ADDRESS:** IFOR, Spoorstraat 38,
  1815 BK Alkmaar, The Netherlands
  TEL: +31 72 512 3014 **FAX:** +31 72 515 1102
  EMAIL: office@ifor.org
  WEBSITE: www.ifor.org

LE CUN DU LARZAC is a centre for conflict resolution working internationally in French. It organises courses on mediation and coordinates specific initiatives.

- **POSTAL ADDRESS:** Le Cun du l'Arzac,
  Route de St-Martin, 12100 Millau, France
  TEL: +5 65 60 62 33 **FAX:** +5 65 61 33 26

LIFE AND PEACE INSTITUTE (LPI) is an international ecumenical centre for peace research and action, which has as its principal aim to support the work of churches and other institutions in the fields of peace, justice and reconciliation.

- **POSTAL ADDRESS:** LPI, PO Box 1520,
  751 45 Uppsala, Sweden
  TEL: +46 18 169 500 **FAX:** +46 18 693 059
  EMAIL: lpi@algonet.se
  WEBSITE: www.nordnet.se/lpi

OXFAM GB is a UK-based international development, relief and campaigning organisation dedicated to finding lasting solutions to poverty and suffering around the world. With offices in over 70 countries, Oxfam has developed policies on many aspects of conflict work and shares its experience in a variety of publications.

- **POSTAL ADDRESS:** Oxfam GB, 274 Banbury Road, Oxford OX2 7DZ, UK
  TEL: +44 1865 311311 **FAX:** +44 1865 312380
  EMAIL: oxfam@oxfam.org.uk
  WEBSITE: www.oxfam.org.uk

PEACE BRIGADES INTERNATIONAL (PBI) is a non-governmental organisation that is exploring nonviolent approaches to peace-keeping and support for basic human rights. By invitation, PBI sends teams of volunteers into areas of political repression and conflict, often to provide protective international accompaniment for individuals and organisations who have been threatened by political violence.

- **POSTAL ADDRESS:** PBI International Office, 5 Caledonian Road, London N1 9DX, UK
  TEL: +44 20 7713 0392 **FAX:** +44 20 7837 2290
  EMAIL: pbiio@gn.apc.org
  WEBSITE: www.igc.apc.org/pbi
  (can be read in English, Spanish, German, French, Italian, Dutch or Swedish)

POST–WAR RECONSTRUCTION AND DEVELOPMENT UNIT (PRDU), based at York University, specialises in research, consultancy and the training of professionals in issues of management and planning of reconstruction after war, humanitarian intervention in complex emergencies, and post-war recovery; it has developed a postgraduate course specifically to cover these areas.

- **POSTAL ADDRESS:** PRDU, The King's Manor, York YO1 2EP, UK
  TEL: +44 1904 433959 **FAX:** +44 1904 433949
  EMAIL: iaas1@york.ac.uk
  WEBSITE: www.york.ac.uk

QUAKER PEACE AND SERVICE is a religious organisation working mainly in the field of mediation, citizen diplomacy and education on conflict prevention and resolution. Its International Relations Section runs a special Reconciliation Programme. The service is also engaged in a number of projects in Sri Lanka, the former Yugoslavia, Lebanon and Northern Ireland.

- **POSTAL ADDRESS:** Quaker Peace and Service, Friends House, 173 Euston Road, London NW1 2BJ, UK
  TEL: +44 20 7663 1000 **FAX:** +44 20 7663 1001
  EMAIL: qps@quaker.org.uk

RESPONDING TO CONFLICT (RTC), a UK-based international agency, offers courses, training, advice and longer-term support to organisations working for peace, rights and development in situations of conflict and violence around the world. Its 10-week international Working With Conflict course provides an opportunity to explore the practical application of many of the tools and strategies in this book, and it has a very diverse international group in which analysis and learning are shared between many contexts and cultures. RTC's programme also offers shorter workshops for the staff of international agencies who are involved in making policy and planning programmes for work in areas of conflict. RTC works with local partners in various countries and regions, using French, German, Russian, Swahili and a number of other languages. RTC has produced a set of video case studies (see 'Selected Videos' in the Resources section).

- **POSTAL ADDRESS:** RTC, 1046 Bristol Road, Birmingham B29 6LJ, UK
  TEL: +44 121 4155641 **FAX:** +44 121 4154119
  EMAIL: enquiries@respond.org
  WEBSITE: www.respond.org

SAFERWORLD is an independent research group committed to alerting governments and educating the public about the need for more effective approaches to tackling and preventing armed conflicts around the globe. Saferworld conducts research on the causes that underlie armed conflict and, in consultation with experts, suggests steps governments can take. Its main programmes deal with conflict management and the arms trade.

- **POSTAL ADDRESS:** Saferworld, 33/34 Alfred Place, 3rd Floor, London WC1E 7DP, UK
  TEL: +44 20 7580 8886 **FAX:** +44 20 7631 1444
  EMAIL: Sworld@gn.apc.org

SEARCH FOR COMMON GROUND (WASHINGTON) and **THE EUROPEAN CENTRE FOR COMMON GROUND (BRUSSELS)** are related organisations carrying out programmes which aim to resolve conflict and prevent violence, with decentralised activities on four continents and offices in nine countries. Their media unit, Common Ground Productions, has produced a documentary video series, *Africa: Search for Common Ground* (see 'Selected Videos' below).

- **POSTAL ADDRESSES:**

    Search for Common Ground,

    1601 Connecticut Avenue NW, Suite 200,

    Washington, DC 20009, USA

    TEL: +1 202 265 4300 **FAX:** +1 202 232 6718

    EMAIL: search@sfcg.org

    WEBSITE: www.sfcg.org

    European Centre for Common Ground,

    Avenue de Tervuren, 94, B-1040 Brussels, Belgium

    TEL: +32 2 736 7262 **FAX:** +32 2 732 3033

Resources

Like the Organisations section, the lists below represent only a small selection of the many books, directories, journals, videos and websites that might be relevant or useful to you. We have chosen those we know and have used.

SELECTED BOOKS

We have listed our 60 most useful books under the relevant chapter headings. However, many of them cover a range of issues relating to more than one chapter. If you wish to order books, we have found the **QUAKER BOOKSHOP** very efficient and helpful:

- **POSTAL ADDRESS:** Quaker Bookshop, Friends House, 173 Euston Road, London NW1 2BJ, UK

    TEL: +44 20 7663 1000 **FAX:** +44 20 7663 1001

    EMAIL: bookshop@quaker.org.uk

CHAPTERS 1 & 2: UNDERSTANDING CONFLICT and TOOLS FOR CONFLICT ANALYSIS

Burton, John, *Conflict: Resolution and Provention*, Macmillan, London, 1990. Approaches to conflict resolution based on the Human Needs Theory.

Curle, Adam, *Another Way: Positive Response to Contemporary Violence*, Jon Carpenter, 1997. Draws on experience in 35 countries to analyse the crisis of violence in the world.

Galtung, Johan, *Peace by Peaceful Means: Peace and Conflict, Development and Civilization*, Sage Publications, London, Thousand Oaks and New Delhi, 1996. Conceptual and theoretical frameworks related to these four themes: peace, conflict, development and civilisation.

Miall, Ramsbotham & Woodhouse, *Contemporary Conflict Resolution*, Polity Press, 1999. Clear and comprehensive overview of different theoretical approaches to conflict resolution.

Mitchell, C.R., *The Structure of International Conflict*, Macmillan, London, 1981. Basic, often-quoted text about conflict analysis and theory.

Reardon, Betty, *Women and War*, Zed Books, London, 1993. Outlines clearly the interrelationship between the condition of women and all forms of human aggression.

Sandole, Dennis J.D. & Hugo van der Merwe (eds), *Conflict Resolution Theory and Practice: Integration and Application*, Manchester University Press, 1993. Summary of some conceptual theories of conflict combined with examples that apply these theories to practical cases.

Turpin, Jennifer & Lester Kurtz, *The Web of Violence: From Interpersonal to Global*, University of Illinois Press, 1997.

CHAPTER 3: CRITICAL ISSUES

Ashafa & Wuye, *The Pastor and the Imam: Responding to Conflict*, Muslim/Christian Youth Dialogue Forum, 1999. Links powerful personal stories of the authors' reconciliation with Christian and Islamic quotations on peace and cooperation.

Bennet, Olivia, Jo Bexley & Kitty Warnock (eds), *Arms to Fight, Arms to Protect*, Panos, London, 1995. First-hand accounts of the impact of armed conflict on women from many countries, including problems about rebuilding communities and coping with the consequences of violence.

Curle, Adam, *To Tame the Hydra: Undermining the Culture of Violence*, Jon Carpenter, 1999. Very readable account of how to subvert a world system built on profit and power.

Ignatieff, Michael, *Blood & Belonging: Journeys into the New Nationalism*, Chatto & Windus, 1993. Explores issues related to ethnic identity and nationalism.

Oxfam, 'Focus on Gender: Perspectives on Women and Development', *Oxfam Journal*, 1993, vol.1, no.2. Case studies and reflections on gender-related conflict.

Ross, Marc Howard, *The Culture of Conflict: Interpretations and Interests in Comparative Perspective* and *The Management of Conflict*, Yale University Press, New Haven & London, 1993. These two books explore culture and conflict, and the 'culture of conflict'.

Salmi, Jamil, *Violence and Democratic Society: New Approaches to Human Rights*, Zed Books, London, 1993.

South African Council of Churches (SACC), *Human Rights Trainer's Manual*, Johannesburg, 1997. Extensive ideas and activities for teaching about human rights and building a human rights culture.

Stavenhagen, Rodolfo, *Ethnic Conflicts and the Nation-State*, Macmillan, London & New York, 1996. Explores ethnicity, identity and conflict with analysis of cases from around the world.

Williams, Suzanne, with Janet Seed & Adelina Mwau, *The Oxfam Gender Training Manual*, Oxfam, 1994. Good practical manual on gender issues including lots of training activities along with short conceptual pieces on specific issues.

CHAPTER 4: BUILDING STRATEGIES TO ADDRESS CONFLICT

Anderson, Mary B., *Do No Harm: How Aid Can Support Peace or War*, Lynne Rienner, Boulder, Colorado, 1999. Explores the potential negative impact of aid on conflict and suggests ways to remedy this and support peace efforts.

Large, Judith, *The War Next Door: A Study of Second Track Intervention during the War in ex-Yugoslavia*, Hawthorn Press, 1997. Addresses the nature and impact of NGO interventions; based on first-hand research.

Lund, Michael S., *Preventing Violent Conflict: A Strategy for Preventive Diplomacy*, United States Institute of Peace (USIP), Washington, 1996. Ideas, concepts and tools for building strategies for preventing violent conflict.

Schuler, Margaret (ed.), *Freedom from Violence: Women's Strategies from Around the World*, UNIFEM, 1992. Stories of women working to combat gender violence.

CHAPTER 5: INFLUENCING POLICY

Handy, Charles, *Understanding Voluntary Organisations: How to Make Them Function More Effectively*, Penguin, Harmondsworth, 1980. Clear and practical ideas on organisational analysis and change.

Jolly, Ruth (ed.), *Working in Long-Term Conflict: Managing the Organisational Challenge*, INTRAC, Oxford, 1997. Practical ideas, frameworks, tools and activities for strengthening organisational capacity to work in and on violent conflicts.

Gawlinski George & Graessle Lois, *Planning Together: The Art of Effective Teamwork*, Bedford Square Press, London, 1988. Step-by-step guide to cooperative planning; many group activities.

CHAPTER 6: INTERVENING DIRECTLY IN CONFLICT

Acland, Andrew F., *A Sudden Outbreak of Common Sense: Managing Conflict Through Mediation*, Hutchinson Business Books, London, 1990. Practical guide to mediation principles, issues and processes from a Western perspective.

Anstey, Mark, *Negotiating Conflict: Insights and Skills for Negotiators and Peacemakers*, Juta & Co. Ltd [PO Box 14373, Kenwyn 7790, South Africa], 1991. Clear guidance based on wide experience.

Augsburger, Daniel, *Mediation Across Cultures: Patterns and Pathways*, Westminster/Knox Press, 1992. Unusual, fully cross-cultural approach, using many proverbs and folk stories to illustrate themes; explores the mediation process from various cultural perspectives.

Cornelius, Helena & Shoshona Faire, *Everyone Can Win: How to Resolve Conflict*, Simon & Schuster, Brookvale, Australia, 1989. Simple, practical guide for planning and taking action, with exercises and examples.

Creative Associates International, *Preventing and Mitigating Violent Conflicts: A Revised Guide for Practitioners*, Washington, DC, 1997. Comprehensive guide, covering a wide range of different actions for different stages.

Easwaran, Eknath & Badshah Khan, *A Man to Match his Mountains: Nonviolent Soldiers of Islam*, Nilgiri Press, USA, 1985. A biography of a man who raised history's first 100,000-strong nonviolent 'army'.

Fitzduff, Mari, *Community Conflict Skills: A Handbook for Groupwork*, Belfast, 1988. Includes exercises on prejudice and identity written in Northern Ireland context, but adaptable to other situations.

Helps, Vanessa, *Negotiating: Everybody Wins*, BBC Books, London, 1992. Very practical guidelines, with sections on strategy, power and win/win outcomes.

International Alert, *Resource Pack for Conflict Transformation*, London, 1996. Extensive collection of materials on training and facilitation for action.

Mahoney, Liam & Luis Enrique Eguren, *Unarmed Bodyguards: International Accompaniment for the Protection of Human Rights*, Kumarian Press, 1997. Accounts of the use of unarmed accompaniment in different situations, and a rule-of-thumb guide to when to use this approach.

McConnell, John A., *Mindful Mediation: A Handbook for Buddhist Peacemakers*, Buddhist Research Institute, Spirit in Education, Wangsanit Ashram & Foundation for Children, Bangkok, 1995. Mediation and peacemaking processes and examples from a Buddhist perspective.

Otite, Onigu & Isaac Olawale Albert (eds), *Community Conflicts in Nigeria: Management, Resolution and Transformation*, Spectrum Books, 1999. Pioneering account of dealing with conflicts over scarce resources in Nigeria.

Roberts, David Lloyd, *Staying Alive: Safety and Security Guidelines for Humanitarian Volunteers in Conflict Areas*, ICRC, 1999.

Sharp, Gene, *The Politics of Nonviolent Action – Part 1: Power and Struggle* (deals with political power and nonviolent struggle); *Part 2: The Methods of Nonviolent Action* (includes 198 specific methods); *Part 3: The Dynamics of Nonviolent Action* (with discussion of three main mechanisms of nonviolent action: conversion, accommodation and nonviolent coercion), Porter Sargent Publishers, Boston, MA, 1973.

Williams, Sue & Steve, *Being in the Middle by Being at the Edge: Quaker Experience of Non-official Political Mediation*, William Sessions, York, 1994. Analysis of political mediation process from the practitioner's perspective.

CHAPTER 7: ADDRESSING THE CONSEQUENCES

Asmal, Asmal & Roberts, *Reconciliation Through Truth*, David Phillips, Cape Town, 1996.

Eade, Deborah (ed.), *From Conflict to Peace in a Changing World: Social Reconstruction in Times of Transition*, Oxfam Working Papers, 1998. Articles on a range of themes, giving a picture of the moral and practical problems involved in intervention.

Lederach, John Paul, *Building Peace: Sustainable Reconciliation in Divided Societies*, United States Institute of Peace (USIP), Washington, 1997. Includes comprehensive, integrated framework for building peace and reconciliation.

Schmookler, Andrew Bard, *Healing the Wounds that Drive Us to War*, Bantam Books 1988. Explains the socio-psychological sources of aggression and suggests therapeutic insights to healing its effects.

CHAPTER 8: WORKING ON THE SOCIAL FABRIC

Boulding, Elise, *Building a Global/Civic Culture*, Syracuse University Press, Syracuse, New York, 1990. Persuasive and practical case for moving towards empowerment of people at a global level.

European Centre for Conflict Resolution, *People Building Peace: 35 Inspiring Stories from Around the World*, 1999. Many examples of practical action for peace and justice, written clearly and full of hope.

Fine, Nic & Fiona Macbeth, *Playing With Fire: Training for the Creative Use of Conflict*, Youth Work Press, Leicester, 1992. Training activities based on the analogy of fire in relation to the stages of conflict.

Hope, Anne & Sally Timmel, *Training for Transformation: A Handbook for Community Workers*, Mambo Press, Gweru, Zimbabwe, 1984. Three volumes, including many participatory methods for exploring issues and analysing situations.

Potter, Goldblatt, Kiloh & Lewis, *Democratisation*, Polity Press, 1997. Conceptual discussion about definitions and dynamics of democratisation.

Rohr-Rouendaal, Petra, *Where There is No Artist: Development Drawings and How to Use Them*, Intermediate Technology, London. Very accessible guidance on how to use graphics to give messages.

CHAPTER 9: EVALUATION

Hallam, Alistair, *Evaluating Humanitarian Assistance Programmes in Complex Emergencies*, Relief and Rehabilitation Network, ODI 1998. Highly practical guide to good practice.

Hollier, Fiona, Kerrie Murray & Helena Cornelius, *Conflict Resolution Trainer's Manual: 12 Skills*, The Conflict Resolution Network, Chatswood, Australia, 1993. Comprehensive training resource with many materials that can be copied or adapted.

Lederach, John Paul, *Preparing for Peace: Conflict Transformation Across Cultures*, Syracuse University Press, Syracuse, New York, 1995. Comparison of elicitive and prescriptive approaches to training, advocating the former.

Oakley, P., B. Pratt & A. Clayton, *Outcomes and Impact: Evaluating Change in Social Development*, INTRAC, 1998. Case studies and discussion of how to attempt to establish effective methods of evaluating social development programmes and initiatives.

Roche, Chris, *Impact Assessment for Development Agencies: Learning to Value Change*, Oxfam, 1999. Contains a review of tools available to design impact assessments for development, emergencies and advocacy, with case studies, plus a theoretical overview.

Rubin, Francis, *A Basic Guide to Evaluation for Development Workers*, Oxfam, Oxford, 1995. A resource to help groups plan and carry out evaluations as an integral part of their work.

CHAPTER 10: AND FIND OUT MORE...

Prevention and Management of Violent Conflicts: An International Directory, published by European Platform for Conflict Resolution and Transformation, 1998. A global directory of organisations concerned with conflict prevention and resolution, both local and international.

Searching for Peace in Africa: An Overview of Conflict Prevention and Management Activities, European Platform for Conflict Prevention and Transformation, 1998. A survey of conflict-related activities, and details of the various organisations promoting conflict transformation in Africa.

Networks, Organisations and Individuals Working to End Violence Against Women and Girls: A Directory, published by UNICEF Regional Office for South Asia (ROSA), Kathmandu, Nepal, 1999.

SELECTED JOURNALS

TRACK TWO – A quarterly publication of the Centre for Conflict Resolution and the Media Peace Centre in Cape Town, South Africa. It aims to promote innovative and constructive approaches to community and political conflict. Recent issues have also been posted on the Centre's website, below. For subscription information, or to obtain backdated issues that are not electronically available, contact the Track Two Publications Secretary, Selma Walters.

- **POSTAL ADDRESS:** Centre for Conflict Resolution, UCT, Private Bag, Rondebosch, 7701, South Africa
  TEL: +27 21 422 2512 **FAX:** +27 21 422 2622
  EMAIL: sewalter@ccr.uct.ac.za
  WEBSITE: www.ccrweb.ccr.uct.ac.za

RECONCILIATION INTERNATIONAL (RI) – A bi-monthly journal published by the International Fellowship of Reconciliation (IFOR). With reports, interviews, analysis and reflections from activists around the globe, RI brings a deeper understanding of the theory and practice of active nonviolence. IFOR also publishes an occasional paper series under the title 'Patterns in Reconciliation'.

- **POSTAL ADDRESS:** IFOR, Spoorstraat 38, 1815 BK Alkmaar, The Netherlands
  TEL: +31 72 512 3014 **FAX:** +31 72 515 1102
  EMAIL: office@ifor.org **WEBSITE:** www.ifor.org

CONFLICT TRENDS – published by ACCORD, South Africa. This magazine covers peace and conflict issues throughout Africa; available online via their website and in hard copy.

- **POSTAL ADDRESS:** ACCORD, Private Bag X018, Umhlanga Rocks, 4320, Durban, South Africa
  TEL: +27 31 502 3908 **FAX:** +27 31 502 4160
  EMAIL: info@accord.org.za
  WEBSITE: www.accord.org.za

ACCORD: An International Review of Peace Initiatives – published three times a year by Conciliation Resources (CR). Each issue deals with a specific peace process and offers analytical text on the various aspects of the peace initiatives. Previous issues include Sri Lanka, Mozambique, Guatemala, Liberia Cambodia, Mindanao (Philippines), Abkhazia and Northern Ireland. Copies can be accessed and downloaded freely from the website of Conciliation Resources (see below). In addition to English-language issues published in print and on the Internet, local-language versions of the journal are published three times annually by regionally based collaborating institutions. For further details, subscriptions or copies of back issues, contact CR.

- **POSTAL ADDRESS:** Conciliation Resources, PO Box 21067, London N1 9WT, UK
  TEL: +44 20 7359 7728 **FAX:** +44 20 7359 4081
  EMAIL: conres@c-r.org
  WEBSITE: www.c-r.org

CONFLICT PREVENTION NEWSLETTER – published quarterly, this provides up-to-date information about work-in-progress on peace, and the organisations involved.

- **POSTAL ADDRESS:** European Platform for Conflict Prevention and Transformation, PO Box 14069, 3508 SC Utrecht, The Netherlands
  TEL: +31 30 253 7528 **FAX:** +31 30 253 7329
  EMAIL: euconflict@euconflict.org
  WEBSITE: www.euconflict.org

HUMANITARIAN PRACTICE NEWSLETTER – contains features, short articles, updates, news of publications, courses and resources. Published twice a year, it has replaced 'Relief and Rehabilitation Network Newsletter'.

- **POSTAL ADDRESS:** HPN Network, ODI, Portland House, Stag Place, London SWIE 5DP, UK
  TEL: +44 20 7393 1674 **FAX:** +44 20 7393 1699
  EMAIL: rrn@odi.org.uk
  WEBSITE: www.odihpn.org.uk

NEW INTERNATIONALIST – published monthly on topical themes of global interest.

- **TEL:** +44 1865 728181 **FAX:** +44 1865 793152
  WEBSITE: www.newint.org

SELECTED VIDEOS

LINKING PRACTICE TO POLICY This series of four videos has been produced by RTC in collaboration with partners in Africa, with funding from Comic Relief. The videos are aimed primarily at enabling practitioners to learn from each other. Titles in the series describe initiatives in Kenya, Uganda, South Africa and Somaliland. Two further videos are planned, dealing with policy issues.

- **POSTAL ADDRESS**: RTC, 1046 Bristol Road, Birmingham B29 6LJ, UK
  TEL: +44 121 4155641 **FAX**: +44 121 4154119
  EMAIL: enquiries@respond.org

AFRICA: SEARCH FOR COMMON GROUND

A series of 13 videos from countries all over Africa. Varied and often well-told accounts, produced by Common Ground Productions, in collaboration with various partners.

- **POSTAL ADDRESSES**:
  Search for Common Ground,
  1601 Connecticut Avenue NW, Suite 200, Washington, DC 20009, USA
  TEL: +1 (202) 265 4300 **FAX**: +1 (202) 232 6718
  EMAIL: search@sfcg.org
  WEBSITE: www.sfcg.org
  European Centre for Common Ground,
  Avenue de Tervuren, 94, B-1040 Brussels, Belgium
  TEL: +32 2 736 7262 **FAX**: +32 2 732 3033

SELECTED WEBSITES

CONFLICT DATA SERVICE (CDS) is an automatic entry point to an information network in the field of Conflict Resolution and Ethnicity, providing quick and user-friendly access to quality information. The information is organised by country and by theme. CDS also offers an extensive Information Bank, which acts as a host to information on the various academic programmes, training programmes, organisations and institutes concerned with issues relating to conflict and ethnicity, and as a more general guide to the subject. Additional resources include a bibliographic database and a researcher database. CDS is a project of the Initiative on Conflict Resolution & Ethnicity (INCORE), which is a joint programme of the United Nations University and the University of Ulster.

- **POSTAL ADDRESS**: INCORE, Aberfoyle House, Northland Road, Londonderry BT48 7JA, Northern Ireland, UK
  TEL: +44 28 71 375500 **FAX**: +44 28 71 375510
  EMAIL: INCORE@incore.ulst.ac.uk
  WEBSITE: www.incore.ulst.ac.uk/cds/

ONE WORLD NET is an Internet community of 478 organisations leading the way for human rights and sustainable development worldwide. You can use their web pages to search or browse through all the partners' websites by country, type of organisation, field of interest or native language. For further information, contact One World's UK office.

- **POSTAL ADDRESS**: One World, Hedgerley Wood, Red Lane, Chinnor, Oxon OX9 4BW, UK
  TEL: +44 1494 481629 **FAX**: +44 1494 481751
  EMAIL: justice@oneworld.org
  WEBSITE: www.oneworld.net

UN HIGH COMMISSIONER FOR HUMAN RIGHTS (UNHCHR) is a valuable source of information and documents relating to international conventions and treaties on human rights, and proceedings of the various United Nations committees that have been set up to monitor these conventions and treaties. The website can be read in French, Spanish or English, and all the documents are accessible for downloading in any of these languages. This website has direct links to other relevant UN websites. For further information, contact the Office of the High Commissioner for Human Rights at the following address.

- **POSTAL ADDRESS**: OHCHR-UNOG, CH 1211 Geneva 10, Switzerland
  TEL: +41 22 917 9000
  EMAIL: webadmin.hchr@unog.ch
  WEBSITE: www.unhchr.ch

✪ INDEX

THIS BOOK IS AVAILABLE IN THE FOLLOWING COUNTRIES:

FIJI
University Book Centre
University of South Pacific,
Suva

Tel: 679 313 900
Fax: 670 303 265

GHANA
EPP Book Services
P O Box TF 490
Trade Fair
Accra

Tel: 233-21 773087
Fax: 233-21 779099

INDIA
Segment Book Distributors
B-23/25 Kailash Colony
New Delhi

Tel : 91 11 644 3013
Fax: 91 11 647 0472

KENYA
Binti Legacy
PO Box 68077
Nairobi

Tel: 57 3 991
Fax: 57 3 992

MOZAMBIQUE
Sul Sensacoes
PO Box 2242,
Maputo

Tel: 258 1 421974
Fax: 258 1 423 414

NEPAL
Everest Media Services
GPO Box 5443, Dillibazar
Putalisadak Chowk
Kathmandu
Nepal

Tel: 977 1 416 026
Fax: 977 1 250 176

PAKISTAN
Vanguard Books
45 The Mall,
Lahore

Tel: 92 42 735 5079
Fax: 92 42 735 5197

PAPUA NEW GUINEA
Unisearch PNG Pty Ltd
Box 320, University
National Capital District

Tel: 326 0130
Fax: 326 0127

RWANDA
Librairie Ikirezi
PO Box 443,
 Kigali

Tel/fax: 250 71314

SOUTH AFRICA
Institute for Policy & Social
Research
41 Salt River Road
Salt River 7925
Cape Town

Tel: 2721 448 7458
Fax: 2721 448 0757

TANZANIA
TEMA Publishing Co Ltd
PO Box 63115
Dar Es Salaam

Tel: 255 51 113608
Fax: 255 51 110472

THAILAND
White Lotus
GPO Box 1141
Bangkok 10501

Tel: 66 2 741 6288
Fax: 66 2 741 6607

ZAMBIA
UNZA Press
University of Zambia
PO Box 32379
Lusaka
Zambia

Tel: 260 1 290409
Fax: 260 1 253 952

Ⓩ ZED BOOKS
TITLES ON CONFLICT AND CONFLICT RESOLUTION

The hopes that conflicts within societies might decrease markedly with the demise of the Cold War have been cruelly disappointed. Zed Books has published a number of titles which deal specifically with the diverse forms of modern conflict, their complex causes, and some of the ways in which we may realistically look forward to prevention, mediation and resolution.

■ Adedeji, A. (ed),
COMPREHENDING AND MASTERING AFRICAN CONFLICTS: the Search for Sustainable Peace and Good Governance

■ Allen and Seaton (eds.),
THE MEDIA OF CONFLICT: War Reporting and Representations of Ethnic Violence

■ Cockburn, C.,
THE SPACE BETWEEN US: Negotiating Gender and National Identities in Conflict

■ Fisher, S. et al,
WORKING WITH CONFLICT: Skills and Strategies for Action

■ Gopal, S.,
ANATOMY OF A CONFRONTATION: Ayodhya and the Rise of Communal Politics in India

■ Guyatt, N.,
THE ABSENCE OF PEACE: Understanding the Israeli-Palestinian Conflict

■ Hartmann, B. and Boyce, J.,
A QUIET VIOLENCE: View from a Bangladesh Village

■ Jacobs, S., Jacobson, R. and Marchbank, J. (eds.),
STATES OF CONFLICT: Gender, Violence and Resistance

■ Jayawardena, K. and De Alwis (eds.),
EMBODIED VIOLENCE: Communalising Female Sexuality in South Asia

■ Koonings, K. and Kruijt, D. (eds.),
SOCIETIES OF FEAR: The Legacy of Civil War, Violence and Terror in Latin America

■ Lumpe, L. (ed.),
RUNNING GUNS: The Black Market in Small Arms

■ Mare, G.,
ETHNICITY AND POLITICS IN SOUTH AFRICA

■ Linda Melvern,
A PEOPLE BETRAYED: The Role of the West in Rwanda's Genocide

■ Salmi, J.,
VIOLENCE AND DEMOCRATIC SOCIETY

■ Shiva, Vandana,
THE VIOLENCE OF THE GREEN REVOLUTION

■ Suliman, M. (ed.),
ECOLOGY, POLITICS AND VIOLENT CONFLICT

■ Turshen, M. and Twagiramariya (eds.),
WHAT WOMEN DO IN WAR TIME: Gender and Conflict in Africa

■ Vickers, J.,
WOMEN AND WAR

For full details of this list and other subject or general catalogues please write to:
The Marketing Department, Zed Books, 7 Cynthia Street, London N1 9JF, UK

or email: Sales@zedbooks.demon.co.uk

Visit our website at:
http://www.zedbooks.demon.co.uk